Text Production and Word Processing with Mailmerge Level 2

for the OCR Certificate in Text Processing

Sharon Spencer

D0414486

Heinemann Educational Publishers
Halley Court, Jordan Hill, Oxford OX2 8EJ
Part of Harcourt Education

Heinemann is the registered trademark of Harcourt Education Limited

© Sharon Spencer 2004

First published 2004

08 07 06 05 04
10 9 8 7 6 5 4 3 2 1

British Library Cataloguing in Publication Data is available from the British Library
on request.

ISBN 0 435 45367 X

Copyright notice
All rights reserved. No part of this publication may be reproduced in any material
form (including photocopying or storing it in any medium by electronic means and
whether or not transiently or incidentally to some other use of this publication)
without the written permission of the copyright owner, except in accordance with
the provisions of the Copyright, Designs and Patents Act 1988 or under the terms of
a licence issued by the Copyright Licensing Agency, 90 Tottenham Court Road,
London W1T 4LP. Applications for the copyright owner's written permission should
be addressed to the publisher.

Typeset by Techtype, Abingdon, Oxon
Printed in the UK by Thomson Litho Ltd

Tel: 01865 888058 www.heinemann.co.uk

051699

Contents

LLYFRGELL COLEG MENAI LIBRARY
LLANGEFNI MÔN ANGLESEY LL77 7HY

Introduction

In today's workplace it would appear that many staff are now expected to produce their own correspondence and do not have access to a secretary or word processor operator. Learning to keyboard and to be able to produce professional looking documents is therefore becoming more important.

If you have to produce your own documents at work, then it is so much more efficient if you can key in text accurately and quickly. If you can produce professional looking documents then this will reflect well on your overall performance. The skills you will learn from this book should serve you well, not just in the examinations but also in the workplace.

About this book

The aim of this book is to provide a step-by-step guide to producing the documents required for each of the following three examinations offered by the OCR Examinations Board at Intermediate Level.

Text Production
Word Processing
Mailmerge

The main features are:

- A step-by-step guide to using Word to create each of the documents required for the examinations.
- Essential English skills to ensure that you produce well-written documents that do not contain grammatical or punctuation errors.
- Consolidation practice for each task to ensure you have thoroughly learned and understood the instructions.
- Examination practice to ensure you are thoroughly prepared for the examination tasks.
- Useful sections on common errors and how to resolve them.
- Recall text provided on CD to use with the exercises for Word Processing and Mailmerge
- Worked examples of all exercises contained in the book. These are provided on the CD.

The book is divided into 4 sections:

Part 1 – Essentials of using Word

This section gives you the basic knowledge to be able to key in text and format documents. You will learn how to save and print your material. These skills are required before you can move on to the examination material.

Part 2 – Text production

This section covers all the knowledge and skills you will require in order to take and pass the Text Production examination at Level 2 (Intermediate). It includes theory and practice exercises on business letters, memos and articles. A consolidation section will help you become familiar with the examination layout. This is followed by a common errors section which will show you the type of errors commonly made in the examination – and how to resolve them. The examination practice contains full length examination style pieces for you to complete within the 1 hour 15 minutes allowed for the examination.

Part 3 – Word processing

This section covers all the knowledge and skills you will require in order to take and pass the Word Processing examination at Level 2 (Intermediate). It includes theory and practice exercises on articles, notices, tables and business letters and memos. A consolidation section will help you become familiar with the examination layout. This is followed by a common errors section which will show you the type of errors commonly made in the examination – and how to resolve them. The examination practice contains full length examination style pieces for you to complete within the 1 hour 45 minutes allowed for the examination.

Part 4 – Mailmerge

This section covers all the knowledge and skills you will require in order to take and pass the Mailmerge examination at Level 2 (Intermediate). It includes theory and practice exercises on creating and amending datafiles and merging with business letters and memos. A consolidation section will help you become familiar with the examination layout. This is followed by a common errors section which will show you the type of errors commonly made in the examination – and how to resolve them. The examination practice contains full length examination style pieces for you to complete within the 1 hour 30 minutes allowed for the examination.

A CD is also provided for your use and contains the following:

Recall text

The Word Processing and Mailmerge examinations require you to recall text saved on disk or the hard drive of your computer. These files are then added to and amended as part of the examination. The CD which accompanies this book contains all the recalled text required for both the Word Processing and Mailmerge examinations.

Worked examples

A worked copy of each exercise is provided on the CD. When you have completed an exercise, check your version with the version contained on the CD. You can either print these or view them on screen, whichever you find easier.

Essentials of using Word

This section shows you the essential basics of using Word. You will need to be able to do all of the items listed below before you can start to work on the examination tasks.

Included in this part is information on:

- Loading Word
- Formatting documents 1
- Proof-reading – types of errors
- Printing and saving documents
- Proof-reading – using the spellchecker
- Essential English skills
- Setting tabs
- Accessing the Help function
- Formatting documents 2

Loading Word

In this section you will learn about:

- loading Word
- changing the document view
- toolbars and menus

To open Word you will need to be in Windows. How you load Windows will depend on whether you are using a networked or stand-alone system. If you use a stand-alone system then the computer will probably automatically load Windows and you will immediately be taken to the desktop, see Figure 1.1 below. If the computer is networked, then you may have to enter a password or a series of logins in order to get to the desktop.

Exercise 1.1

1 Find out whether you are using a networked or stand-alone system.
2 Find out how to load Windows on your system.
3 Load Windows.

Once you have loaded Windows you will see the 'desktop'. This is the main menu from which you move around in Windows. It will look something like Figure 1.1, but the icons may differ according to the programs installed and the setup options that have been defined.

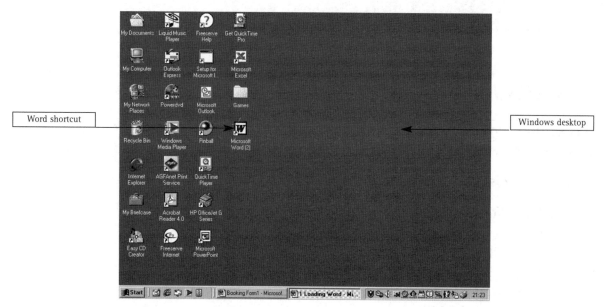

Figure 1.1 Windows desktop

Once you have reached the desktop you will be ready to open Word. You may see a shortcut icon on the desktop which will take you straight to the Word software. If the icon is not on the desktop then you will need to open Word from the Program menu using the Start button.

Exercise 1.2

Load Word.

Method 1

1 Move the mouse cursor over the **Start** button and click the left mouse button – a pop-up menu will appear listing the various programs and applications installed on the computer (see Figure 1.2).

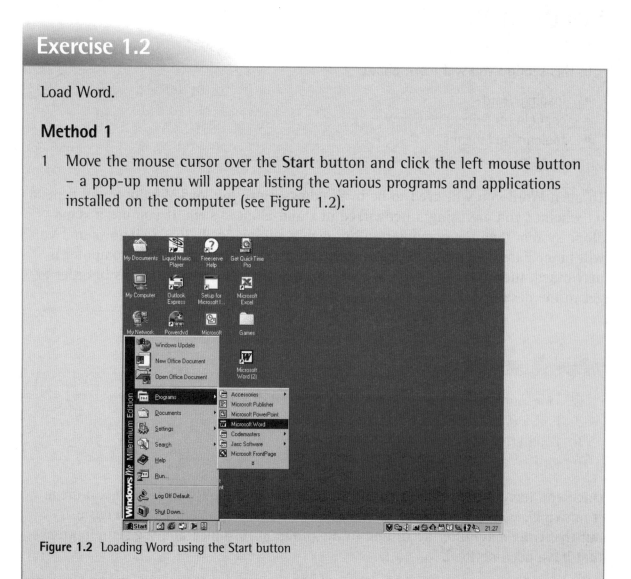

Figure 1.2 Loading Word using the Start button

2 Highlight **Programs** by moving the mouse over it – another menu will appear.
3 **Drag** the mouse across to **Microsoft Word** and click on it. Word will now begin to load.

Method 2

(Use if you have a shortcut icon to Word on your desktop)

1 Click on the **Microsoft Word** shortcut icon (see Figure 1.3).

Figure 1.3 Word shortcut icon

You will be taken to a blank document on which you can start working. The screen should look like Figure 1.4 below. Note however, that the view used here is called **Print Layout**. If you are not in this view then your screen will be different.

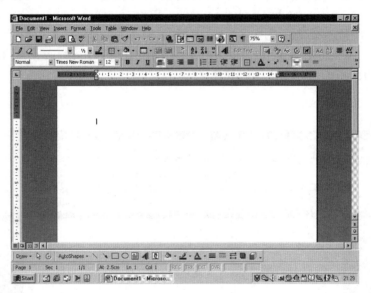

Figure 1.4 Blank document

Exercise 1.3

Change the view to Print Layout – or look at the various views available.

Method 1

1 Go to **View** on the toolbar and choose **Print Layout** from the choices available. (If you cannot find **Print Layout** then click on the arrow at the bottom of the menu. This will now expand and show all the choices available.)

2   Click on **Print Layout**. If your default setting is Print Layout then choose a different view, such as **Normal** or **Outline.** Notice the difference in layout.

Method 2

1   In the bottom left-hand corner of your screen, just before the toolbars, you will find a <u>V</u>iew menu. See Figure 1.5 below.

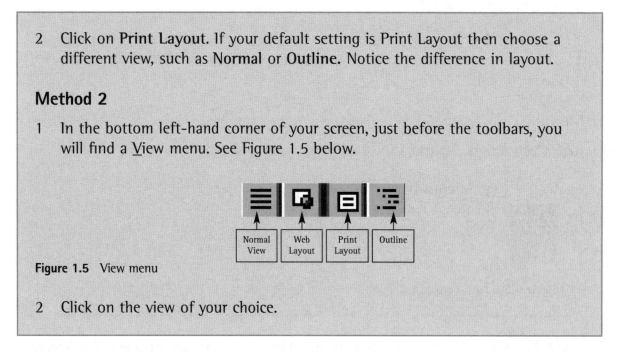

| Normal View | Web Layout | Print Layout | Outline |

Figure 1.5   View menu

2   Click on the view of your choice.

Toolbars and menus

The desktop in Word displays a variety of toolbars and menus. Look at Figure 1.6 below. Your screen may not look the same as Figure 1.6 – it may be displaying more or fewer toolbars. This is because you are able to customise the toolbars displayed in Word. In Figure 1.6 there is a large number of toolbars displayed so that easy access is provided to the various tools available.

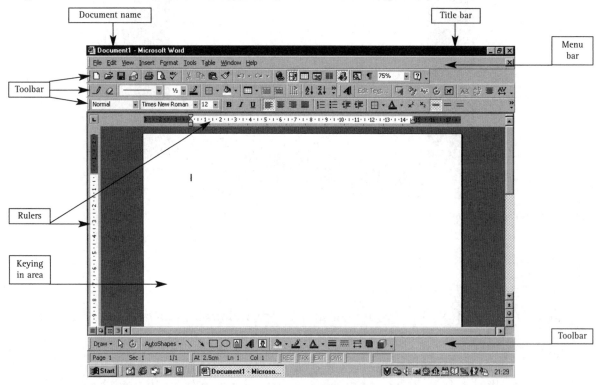

Figure 1.6   Word desktop

Formatting documents 1

In this section you will learn about:

- paper size and orientation
- changing the font and font size
- altering the line spacing

It is important to format your documents correctly so that your work looks neat and tidy. This means that your margins are correctly set, the page orientation is correct and that you use the same font style and size throughout the main body of the text.

If you take care to format your documents correctly your work will have a professional feel to it.

Before you start keying in text you should be able to set the following in Word to ensure your document is correctly formatted.

- Paper size and orientation
- Margins
- Font type and size

Paper size and orientation

The paper size required for most documents is A4, which measures 210 × 297 mm. Look at Figure 1.7 below.

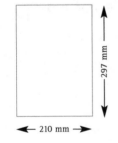

Portrait orientation
(Shortest edge at top)

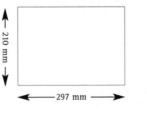

Landscape orientation
(Longest edge at top)

Figure 1.7 A4 paper

You will note that there are two ways of using the paper – portrait and landscape. Portrait has the shortest edge at the top and landscape has the longest edge at the top. It is important that you remember these and use them correctly.

To ensure that Word recognises the correct paper size for your document, you can check the settings by using the following method.

Exercise 1.4

Check the paper size and orientation of your document.

Method

1 Go to **File** and choose **Page Setup**.
2 The following menu will appear (see Figure 1.8).

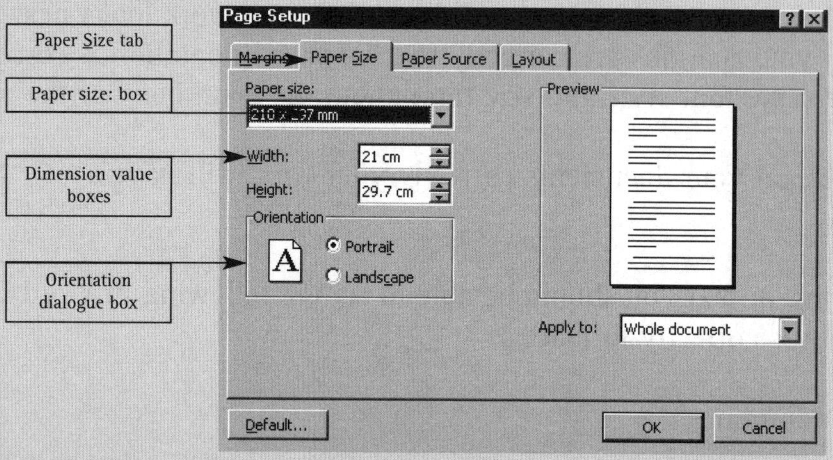

Figure 1.8 Paper Size menu

3 Click on the **Paper Size** tab to bring the menu on screen.
4 Check that the dimensions shown in the **Paper Size** box are correct for A4 paper (210 mm × 297 mm).
5 Check that the **Portrait** button is checked in the **Orientation** dialogue box.
6 Click **OK**.

Margins

The margins relate to the space around the text in a document. In Word, the default margins (i.e. is those pre-set by the software package) are as follows:

Top	2.45 cm
Bottom	2.45 cm
Left	3.17 cm
Right	3.17 cm

These give a reasonable amount of space around the text, making the page easy on the eye. You can, of course, adjust the margins and this is particularly useful if you want to fit just one line of text at the bottom of a page. However, you must be aware that most printers will not allow printing less than 0.5 cm from the edges of the paper.

Exercise 1.5

Change the margins to 3 cm top and bottom and 4 cm left and right.

Method

1   Go to <u>F</u>ile and choose **Page Set<u>u</u>p**.
2   The following menu will appear (see Figure 1.9).

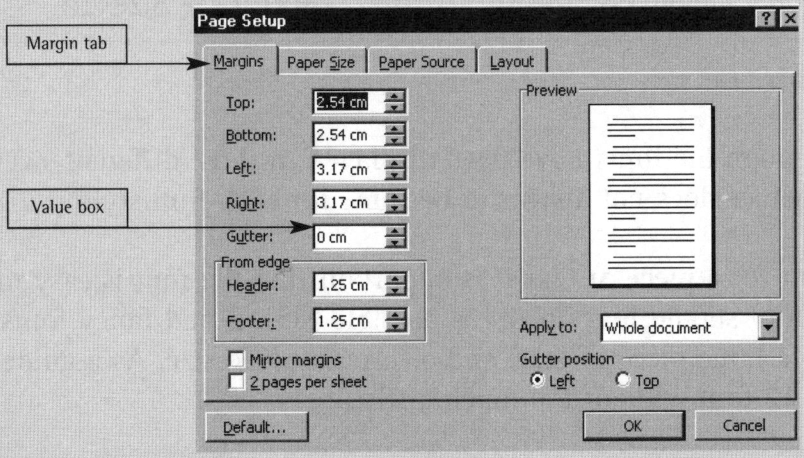

Figure 1.9 Page Setup menu

3   Ensure the tab entitled <u>Margins</u> is uppermost, if not click on it.
4   Click in the **Value** box for the **<u>Top</u>** margin. Either double click so that the existing value is highlighted or drag the cursor to highlight the existing value. Key in 4 cm. Alternatively, use the arrow boxes to the right of the value box to adjust the margin in small units.
5   Repeat the steps for the **<u>B</u>ottom, Le<u>f</u>t and Rig<u>h</u>t** margins.
6   When you have completed all the boxes click **OK**.

Font sizes and styles

The typeface of a document is called the font. You should ensure that you are using a suitable font for your document, one that is easy to read and is neither too large nor too small.

In the workplace your company will probably dictate the font that is to be used for documents as part of its 'house style'. House style means the standard layout, font, size, and other formatting items that are used for all documents throughout the business.

Look at Figure 1.10 below to see some different fonts and sizes.

Times New Roman – Size 10	Times New Roman – Size 12	Times New Roman – Size 14
Arial — Size 10	Arial — Size 12	Arial — Size 14
Ryans Hand – Size 10	Ryans Hand – Size 12	Ryans Hand – Size 14
Comic Sans - Size 10	Comic Sans - Size 12	Comic Sans - Size 14
Garamond – Size 10	Garamond – Size 12	Garamond – Size 14
Tahoma – Size 10	Tahoma – Size 12	Tahoma – Size 14

Figure 1.10 Different fonts and font sizes

You can see that although the fonts have been displayed in three different sizes, the actual size of the typeface does not appear to be same for each font style.

When choosing a font for a piece of text it is important that the font is easy to read. This means that the font should be as plain as possible (scripts and fancy fonts are difficult to read over a large piece of text) and of a reasonable size. As a guide, most people can read size 12 font without too much difficulty.

Exercise 1.6

Change the style and size of the font.

Method 1

1   Go to **Format** on the menu bar and choose **Font**. The following menu will appear.

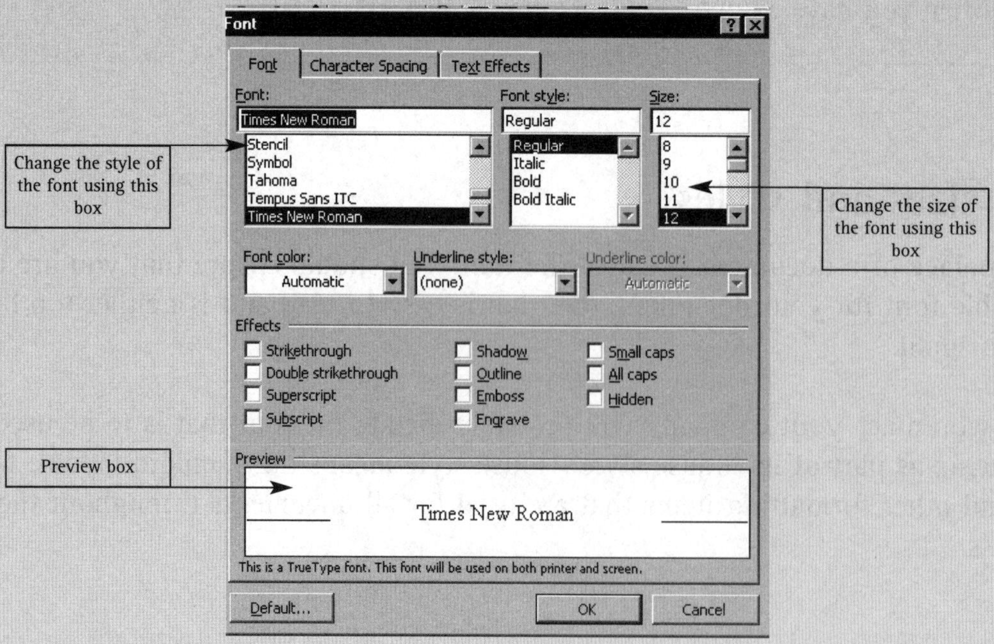

Figure 1.11 Font menu

3   To change the style of the font, use the arrows at the right-hand side of the <u>F</u>ont box to scroll through the styles available. When you have found a suitable font, click on the name. The name should then change in the **Preview** box.

4   To change the size of the font, use the arrows at the right-hand side of the <u>S</u>ize value box until you find the correct size and click on the number. The size of the text shown in the **Preview** box should change.

5   When you have finished making the amendments, click on **OK** to confirm your choice(s).

Method 2

1   On the toolbar you will find the <u>F</u>ont and <u>S</u>ize value boxes. See Figure 1.12 below.

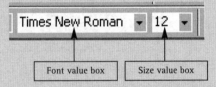

Figure value box   Size value box

Figure 1.12 Font and size value boxes

2   Click on the arrow next to the **Font** box and a drop-down menu showing the various fonts available will appear. Using the arrow, scroll down until you find a suitable font. Click on the name. The name will now change in the value box. Repeat the same steps for the size.

Line spacing

Line spacing is the term given to the white space that appears between the lines of text. Look at Figure 1.13 below.

Single line spacing is the most widely used form of spacing. It is particularly appropriate for business letters and memos. There are no clear line spaces between the lines of text.

One and a half line spacing gives a half line of clear white space between the lines of text. This is useful for drafts and reports.

Double line spacing has spacing of a clear line between lines of text. This means that the space between the two lines of text is equal to that of one line of text.

Figure 1.13 Line spacing

You will use single line spacing for letters and memos, however you may be asked to draft work in one and a half or double line spacing. To set the line spacing, follow the procedure in Exercise 1.7.

Exercise 1.7

Set line spacing to one and a half.

Method

1   Go to the **line spacing** tools on the **Toolbar**. If they are not available, you can add them to your toolbar by going to <u>V</u>iew, <u>T</u>oolbars, Formatting.
2   Choose the one and a half line spacing icon (see Figure 1.14).

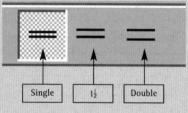

Figure 1.14 Line spacing icons

Exercise 1.8

Key in the following text using one and a half line spacing.

Skincare

It is very important that you look after your skin from an early age. As soon as you start to wear make-up you should start to follow a cleansing and moisturising routine. Each night before you go to bed, you should cleanse your skin with either a facewash or moisturising soap. Pat your skin dry using a soft towel. Then use a light layer of moisturiser so that your skin does not dry out.

If you leave make-up on overnight then your pores will become blocked and there is a much greater chance of spots and blackheads appearing. If you do not moisturise your skin then it may become dry and prone to wrinkles.

Men can also benefit from having a skincare routine. Again, thorough cleansing and the use of moisturiser will help with any dry patches of skin and their skin will also be less prone to spots, blocked pores and eventually fine lines and wrinkles.

Proof-reading – types of errors

In this section you will learn about:

• common errors

This is probably the most important part of any text processing examination and, in fact, of producing documents in the workplace. Many people believe that the skill involved in learning to keyboard is all about the speed at which you can type. This is only part of the skill. The really important thing is to be able to keyboard quickly and accurately. There is no point in being able to keyboard quickly if your work is full of errors. Equally, if you are employed to key in documents, then your employer will want you to produce documents at a reasonable rate of production.

Unfortunately, we are not always able to spot our own mistakes easily. This means that you have to take the time and trouble to read your work very carefully, either on screen or with a printed copy, and amend your errors before producing a final copy. It helps tremendously if, when you are reading your work, you make sense of the text you are keying in. This makes spotting errors much easier as any incorrect words should leap out at you.

The most common errors include:

• Typographical errors – these are pure keying in mistakes, eg *plase* instead of *please*.
• Incorrectly spelt words, eg *proffeshional* instead of *professional*.
• Words used in the wrong context, eg are/our.
• Punctuation and grammar errors.
• Words and/or sentences omitted.

Exercise 1.9

Check the work you have just keyed in (Exercise 1.8) very carefully. Did you find many errors?

Printing and saving documents

In this section you will learn about:

*   printing documents
*   saving documents
*   exiting Word

Printing your work

Exercise 1.10

Correct any errors you may have found in the exercise entitled Skincare (Exercise 1.8). Print a copy of this document.

Method

1   Go to **File**, choose **Print**. The following menu will appear (see Figure 1.15).

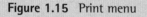

Figure 1.15   Print menu

2   In the **Page range** dialogue box, ensure that the correct pages are selected. For this exercise, the default setting of **All** is fine.
3   In the **Copies** dialogue box, ensure that the number in the **Number of copies** dialogue box is set at 1.
4   Click **OK**.

Note: The print menu may vary depending on the type of printer you are using and, if you are using a networked PC, the network settings.

Saving your work

You will need to save the documents you produce so that they can be retrieved at a later date. It is a good idea to save your work as often as possible. This will ensure that if anything goes wrong, such as the computer crashing, your work will not be totally lost.

To save your work, follow the procedure in Exercise 1.11.

Exercise 1.11

Save the document as Skincare.

Method

The first time you save a document you will need to give it a name. After that you just need to save the work, usually without renaming it.

1   Go to **File** and choose **Save As**. The following menu will appear (see Figure 1.16).

Figure 1.16 Save As menu

2   If the name of the folder in which you are going to save the work is on screen, then double click on the name to open it.
3   If the name of the folder in which you are going to save the work is not on screen then you will need to find it. You can do this by clicking on the arrow shown in Figure 1.16. This will show you the various components on the computer, such as the hard drive, a floppy drive (to take discs) or a CD drive. Click on the correct one and then using the same method move around to find the folder you want.
4   You may also use the **Up One Level** icon which will move you around the existing folders and then the computer elements.

5   Once you have found and opened the correct folder, make sure the cursor is flashing in the **File name** box. Key in the name of the document – for this exercise it is Skincare.
6   Click the **Save** button to save your work.

Exiting Word

Practice closing down and exiting Word.

Exercise 1.12

Close down and exit Word.

Method

1   Ensure you have saved your work using the method given above.
2   Go to **File** and choose **Exit**. Word will now shut down safely.

Proof-reading – using the spellchecker

In this section you will learn about:

• using the spellchecker in Word

Exercise 1.13

The following exercise contains a number of errors. See if you can find them. When you have finished proof-reading the document, load Word and key in a correct copy using a blank document and double line spacing. The answers to this exercise can be found in the worked examples on the CD-ROM that accompanies this book.

Digital Photography

With the advent of the new digitel camera's almost anyone can produce very proffesional looking photographs at very little expence. New digital cameras can cost from as little as £50 and are capable of producing very good quality prints. There our several ways in which you can develop your pictures. You can send them of to a specialist laboratory which will produce prints of a usual size and quality. If you prefre you can download the images onto your computor and print them onto photographic quality paper yourself.

As well as producing good quality images straight from the camera, you can also use some of the photo editing software packages that are availible to enhance your snaps. You can alter the color, brightness and contrast of the image as well as cropping out, that is remove aresas that you do not want in the photo.

There our many specialist classes on offer that can teach you the basic skills of digital photography. Ask at your local college or adult education center.

Using the spellchecker facility

Word has a spellchecker facility that can help you find spelling and typographical errors. However you should not rely entirely on the spell check as it will not pick up the following errors:

- If you use an incorrect but real word, for example if you key in *cheque* instead of *check*.
- If you are keying in names and addresses, or technical words.
- If you omit a word or sentence.

The English language contains many words that sound the same but mean different things and are spelt in different ways. Take 'sew' for example. Spelt this way it means to stitch. Spelt 'sow' it means to plant seeds, but also, depending on the pronounciation, it can mean a female pig. To add to the confusion we also have the word 'so'. The spellchecker has no way of knowing the context in which you are using the word and it would mark any of these as correct.

To use the spellchecker facility follow the procedure in Exercise 1.14.

Exercise 1.14

Key in the following document and then use the spellchecker to find any errors.

> The see views from the property are wonderful. You will sea many boats and yachts as they sale into the harbour. The seen is very picturesque and artists often spend a weak or sow painting harbour scenes. These pictures often end up as greetings cards and postcards. It can be very interesting to watch the artists and compare the different approach each won takes.

Method

1 Check the text you have keyed in against the exercise to ensure that nothing has been missed.
2 Ensure that the cursor is flashing in the text. Go to **Tools** and choose **Spelling**. Alternatively, press **F7**. The spellchecker will automatically check your document. Unless you have made any typographical errors the spellchecker should not find any mistakes in the text you have just keyed in.
3 If you have made an error, check the options you are given (see Figure 1.17). Choose the correct option – be careful here, the correct option is not always the first option. To choose an option, click on the word you wish to use.

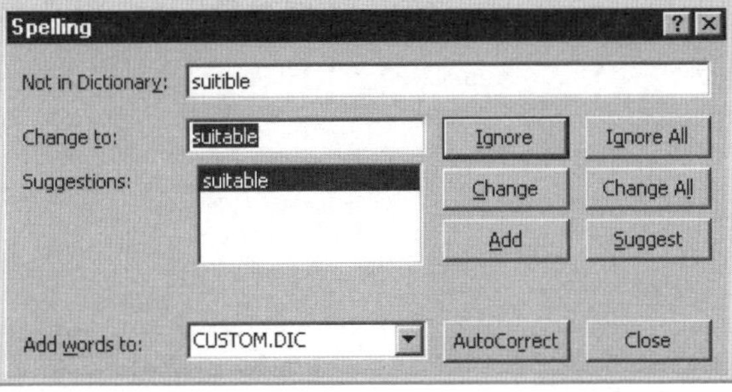

Figure 1.17 Spelling options

> 4 When you are sure you have chosen the correct word, click on <u>C</u>hange.
> 5 Once you have finished spellchecking your document, click **Close**.
>
> The correct version of this exercise can be found on the CD-ROM.

Essential English skills

> **In this section you will learn about:**
> * using capital letters

Capital letters

There are a few rules you need to know when using capital letters. If you are in any doubt then follow the draft given to you. The rules are as follows:

* Sentences should always start with a capital letter.
* A capital I should always be used if talking about yourself.
* Use a capital at the start of direct speech.
* Use initial capitals for names of people, places and proper nouns.
* Use capitals for days of the week and months of the year.
* Do not use capital letters for seasons.

Exercise 1.15

Key in the following text applying capital letters as appropriate. The correct version is given in the worked examples on the CD-ROM. Note how difficult it is to read without capital letters breaking up the sentences.

> phoebe stack wrote a very interesting book called a may romance. it is set in elizabethan times with most of the action taking place in plymouth. the story is a romantic tale involving sir walter raleigh and a young woman named betty house. the romance takes place in spring and lasts for the month of may. the book is very cleverly written and the author manages to convey a whole range of emotions. we will, in turn, feel sorrow, happiness, passion, humour and heartbreak. this book may well become a best seller and i would recommend you to read it.

Setting tabs

In this section you will learn about:

- using tabs
- setting tabs

You may need to set tab points so that you can line up work neatly. Look at Figures 1.18, 1.19 and 1.20 below. This is a useful method of ensuring your work looks neat and tidy. For column work and tables it is suggested you use the table editor, information on which can be found on page 116.

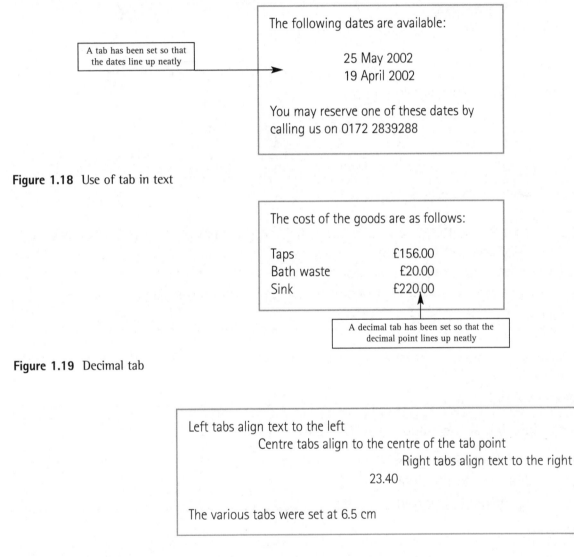

A tab has been set so that the dates line up neatly

The following dates are available:

25 May 2002
19 April 2002

You may reserve one of these dates by calling us on 0172 2839288

Figure 1.18 Use of tab in text

The cost of the goods are as follows:

Taps   £156.00
Bath waste   £20.00
Sink   £220.00

A decimal tab has been set so that the decimal point lines up neatly

Figure 1.19 Decimal tab

Left tabs align text to the left
            Centre tabs align to the centre of the tab point
                        Right tabs align text to the right
            23.40

The various tabs were set at 6.5 cm

Figure 1.20 Alignment of tabs

Exercise 1.16

Set a left-hand tab 2 cm from the left-hand margin and key in the following text exactly as shown.

>   Left hand tabs
>   align text to the
>   left of the tab
>   setting

Method

Ensure the tab icon is on **left tab** (see Figure 1.22).

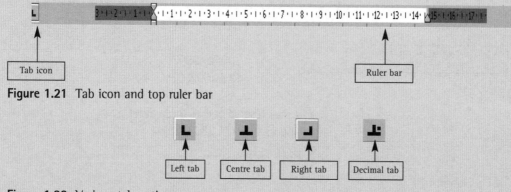

Figure 1.21 Tab icon and top ruler bar

Figure 1.22 Various tab options

2   Click on the **Left tab** icon and then click on the ruler bar at the 2 cm mark. A left tab icon will appear on the ruler bar.
3   Press the Tab key on the keyboard to move to the tab point.
4   Key in the text for the first line and then press the Return key. Repeat steps 3 and 4.

Exercise 1.17

Set a right tab at 5 cm and key in the following text.

>   Right hand tabs
>   align text to the right
>   of the tab setting

Method

1   Ensure that the **Tab** icon, which can be found in the left corner, is on **right tab**.
2   Click on the **Right tab** icon and then click on the ruler bar at the 5 cm mark. A right tab will appear on the ruler bar.
3   Press the Tab key on the keyboard to move to the tab point.
4   Key in the text for the first line and then press the Return key. Repeat steps 3 and 4.

Exercise 1.18

Set a decimal tab at 6.5 cm and key in the following text.

12.53
1920.66
1.20000
1,000,000.00

Method

1   Ensure that the **Tab** icon, which can be found in the left corner, is on **decimal tab.**
2   Click on the **Decimal tab** icon and then click on the ruler bar at the 6.5 cm mark. A decimal tab will appear on the ruler bar.
3   Press the Tab key on the keyboard to move to the tab point.
4   Key in the text for the first line and then press the Return key. Repeat steps 3 and 4.

Exercise 1.19

Practise setting tabs by keying in the following tables in this exercise and in Exercise 1.20.

Chocolate	Boiled Sweets	Toffees
Sherbet	Liquorice	Humbugs
Pear Drops	Mints	Wine gums

Exercise 1.20

1.99	19.99	199.99
0.760	000.760	00000.76000
43.85	438.5	43800000.00

Accessing the Help function

In this section you will learn about:

*   the Help function in Word
*   Undo and Redo buttons

The Help function

At some point you may need to access the various Help options. To access the **Help** function, do the following:

Exercise 1.21

Access the **Help** function using various methods.

Method 1

1   Press the **F1** button at the top of the keyboard. The **Help** assistant will appear on screen. Key in a question relating to the help you require.

Method 2

1   Click on the **Help** button on the toolbar. [?]

Method 3

1   Click on the **Help** button on the menu bar.

Undo/Redo

If you have made a mistake and wish to go back to where you were, you can use the Undo/Redo buttons which are situated on the toolbar.

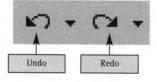

Figure 1.23 Undo and Redo buttons

The **Undo** button will remove the last action one by one to a maximum of 20. (The number of undo actions can be changed by choosing **Options** on the **Tools** menu – go to the **Edit** tab.)

The **Redo** button will redo an action that has been undone.

Formatting documents 2

In this section you will learn about:

- sub or shoulder headings
- text alignment

Use sub or shoulder headings

Sub or shoulder headings appear within the text to separate pieces of information or topics and make reading the article easier and clearer.

Look at Figure 1.24 below.

MAIN HEADING

<u>Sub Headings</u>

These are often underlined, however other types of emphasis that can be used include bold with initial capitals, italic or any other combination.

<u>Sub Headings</u>

You must be consistent with the headings – they should be in the same style and font all the way through the document. The spacing before and after the headings must also be consistent.

Figure 1.24 Headings

You can see that there is a clear line space before and after the sub or shoulder headings and that emphasis has been used to clarify the heading. You must ensure that you are consistent with the display of sub or shoulder headings. Check the following very carefully:

- Font
- Font size
- Capitalisation
- Spacing – before and after the heading

Text alignment

The alignment of the text can also vary. Look at Figure 1.25 below.

This text is left aligned and has a ragged right-hand margin. This means that all the lines start at the left-hand margin. The right-hand margin is allowed to occur naturally. You should not press enter at the end of each line.

This text is centred.
This means that each line is centred between the margins.
The enter key has been pressed at the end of each line.

This text is right aligned. This means the text flows from the right-hand margin to the left. The enter key has not been pressed at the end of each line, so that the text will flow naturally. This type of text is normally only used for headings or when creating a piece of display work.

This text is justified. This means the text is aligned to both the left and right margins. The software will automatically add extra space to the text in order to ensure the lines end at the same place. It can be difficult to read large blocks of text that have been justified. The ragged edge helps guide the eye. This display is often used for reports.

Figure 1.25 Text alignment

Exercise 1.22

Key in the following text. Use single line spacing, and a justified right margin. Centre the heading. Correct any spelling or typographical errors you might find. Save the document as Exercise 1.22. The correct version is given in the worked example on the CD.

PHOENIX GROUP PLC

WHO ARE WE?

Phoenix Group plc is a large public limited company with business interests in many areas. Founded in 1959 by Alex Cross and Sara Davies, It has grown into one of the country's largest and most popular limited companies.

WHAT DO WE DO?

Phoenix Group plc has many and varied business interests. From corporate hospitality, through retail and Internet shopping to travel agencies and holiday operators. We believe diversification is the key to a successful business.

HOW WELL DO WE DO IT?

Our market share is large and our stock price has shown consistent growth over the past five years. Our shareholders have enjoyed dividend increases during this period. Our profit forecast for this year shows a 16% increase. We feel justifiably proud of our achievements.

Method

1   Go to the text alignment tools on the **Toolbar**. If they are not available, you can add them to your toolbar by going to **V**iew, **T**oolbars, **Formatting**.

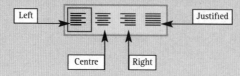

Figure 1.26 Text alignment icons

2   Click on the **Centre** icon and then key in the heading. Press the Return key twice to leave a clear line space after the heading.
3   Click on the **Justified** icon so that the body of the text is fully justified.

Text production

The Level 2 Text Production (Intermediate) examination offered by OCR consists of three tasks:

1 A letter keyed in on headed paper
2 A memo keyed in using a memo form
3 A report or article

You may use either a typewriter or a word processor and will be allowed 1 hour and 15 minutes to complete the examination.

You will be asked to demonstrate a number of skills, by using the keyboard and your knowledge and application of English. Each of the three tasks will contain one or more of the following:

- Words that need to be corrected (these will be circled), including spelling errors, punctuation, apostrophes, omitted full stops and errors of agreement
- Abbreviations which need to be expanded
- Emphasis of headings
- Amendments using correction signs
- Information to be transferred from one document to another
- Information which must be keyed in using a consistent format
- A continuation sheet
- Use of double and single line spacing

In this section you will learn about the following:

- Business letters
- Essential English – correction signs
- Essential English – spelling
- Articles and reports
- Essential English – errors of agreement
- Consolidation practice
- Essential English – abbreviations
- Memos
- Consistency
- Essential English – apostrophes
- Checking details to provide information
- Taking the examination

Business letters

In this section you will learn about:

- headed paper
- templates
- references
- dating and postdating letters
- using special marks
- name and address block
- salutation
- paragraphs
- complimentary close
- enclosures
- continuation sheets
- consistency

You will need to know how to set out a business letter correctly. Look at Figure 2.1 below.

| Headed paper | → | ANGEL SOUNDS
12 Fore Street
CHELTENHAM
Glos GL1 2NO |

Telephone: 01221 283910   Fax 01221 282947
E-mail info@angelsounds.co.uk

Reference → Our Ref ANG/SA/1

Date → 2 May 2003

Special mark → PRIVATE AND CONFIDENTIAL

Name and address block →
Ms K Lewis
8 Apsley Road
CHELTENHAM
Glos
GL2 8NL

Salutation → Dear Ms Lewis

Thank you for your application form for the above position. We would like you to attend for interview at the store on 19 May at 2.00 pm. A short job description is enclosed for information.

Paragraphs of text →
Please confirm you are able to attend for interview by contacting Leila Grant on the above telephone number.

Mrs Patti Mansell, the store manager, looks forward to meeting you.

Yours sincerely

Complimentary close → Leila Grant
Personal Assistant

Enclosure → Enc

Figure 2.1 Business letter

This letter has been displayed in a **blocked** style – this means all the lines start at the left-hand margin. The punctuation is **open punctuation** – ie the standard items such as name and address block, salutation, heading and complimentary close do not contain punctuation. The main text does of course contain punctuation.

Headed paper

Business letters should always be keyed in on headed paper. This may be provided as **pre-printed paper** that you feed into the computer printer, or may be a **template** saved on the computer.

Pre-printed paper is more common in the workplace. If you use this you will need to do the following:

- Set the top margin of the page to allow for the heading at the top of the paper. To do this, you will need to measure the amount of space taken up with the pre-printed heading. Now alter the top margin using the page setup method (see page 7) by that amount.
- Work out how the paper is loaded into your printer. This varies from printer to printer, so you will need to ask your tutor.

Template

You may use a template that has been loaded onto your computer. If this is the case, you will need to do the following:

- You will need to know the name of the template. Each time you want to key in a letter you will need to open that file.
- Once you have used the template to key in the letter, you must ensure that you save the document using a different name. If you do not and just save the letter after keying in then the new text will be saved onto the template.

There is a letter template provided on the CD-ROM that accompanies this book.

Exercise 2.1

Open the letter template called Headed Paper Template on your CD-ROM.

Method

1 Ensure the CD-ROM is inserted into the drive.
2 Go to **File** and choose **Open**. The following sub-menu will appear.

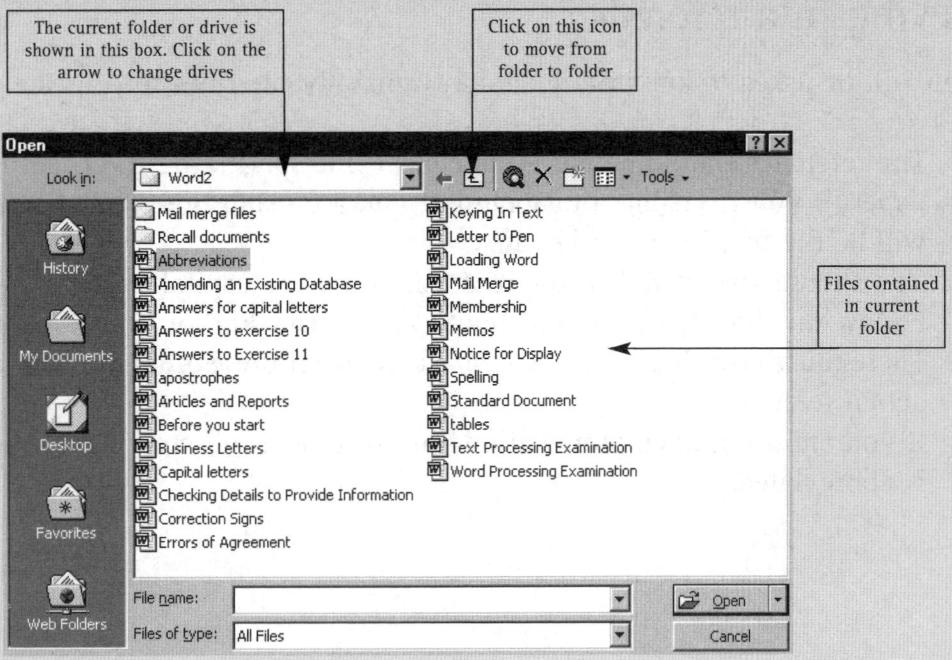

The current folder or drive is shown in this box. Click on the arrow to change drives

Click on this icon to move from folder to folder

Files contained in current folder

Figure 2.2 Open sub-menu

3   Click on the arrow next to the **Look in** box to see a list of drives and folders.
4   Click on the CD drive (the name of this may vary from PC to PC). The folders and files contained on the CD should appear.
5   Click on the folder called **Recall Documents**.
6   Click on the template called Headed Paper Template.
7   Click **Open**.

The template should now be on screen (see Figure 2.3).

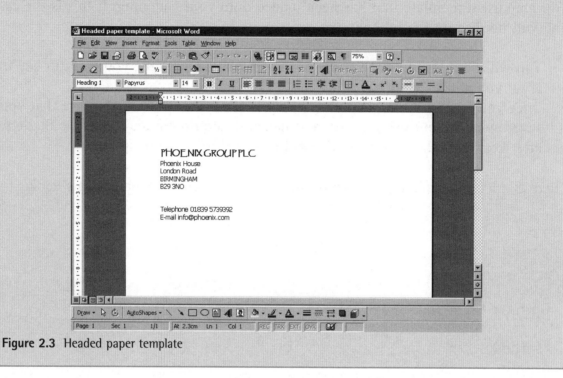

Figure 2.3 Headed paper template

Keying in a reference

You will be asked to key in a reference. Generally the rules for this are as follows:

*   The reference should be placed one clear line space after the heading on the paper (if you are using a template). If you are using pre-printed paper then it will be the first item you key in.
*   You should always follow the draft to ensure the capitalisation is correct.
*   Follow the draft to see if you should key in 'Our Ref' or 'Our Reference' in full.
*   There must be at least one clear space between the words 'Our Ref' and the actual reference.
*   If you are using open punctuation, do not type a full stop if the word 'reference' is abbreviated.

Exercise 2.2

Using the letter template you opened in Exercise 2.1, key in the reference Our ref SLS/12/DP.

Method

1 Click at the bottom of the headed paper as shown in Figure 2.3.
2 Press the Return key twice to ensure that there is at least one clear line space between the headed paper and the reference.
3 Key in the reference exactly as shown, starting at the left-hand margin.

Date

All letters must have a date. The exam paper will not tell you to insert the date – you will be expected to remember this. It is important that you do insert the date, because if you forget you will lose 3 marks. The rules are as follows:

- Leave a clear line space between the reference and the date (press **Enter** twice).
- Key in the date in full, eg 25 June 2003.
- If using open punctuation, do not type in 'th', 'rd', etc. and do not use commas to separate the month and the year.

You may use the automatic **date and time** insertion available on Word. To use this, do the following:

Exercise 2.3

Continue using the letter template from Exercise 2.2. Insert today's date in the correct position (see Figure 2.1).

Method

1 Ensure that there is a clear line space between the reference and the date insertion point.
2 Go to <u>I</u>nsert on the toolbar and choose Date and <u>T</u>ime. The following sub-menu will appear.

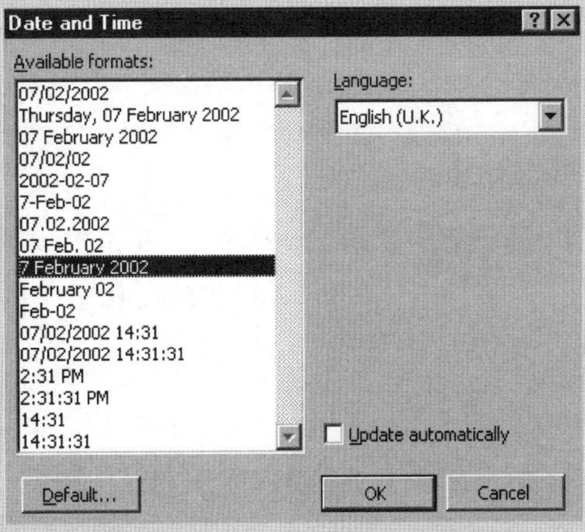

Figure 2.4 Insert date and time menu

3 Check that the <u>L</u>anguage box on the right-hand side of the dialogue box is set to English (UK).
4 Choose a format from the <u>A</u>vailable Formats box on the left-hand side by clicking on the style of date you wish to use. Remember that the date must be in date, month, year order. If you use an American style (ie month, date, year order) you will be penalised in an examination. The best choice for examination purposes is date, month in full, year in full – 20 March 2003.
5 Click OK.

Postdating

You may be asked to postdate a letter or memo during the examination. The instruction will read something like 'insert the date for the first Monday of next month'. You will need to use a calendar to ensure you insert the correct date. It is perfectly acceptable to take a calendar into the examination and is in fact essential as failure to use the exact date will result in marks being lost.

Special mark

A special mark is a word or phrase such as 'Urgent', 'Private and Confidential' and 'For the attention of ...'. It should be keyed in as follows:

- Key in a special mark after the date, leaving one clear line space between.
- Follow the draft for capitalisation, although it is usual to key in a special mark in closed capitals – ie blocked capitals.
- If you are using 'For the attention of' you will need to add the name of the person who will be receiving the letter.
- If you are using 'For the attention of' you should **not** repeat the name of the person in the address block. If you do repeat the name in an examination, you will lose 3 marks.

Exercise 2.4

Continue using the exercise you started in Exercise 2.3. Key in URGENT after the date.

Method

1 Ensure that there is a clear line space after the date.
2 Key in the special mark, following the capitalisation as shown, at the left-hand margin.

Name and address block

It is very important to key this in accurately otherwise the letter might not reach its destination! To key in the name and address block do the following:

- Key in the block after the date or special mark if there is one, leaving a clear line space.
- If you are using open punctuation, do not type a full stop after any capitals or insert a comma at the end of each line.
- The town must be keyed in in CAPITALS.
- Key in any abbreviations, such as Rd, Ave, Grdns, etc. in full.
- County names may be kept as abbreviations.
- Always use a separate line for the postcode. This should be displayed in two separate blocks, eg BA1(space)8QP.

Exercise 2.5

Continue using the letter from Exercise 2.4. Key in the name and address block as follows:

Mr J Rashid
49 Bolton Ave
LEEDS
LS1 3NO

Method

1 Ensure that there is a clear line space after the special mark.
2 Key in the name and address block, remembering to expand any abbreviations. Ensure that each line of text starts at the left-hand margin.

Salutation

This is the opening of the letter, for example Dear Mr Stevens etc. Remember the following:

- Key in the salutation after the name and address block, leaving one clear line space.
- Do not use the person's initials in the salutation.
- Remember to use initial capitals.
- If using open punctuation, do not add a comma to the end of the line of text.

Exercise 2.6

Continue using the letter from Exercise 2.5. Key in Dear Mr Rashid in the appropriate place.

Method

1 Ensure that there is a clear line space after the name and address block.
2 Key in Dear Mr Rashid at the left-hand margin, using the capitalisation as shown. Do not enter the initial J in the salutation. If you are using open punctuation, do not add a comma at the end of the salutation.

Paragraphs of text

These form the main body of the letter. The rules are as follows:

- Leave a clear line space between the salutation and the paragraphs of text.
- Leave a clear line space between each paragraph.
- Ensure that all paragraphs start at the left-hand margin. Unless specified, you should use a ragged right-hand margin for business letters.
- Do not forget to use punctuation in the text, even if you are using open punctuation.

Exercise 2.7

Continue using the letter from Exercise 2.6. Key in the following paragraphs of text.

Thank you for your recent enquiry. I am pleased to enclose a copy of our latest catalogue, together with a price list.

Please note that you may order by phone, fax, e-mail or post. Orders are normally despatched within 4 working days.

I look forward to receiving your first order.

Method

1 Ensure there is a clear line space between the salutation and the start of the text.
2 Key in the text, allowing it to wrap at the end of the line. This means you do not need to press return at the end of each line.
3 Ensure there is a clear line space between each paragraph of text.

Complimentary close

The complimentary close consists of 'Yours sincerely' or 'Yours faithfully', followed by a space large enough to put a handwritten signature. The name of the person who drafted the letter follows, often accompanied by their job title.

- Leave a clear line space after the paragraphs of text.
- The first word of the complimentary close should always have an initial capital.
- Remember, if you addressing the letter to a named person the close should be 'Yours sincerely'.
- If you are addressing the letter to 'Dear Sir' or 'Dear Madam' then you should use 'Yours faithfully'.
- Leave a minimum of 5 clear line spaces to ensure there is sufficient room for the signature.
- If asked to type the name of the person drafting the letter, or the name of the company, then follow draft for capitalisation.

- If keying in the name of the person, together with their job title, then put each on a separate line, but do not leave a clear line space between.

Exercise 2.8

Continue using the letter from Exercise 2.7. Key in Yours sincerely Debbie Kingston Mail Order Manager as a complimentary close.

Method

1   Ensure there is a clear line space between the end of the text and the start of the complimentary close.
2   Key in Yours sincerely, following the capitalisation as shown.
3   Press the return key 6 times in order to leave 5 clear line spaces.
4   Key in Debbie Kingston, press return.
5   Immediately under the name, key in Mail Order Manager. Again, the capitalisation should be exactly as shown.

Enclosure(s)

If you are enclosing additional documents with a letter then you should indicate this at the bottom of the letter, after the complimentary close. You must check the draft of the document to see if there are to be any enclosures yourself as it will not be written on the examination paper.

As a general rule, you should do the following:

- Check the letter to see if it states 'we are enclosing' or 'attached is a ...'.
- Leave a clear line space after the complimentary close.
- Key in Enc or if there is more than one enclosure Encs.
- Do not key in a full stop after the abbreviation.

Exercise 2.9

Continue using the letter from Exercise 2.8. Key in Encs to indicate that there are enclosures with the letter.

Method

1   Ensure you have a clear line space between the complimentary close and the start of the enclosure indicator.
2   Key in Encs exactly as shown at the left-hand margin.

Your letter is now complete. A worked example of this letter appears in the worked example on the CD-ROM.

Continuation sheets

You will need to use a continuation sheet if the work carries on to a second page. Do the following:

- You must number the continuation sheet.
- There is no need to add the date and the name of the addressee. If you do you must ensure you key this in accurately, otherwise marks will be lost in the examination.
- Do not have 'widows' and/or 'orphans' in your document. This means just one line of text at the bottom of the first page or the top of the second page. See Figure 2.5.

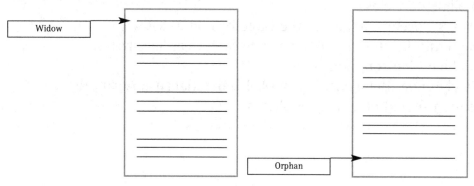

Figure 2.5 Widows and orphans

You can set widows and orphans control in Word to stop this happening. To do this use the following method.

Exercise 2.10

Set widows and orphans control.

Method

1 Open the letter template provided with the CD-ROM.
2 Go to the **Format** menu on the toolbar and choose **Paragraph**. The following menu will appear (see Figure 2.6).

Figure 2.6 Paragraph menu

4   Click on the **Line and Page Breaks** tab and then ensure that there is a tick in the **W**idow/Orphan control box.

5   Click OK.

Note: If you do find you have a widow or orphan in your document and haven't got time to put it right, then don't worry, you will not be penalised in the examination. However, in order to make your work look neat and professional it is a good idea to always ensure you have set the Widow/Orphan control box.

Exercise 2.11

Key in the following letter using the methods given above. Check your work carefully, amend any errors and print one copy. A correct version of this exercise appears in the worked examples on the CD-ROM.

Our ref SG/FL12

Mr J Neale
41 Lighthouse Close
BRIGHTON
BN1 2AD

Dear Mr Neale

Further to our recent telephone conversation, I was pleased to hear that your holiday in the Maldives was a great success. I can now confirm that Sally Greene, our Features reporter, will be calling on you at 10.30 am on Tuesday 21 March.

Sally would like you to tell her about the holiday you won in our Luxury Travel competition. She will be joined at 11am by Felix Legg, a free lance photographer, who would like to take some photographs of you and your family.

If you have any interesting memorabilia bought on the holiday, or family photographs that could be featured in the article, please have these ready. The entire interview should not take longer than an hour and a half.

If you have any questions regarding the interview, please do not hesitate to contact me.

Yours sincerely

Evelyn Wright
Travel Editor

Consistency

You must ensure that when you are keying in text that you do so in a consistent style. This means that the formatting of the text, ie the font, font size, etc. is the same throughout the document. This gives your work a neat, tidy and professional appearance.

Areas of work that must be consistent include:

Punctuation

You may use either open or full punctuation, however you must keep to the same style throughout. Do not mix the two or you will be penalised in an examination. It does not matter whether you leave one or two spaces after a full stop, but again, whichever style you choose, keep to it throughout a document.

Words and figures

You may use either words or figures for keying in numbers in documents, but not both. It doesn't matter which you choose, but there are one or two exceptions:

- Never start a sentence with a figure.
- Never use the figure 1 when it is not referring to a measurement. For example, if you were to key in the sentence *it is annoying when one is late for an appointment.* It would be inappropriate to use the figure 1 in this sentence.

Money

The rule for numbers also applies to sums of money. Once you have chosen a style you should keep to it, however you should quickly read through the document to see if there are any other numbers to be keyed in. For example, if you keyed in one pound (£1) in words but later found you had to key in sixty five thousand, seven hundred and forty two pounds (£65,742) then it would look better in figures.

You must also display sums of money consistently with regard to decimal places. For example, £10.00 and £5270.00 – they are both displayed with two decimal places.

If you are keying sums of money in columns then the decimal point must always be lined up and therefore hundreds, tens and units are also directly underneath each other. This will involve using the decimal tab, instructions on which can be found on page 17.

You should always ensure that you copy the text in your examination paper exactly as shown, otherwise you may lose marks. However, when keying in documents in the workplace you should check for words and figures, etc. before starting to ensure you make your work as consistent as possible.

Exercise 2.12

Key in the following letter using the headed paper template found on the CD. Display any numbers and figures consistently. Save the exercise as Douglas and print one copy. A correct version of this exercise appears in the worked examples on the CD-ROM.

Our ref KD/1249

Ms Kerry Douglas
Purchasing Manager
Paws Direct Ltd
P O Box 124
EXETER
EX2 9PU

Dear Ms Douglas

Thank you for your recent order, reference number 19425. We can confirm that the items you requested are in stock and are available for delivery within three working days. Unfortunately, the prices quoted on the order are out of date. There have been some increases to our stock prices within the last two months. [The dog name tags are now sixty-seven pence each with a retail price of £2.20. The cat toys are 99p each with a retail price of one pound seventy five pence. All prices are subject to 17.5% VAT.

Please let us know as soon as possible if you would like to continue with your order.

We look forward to hearing from you.

Yours sincerely

Lewis Granger
Sales Manager

Essential English – abbreviations

In this section you will learn about:

- common abbreviations

When people are drafting documents, they often use abbreviations. It will be part of your work to know when to expand these abbreviations and to do so correctly.

At Level 2 you will need to know the following abbreviations and be able to expand them correctly.

Abbreviation	Expansion	Abbreviation	Expansion
a/c(s)	account(s)	opp(s)	opportunity/ies
approx	approximate(ly)	org	organisation
cat(s)	catalogue(s)	poss	possible
co(s)	company(ies)	ref(s)	reference(s)
dr	dear	ref(d)	refer(red)
gntee(s)	guarantee(s)	sec(s)	secretary(ies)
immed	immediate(ly)	sig(s)	signature(s)
info	information	temp	temporary
mfr(s)	manufacturer(s)	yr(s)	year(s)
misc	miscellaneous	yr(s)	your(s)
necy	necessary		

There are also the more common abbreviations that you should know:

Days of the week – for example, Mon, Sat
Months of the year – Aug, Sept

Others include:

Complimentary closes

Abbreviation	Expansion
ffly	faithfully
sncly	sincerely

Words used in addresses

Abbreviation	Expansion	Abbreviation	Expansion
rd	road	sq	square
st	street	cres	crescent
ave	avenue	pl	place
dr	drive	pk	park

Exceptions

There are some words that will appear in an abbreviated format that you should not expand.

NB, PS, plc, Ltd and the & when used in company names only. You should not expand Our Ref or Your Ref when it appears in a letter or memo heading.

Exercise 2.13

Key in the following letter, expanding the abbreviations where necessary. Save as Linnington and print one copy. A correct version of this exercise appears in the worked examples on the CD-ROM.

Our ref CAT/KL

Mrs K Linnington
165 Park Sq
BRADFORD
BR6 9TW

Dr Mrs Linnington

Thank you for requesting a copy of our latest cat. I have arranged for this to be sent to you immed.

We would like to offer you the opp of opening an a/c with our co. There are many advantages to becoming an a/c holder. These include receiving a small discount on all orders and free packing and postage on all orders over £60.

We believe our org offers an excellent service. We carefully select the mnfrs of goods to ensure they are of the highest quality. Naturally all our goods carry a full 2 yr gntee.

If you would like more info on becoming an a/c holder please contact my sec Lucy Richmond quoting ref 621.

I look forward to receiving yr first order.

Yrs sncly

Mark Andrews
Managing Director

Essential English – correction signs

> **In this section you will learn about:**
>
> • correction signs

These correction signs are used in the workplace to show where errors and omissions must be amended. These may also be called proof marks or typescript signs and there are many of them. For the Text Production examination you will only be expected to learn a few. You must ensure that you understand what is meant by each of them and that you learn these thoroughly.

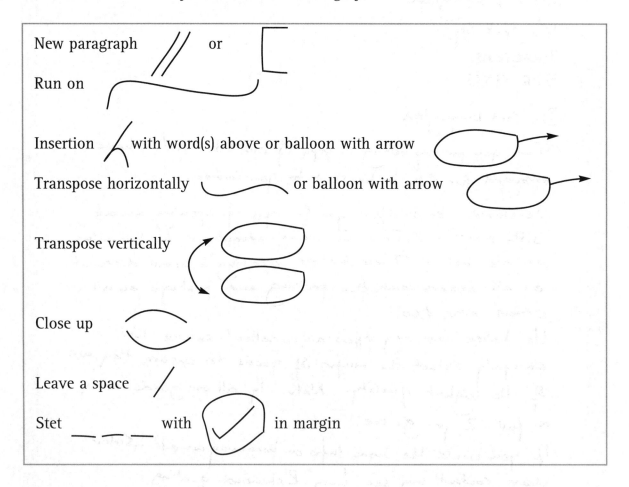

New paragraph

This means you should start a new paragraph. Remember to leave a clear line space between the two paragraphs.

Run on

This sign means you should join two paragraphs together, making one larger one. It is important that you remember to leave the correct number of spaces after the full stop of the first paragraph.

Insertion

You will need to insert the word or words exactly where the insertion sign appears. The words to be inserted are either written above the existing text or in a balloon that is situated elsewhere on the page. Check your work very carefully to ensure that you have inserted the text in the correct place.

Transpose horizontally or vertically

This means you need to move the text to a different location. For example, if you were asked to move the text horizontally then the sentence might look like this.

The basket of fruit contained, pears, apples, bananas, oranges and a pineapple.

The sentence should, after you have made the alteration look like this:

The basket of fruit contained pears, apples, bananas, oranges and a pineapple.

If you are asked to move text vertically then you should swap the paragraphs so that they appear in different places. The most important thing to check is that you have moved all of the text requested.

Close up

This is where a large space has been left, for example after a full stop, in between two words or within a word. You should close up the space, but remember if you are doing this after a full stop, you must still leave the correct number of spaces.

Stet

This means to use the original word. You will see this sign where the editor has crossed out a word and then replaced it with a different word. The second word has also been crossed out. The editor will then put a row of dashes under the word that is to be used in the text. For example

The dog has a glossy ~~black~~ coat.

In this sentence the correct word is black.

Exercise 2.14

Key in the following letter, making corrections as indicated. Save as Richards and print one copy. A correct version of this exercise appears in the worked examples on the CD-ROM.

Our ref MR/MB

Ms M Richards
64 Roseberry Lane
PORTSMOUTH
Hants
PO9 8JU

Dr Ms Richards

Thank you for yr recent letter ~~dated 21 March~~. I have now refd yr complaint to our Managing Director and she has agreed that yr a/c will be ~~credited~~ refunded with a full refund of £1280.

We can only apologise for the inconvenience you have been caused. We have ~~on many occasions~~ contacted the mfrs. They have been unable to explain why your fridge has broken. Although ~~yr fridge~~ this item is still under gntee the mfrs are unwilling to provide a replacement item.

We do not feel this is satisfactory and in order to resolve yr problem quickly have decided to refund your money. The fridge will be collected from yr home in due course.

Yrs sncly

~~Madeline~~ Margaret Brookes
Sales Manager

Memos

In this section you will learn about:
• memo layouts
• references
• dating memos
• special marks

A memo, or memorandum as it is sometimes called, is a document used to send messages to colleagues within an organisation. It is never used to send to customers outside the company.

As with letters, you may use either a pre-printed memo form or a template stored on the computer. The layout of the memo form may vary from company to company, but should always contain the following:

- To – where the name of the person receiving the memo is keyed in.
- From – where the name of the person sending the memo is keyed in.
- Ref – the reference of the person sending the memo is keyed in here.
- Date – all business documents should contain a date.

A typical memo layout will look like Figure 2.7.

Memorandum
To
From
Ref
Date
Paragraphs of text to follow on from here.

Figure 2.7 Typical memo form

When practising the exercises given in this book, use the MEMO template that is stored on the CD-ROM.

Exercise 2.15

Open the document called MEMO stored on the CD and key in the details as shown.

Method 1

1 You can, if you wish, line the cursor up with the 'o' in 'To' and then press the space bar twice in order to leave a clear space.
2 Now key in the words Amanda Green. However, this gives a rather untidy appearance and it is strongly recommended that you use the tab method shown on page 17. Figure 2.8 shows the appearance of the text using the tab method.

To	Amanda Green
From	Kathy Spraggs
Ref	
Date	

Figure 2.8 Memo

You can see that each line starts in the same place giving a uniform appearance and that there is a small clear space between the longest line of the template (From) and the start of the name (Kathy Spraggs).

3 Now key in Kathy Spraggs lined up with the **From** line.

Reference

It is usual to give a reference in the memorandum. When you are keying in a reference, particularly for examination purposes, it is important that you follow the draft carefully to ensure that capitalisation is correct. You should use capital letters only where they are shown in the draft. The parts of the reference are separated using a forward slash /, or oblique as it is called. Do not use a backward slash \ or you will lose marks.

You should not add your own initials to the reference given in the examination.

Exercise 2.16

Continue using the memo you opened in Exercise 2.15, and key in the reference KS/AG/121.

Date

There must be a date on the memorandum. If a date is not given in the examination paper then you must insert the current date. For information on how to insert a date into your document see page 27.

Exercise 2.17

Using the memo from Exercise 2.16, insert today's date in the appropriate place.

Special mark

You may be asked to include a special mark on the memo. This should be keyed in one clear line space after the date. It is usual to use blocked capitals for the special mark.

Exercise 2.18

Continue using the memo from Exercise 2.17, and key in URGENT in the correct place.

Exercise 2.19

Continue using the memo from Exercise 2.18. Key in the main text of the memo as shown below. Save the exercise as **credit cards** and print one copy.

It has been brought to our attention that there has been a large increase in the number of stolen credit cards used in this area recently. We must be extra vigilant in order to minimise our losses incurred when accepting stolen credit cards.

Please ensure the shop staff are aware of this increase. They must be aware of the procedures we have in place, together with those of the credit card cos. The staff must follow the procedures carefully each time they accept a credit card. If they are given a stolen credit card, they must leave the shop floor with the card and bring it to the manager. They must not endanger their safety or that of other customers. If they encounter a dangerous situation they must not hesitate to use the panic buttons located under the counters.

It would be helpful if you could go through the various procedures with the staff tomorrow morning during the staff training hour.

Thank you for your co-operation in this matter.

A correct version of the completed memo can be found in the worked examples on the CD-ROM.

Enclosure(s)

As with business letters, if you are enclosing additional documents with a memo then the enclosure(s) must be indicated. You must check the draft of the document to see if there are to be any enclosures yourself as it will not be written on the examination paper.

As a general rule, you should do the following:

- Check the memo to see if it states 'we are enclosing' or 'attached is a ...'.
- Leave a clear line space after the last line of text.
- Key in Enc or if there is more than one enclosure Encs.
- Do not key in a full stop after the abbreviation.

Essential English – spelling

In this section you will learn about:

- spelling of some difficult words

The examination requires you to be able to spell correctly words taken from the list below. You will also be expected to know and be able to spell their derivatives. These are the different endings of the same word, for example accommodate has the following derivatives: accommodated, accomodating, accommodative, accommodator, accommodation.

In order to select the correct derivative, you must read the text very carefully – read for meaning and then the required word should be obvious.

You will need to learn the following list:

Access	Accommodate	Achieve	Acknowledge
Accessed	Accommodated	Achieved	Acknowledged
Accessing	Accommodating	Achiever	Acknowledging
	Accommodation	Achieving	
		Achievable	

Advertisement	Although	Apparent	Appreciate
Advertised		Apparently	Appreciated
Advertising			Appreciating
Advertiser			

Believe	Business	Client	Colleague
Believed	Businesses	Clients	Colleagues
Believing			
Believer			
Believable			

Committee	Correspondence	Definite	Develop
Committees		Definitely	Develops
			Developed
			Developing

Discuss	Expense	Experience	Financial
Discussed	Expenses	Experienced	Financially
Discussing		Experiencing	

Foreign	Government	Inconvenient	Receipt
Foreigner	Governments	Inconveniently	Receipts
	Governmental	Inconvenience	
		Inconveniencing	
		Inconvenienced	

Receive	Recommend	Responsible	Separate
Receiving	Recommendation	Responsibly	Separated
Received	Recommends	Responsibility	Separates
			Separating
			Separately

Sufficient	Temporary	Through
Sufficiently	Temporarily	

Exercise 2.20

Key in the following memo, checking that all words are spelt correctly and amending any that are incorrect. Save as Webster and print one copy. A correct version of this exercise appears in the worked examples on the CD-ROM.

Ref   JC/PW

From June Chisholm

To Peter Webster

(Please mark this URGENT)

I have now (receiveed) the following text for the travel article that will appear in next week's holiday supplement. Please edit this as a matter of some urgency and send the corrected version to Cattel. He needs to have this by 4.00pm at the latest.

'We (recomend) that you find (acomodation) before you start yr travels. Greece is very busy during the summer months and in our (experence) most hotels, especially budget hotels, are fully booked months in advance.'

'You can often find bargains by looking at the (advertisments) on the Internet. The only drawback is that the sites appear in a (foriegn) language. However, if you look at some of the specialist sites for travellers, they may (recomend) good quality (accomodation.)'

'When booking (acommadasion) check yr booking will (difinitely) be held until the hotel (recceives) yr deposit. The transfer of (financail) sums can be difficult and can incur extra (expence) such as bank transfer fees. There/add a substantial sum to the total cost. If it is (possable), it may be more economic to use a credit card.'

Consistency

In this section you will learn about:

- measurement and weights
- time
- percentages

You looked at some areas where consistency is essential in the letters section. Other areas where you need to ensure your work is consistent include:

Measurements/Weights

You can display these in words or figures as long as you keep to the same style. It is worth remembering that it is often easier to read figures as long measurements can become confusing in words. Look at the following example:

Twenty two centimetres multiplied by one metre seven centimetres OR
0.22 m × 1.7 m

It is best to leave a space after the number and before the measurement. For example, 165 mm, 27 ltrs, 121 kg. Use the lower case letter × instead of the word **multiply** or **times**.

Time

You should always follow the draft given in the examination paper to see whether you are going to use the 12 or 24 hour clock. For the 12 hour clock, you will also need to be consistent in the display of hours and hours and minutes.

If you are going to be keying in both hours and hours and minutes the display should have a point (full stop) followed by the two minute figures (or zeros in the case of a full hour). If you are going to key in just hours then you do not need to key in the two zeros, the hour on its own will be sufficient. There should always be a space between the figures and the am/pm indicator. Look at the following examples:

5 pm, 8.30 am, 12 noon, 4.21 pm

For the 24 hour clock you must remember to key in the abbreviated form of hours (hrs) after the figures. There is no point in the 24 hour clock. It is usual to place a zero at the front of single figure times so that the display remains consistent. Look at the following examples:

1500 hrs, 2400 hrs, 0130 hrs, 0620 hrs

Percentages

If you are required to key in percentages you should always follow the draft on the examination paper. In the workplace, you could use any of the following styles:

25%   twenty-five per cent   25 per cent

Remember that if you are keying in other numbers in the same document, then you should use the same style for any percentages.

You should always ensure that you copy the text in your examination paper exactly as shown, otherwise you may lose marks. However, when keying in documents in the workplace you should check for words and figures, etc. before starting to ensure you make your work as consistent as possible.

Exercise 2.21

Key in the following memo ensuring that your work is consistently displayed. Save as Drimmin and print one copy. A correct version of this exercise appears in the worked examples on the CD-ROM.

To   Sandra Lopez

From   Matt Drimmin

Ref   MD/SL

PRIVATE AND CONFIDENTIAL

I have now received the sales figures for last month. They are not particularly good, in fact we are down 14.6% on target for this month. This means that we are now operating at twenty-eight per cent below target for the financial yr. This translates to a drop in profit of around £85,000. Obviously the Board will have to make some far-reaching decisions if we are to stay in business. Job losses may have to occur within the next few weeks. I am enclosing a copy of a confidential report prepared by Jon Champion. This shows possible savings of £24,750 in staff salaries.

We need to meet as soon as possible to discuss these recommendations. I am available on Friday at 11am. Please let me know if this is convenient for you. We will need to go through the recommend Jon has made and develop a plan to take to the next board meeting.

Exercise 2.22

Key in the following memo using the memo template on the CD. Save as **Churston** and print one copy. A correct version of this exercise appears in the worked examples on the CD-ROM.

To   Emily Churston

From   Ian Fisher

Please mark this URGENT

Ref   EC/IF/VEGAN

The proof copies of the new cookery book Vegan Dinner Parties have arrived today. I would be greatful if you could check the attached copy to ensure that all the amendments have been made. you requested

It would be extremely helpful if you could let me have yr comments, together with any final amendments, by the end of next week.

The choice of photographs has now been decided and these have been included in yr copy. Please ensure that they meet yr requirements.

We now need to discus the launch for this book. Please let me know yr availability for a half-day meeting. It would be useful if this could take place within the next two weeks.

Exercise 2.23

Key in the following memo using the memo template on the CD. Save as **Herzog** and print one copy. A correct version of this exercise appears in the worked examples on the CD-ROM.

To Marc Le Bon

From Janine Herzog

The report you submitted regarding the new office layout and refurbishment for Lifestyle Magazine has now been considered by the Board. They were very enthusiastic about yr ideas and have made a small no of suggestions. These have been marked on the report, a copy of which is attached.

Please consider there suggestions and let me have your comments as soon as poss.

You will see that a budget figure has been suggested for the refurbishment. I will need to know if you can complete all the necy work within this budget. If this is not poss, please suggest ways of cutting costs to ensure the final total is not too much higher than the stated amount.

Once agreement has been reached then work may begin. You will need to speak to the contractors regarding a firm start date. I would hope this could be the beginning of June. I look forward to receiving yr comments.

Articles and reports

In this section you will learn about:

- changing line spacing
- adding emphasis
- numbering continuation sheets
- inserting paragraphs

You will also need to key in an article or report. This is straightforward copy typing, but you will need to incorporate various instructions and amendments which are placed throughout the draft.

As well as expanding abbreviations and correcting errors you will also need to be able to do the following:

- Change line spacing from double to single or vice versa
- Emphasise words or sentences
- Use sub or shoulder headings
- Number continuation sheets
- Insert paragraphs of text where indicated

Changing line spacing

You have already looked at setting line spacing on page 9. However if you are changing from single to double (or double to single) there are a few rules to remember.

Exercise 2.24

Key in the following text using single line spacing. The second paragraph only should be keyed in double line spacing. A correct version of this exercise appears in the worked examples on the CD-ROM.

CAT SANCTUARY

Feline Friends is a rescue centre for cats that have been abandoned or abused. We work closely with the RSPCA and often care for cats that they have rescued and need long term care. Our cattery can accept up to fifty cats at any time.

In order to continue with our much-needed service, we need to raise over £25,000 per year. We do not receive any grants from local or central government. To enable us to raise these funds we lease a second-hand goods shop in the centre of the town. This is run purely by volunteers and we rely on the generosity of the public to provide good quality second-hand goods for us to sell.

If you would like to help such a worthy cause and can spare a little of your time, even just an hour each week, we would be delighted to hear from you. Please contact Joyce on 01803 429176 between the hours of 10 am and 5 pm.

Method

1   Key in the first paragraph of text. After you have finished keying in press the **Return** key twice **whilst still in single line spacing** to start the second paragraph.

2   Now click on the **double line spacing** icon ▬

3   Key in the text for the second paragraph. Press return just once – remember you are in double line spacing. Now click on the **single line spacing** icon ▤ and key in the remaining paragraphs.

Note: If you use the above method the space between the paragraphs of text will be roughly equal. If you use any other method the space between the paragraphs will be unequal thus giving an inconsistent appearance.

Emphasis

You may be asked to emphasise a word or sentence. The most usual form of emphasis is to embolden the text. Look at Figure 2.9 which gives examples of common forms of emphasis.

Embolden – This makes the characters darker and slightly thicker. It is the most common form of emphasis.
<u>Underscore</u> or <u>underline</u> – Before computers this was the only form of emphasis. Nowadays it is not used as much as a main form of emphasis but is often used together with bold or italics.
Italic – The letters slope to the right. It is not the most suitable form of emphasis for headings as, unless you use italic and bold together, it does not stand out very well.

Figure 2.9 Common types of emphasis

You can, of course, use more than one type of emphasis at a time. For example, *Italic and Bold* work well together, as does <u>*Italic and Underline*</u>. <u>**Underline and Bold**</u> can also be used, but appears rather heavy on the page.

Exercise 2.25

Using Exercise 2.24, emphasise the text exactly as shown below.

CAT SANCTUARY

<u>Feline Friends</u> is a rescue centre for cats that have been abandoned or abused. We work closely with the **RSPCA** and often care for cats that they have rescued and need long term care. Our cattery can accept up to *fifty* cats at any time.

In order to continue with our much-needed service, we need to raise over *£25,000 per year.* We do not receive any grants from local or central government. To enable us to raise these funds we lease a second-hand goods shop in the centre of the town. This is run purely by volunteers and we rely on the generosity of the public to provide good quality second-hand goods for us to sell.

If you would like to help such a worthy cause and can spare a little of your time, even just an hour each week, we would be delighted to hear from you. Please contact Joyce on **01803 429176** between the hours of 10 am and 5 pm.

Method 1

1   Go to the emphasis icons that appear on the toolbar.

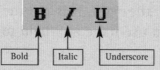

Figure 2.10 Emphasis icons

2   Choose the type of emphasis you wish to use by clicking on the icon.
3   Key in the text you wish to emphasise.
4   Click on the icon again to switch off the emphasis.

Note: You can also use this method after you have keyed in the text. To do this, key in the text, then highlight it. Now, click on the relevant icon and the text will be emphasised.

Method 2

1   Go to **F**ormat on the menu bar. Select **F**ont, and the following sub-menu will appear.

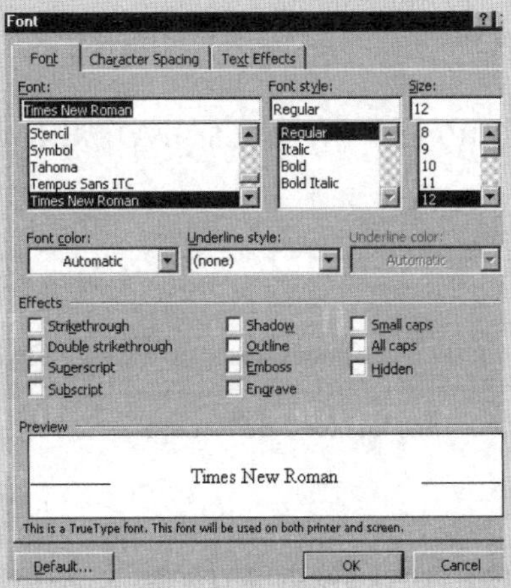

Figure 2.11 Font sub-menu

2   In the **Effects** menu check the appropriate box(es) and click **OK**.

Method 3

1   Hold down the **Ctrl** key and press the relevant emphasis shortcut key – B for **Bold**, **I** for Italic and **U** for Underscore.
2   Key in the text – the text will be automatically emphasised.
3   To switch off the emphasis, hold down the **Ctrl** key and press the relevant shortcut key again. This is known as the **toggle switch**.

Be very careful when emphasising text in the examination that you do not emphasise too much or too little as marks will be lost.

Number continuation sheets

Whenever you use a second page in a letter, memo or article, the second and subsequent pages should always be numbered. Word has an automatic page numbering facility that you can use. The following method is to be used for Exercise 2.26 on page 58.

Method

1   Go to **Insert** and choose **Page Numbers**. The following dialogue box will appear on screen.

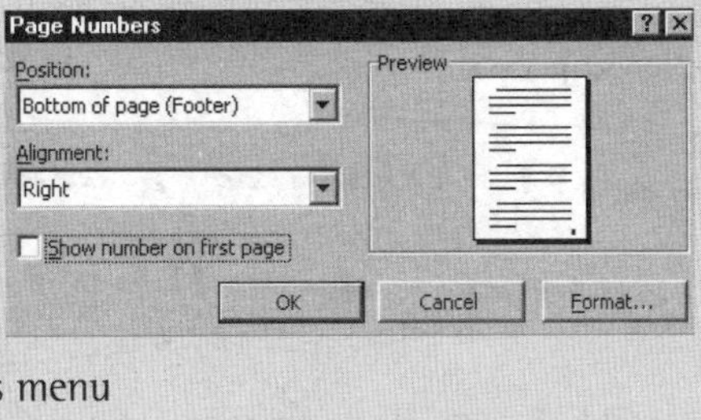

Figure 2.12 Page numbers menu

2   Ensure that the **Show number of first page** box is clear (no tick appears).
3   Check that the page number is set to start at the **Bottom of page (Footer)**. If it is not then click on the arrow to see the various options.
4   Click **OK**.

Exercise 2.26

Key in the following text. Using the methods given above, amend it as indicated. Number the second page.

SAILING HOLIDAYS

For a unique sailing holiday why not try one of our cruises on a gagg-riffed sailing boat. We offer a variety of destinations and our trips last for 7 or 10 days.

During the holiday you can ~~either~~ relax and enjoy the excellent food and wine, making the most of the sun and the sea air. If you are more adventurous you can become an honorary crew member and try your hand at sailing. For the most enthusiastic we offer basic <ins>RYA</ins> qualifications in navigation and seamanship. An interesting and enjoyable way to (develep) your skills.

The (aconodation) cannot be described as luxurious. However the 1 or 2 berth cabins are [well equipped,] [comfortable] and provide plenty of storage space. There are two (Seperate) shower rooms on board.

This paragraph in single linespacing

This year we are offering cruises to the Isles of Scilly, France and Scotland. Our full programme will be published shortly. Please call us to request our latest price list and brochure.

We do not plan an exact itinerary for our trips. Flexibility is one of our charms. We take into account the weather and sailing conditions and plan our journeys as we go. Our promise is that you will enjoy your trip wherever we ~~end up~~ <ins>land</ins>.

If you would like to holiday with a group of friends or family it is possible to charter one of our boats. The prices for these special trips are very ~~reasonable~~ <ins>inexpensive</ins>. You may charter a boat for a ✓ weekend break as well as for longer periods.

These holidays need to be booked a minimum of two months in advance. ← (Emphasize this sentence)

For further information call Penny or Kristian on 024 892 1676. We would be delighted to (disscuss) your requirements with you.

Insert paragraphs of text where indicated

During the examination you will be handed a separate piece of paper containing some handwritten paragraphs of text that must be inserted into the report or article. This will happen between 15 and 30 minutes into the examination.

You must ensure that you enter the extra paragraphs in the correct position otherwise you will lose marks.

Essential English – apostrophes

> **In this section you will learn about:**
> - apostrophes showing possession
> - apostrophes showing omission
> - its/it's
> - your/you're

You are expected to ensure that apostrophes are used correctly in the examination. The rules for learning when to use an apostrophe are simple, but sometimes it can be difficult to see exactly where an apostrophe should be.

Keep in mind there are only two reasons for using an apostrophe – to show possession and to show omission of a letter or letters.

Showing possession

This is often the most difficult to decide. Basically, the apostrophe should be used when the item 'belongs' to something. For example, *the dog's food bowl was empty.* Here the *food bowl* 'belongs' to the dog. Another example would be: *the manager's diary.* You could turn this round and say, *the diary belonging to the manager.*

The only tricky decision to be made is when you are dealing with singular nouns that end in s. For example, if you wanted to say *the bike belonging to James*, where would the apostrophe be?

In this example, you would place the apostrophe at the end of James and then add an s – *James's bike.* However, if applying this rule means that there is a complicated sound, or a double or treble s, then add the apostrophe at the end of the word.

These rules are simple enough, but it does get more complicated when dealing with plurals. For example: *the ladies' coats were stolen from the cloakroom.* Here the coats (plural) belong to the ladies (plural). The apostrophe should be placed at the end of the word ladies.

When looking at possession remember the following:

- If there is only one owner (eg lady, cat, girl, man) then add an **apostrophe + s**.
  For example, lady's, cat's, girl's, man's.
- If there is more than one owner (eg ladies, cats, girls) then just add the **apostrophe**.
  For example, ladies', cats', girls'.

Some words, however, change completely when they move from singular to plural. For example, *child/children, man/men*. Certain words change their endings, for example: *lady/ladies, company/companies*. These will still need an apostrophe if they relate to possession. You should remember the following when dealing with plurals:

- If the plural does not end in 's' add an **apostrophe + s**.
  For example, children's toys, men's overcoats.
- If the plural ends in s, then add the **apostrophe**.
  For example, ladies' handbags, nurses' uniforms.

To show omission

An apostrophe can also be used to shorten certain words, for example *don't, can't wouldn't, you're*. The rule for this is quite simple:

- When showing omission, place the apostrophe at the point where the letters are missing.

This is relatively straightforward, however there are two pairs of words that are often used incorrectly. These are *it/it's* and *your/you're*.

Its/It's

The way to test whether an apostrophe is needed is to see if you can substitute the words 'it is' instead of 'it's'. For example, if you said *It's a lovely day*, it would also make sense to say *It is a lovely day*. However, if you tried this with *the dog has finished its dinner*, then it would not make sense (*the dog has finished it is dinner*), so an apostrophe is not needed.

- If you can substitute the words 'it is' then an apostrophe is required.

Your/You're

These two can cause trouble, but you can think about them in the same way as its/it's. If you can substitute 'you are' in the sentence then an apostrophe is needed. For example, if you said *your hair looks nice today*, substituting *you are* for 'your' would not make sense ('you are hair looks nice today'), but substituting 'you are' for 'you're' in the sentence *you're the first to arrive* would make sense.

- If you can substitute the words 'you are' then an apostrophe is required.

Exercise 2.27

Key in the following article, making the amendments as shown. A correct version of this exercise appears in the worked examples on the CD-ROM.

Use double linespacing except where indicated.

CARING FOR YOUR DOG

Owning a dog can be great fun, but (its) a big (committment.) You need to have spare time, money and energy in order to keep your pet healthy and happy.

The cost of owning a dog must be taken into consideration before you purchase an animal. Firstly, there is the cost of actually buying the dog. Pedigree (animal's) can cost from around two hundred and fifty pounds to £1,000. Rescue centres often charge around £100 to one hundred and fifty pounds for re-homing a dog. This is to cover the cost of any veterinary fees ~~together with day to day living expenses~~

Secondly, you may need to make alterations to your home and/or garden. The (boundary's) of your property must be secure. You may need to purchase new fence panelling or gates. This can prove to be very expensive.

Please emphasise this sentence

The breed of dog you choose will also affect (it's) cost. Generally the larger the dog, the more it will eat. It will also need accessories such as dog leads, collars, grooming equipment etc.

If you own a dog with long hair, then the cost of regular cutting /and grooming must be included in (you're) reckonings. This can cost around £30 per cut and the dog will need grooming every two months or so.

Dont forget that your pet may need medical treatment on a regular basis. As your pet gets older this can be a substantial sum each month. You can purchase specialist pet (ensurance) plans to cover the cost of any treatment. These cost in the region of ten to fifteen pounds each month.

This paragraph only in single linespacing

Exercising the animal must also be taken into consideration. You will need to take your pet for regular walks. Again, depending on the type of breed you choose, this might be a short walk of 15 minutes duration once a day or a longer exercise of an hour or so twice a day.

Once you have decided you can afford to keep a pet then you need to think about (it's) well-being. Dogs do not really enjoy being left ~~at home~~ alone all day. They need companionship and may bark or become destructive if left alone for long periods.

If, however, you do decide to keep a pet dog, you will find it repays you in so many ways. (Youre) never alone, you will be forced to take regular, healthy exercise and you will have a friend for life.

Insert extra paragraph here

One way around this problem is to employ a dog sitter. They will either collect yr dog from home and take it to their own house or will sit with it at yr property. They will also take the dog for a walk for you. This option can be expensive and you must ensure that you find someone who is trustworthy and reliable.

Essential English – errors of agreement

In this section you will learn about:

• errors of agreement

An error of agreement is a grammatical error. For example, if you said 'We is going to the cinema later', then you have made an error of agreement as the subject and verb do not agree.

Look at the following sentence:

The dog are having its tea.

This is obviously incorrect. There is only one dog and therefore the sentence should read *The dog is having its tea.* If there were two or more dogs then the sentence should read *The dogs are having their tea.* This is a very easy example. It becomes more confusing with sentences such as the one below:

The party of tourists are late.

On the surface this may sound correct, but in fact it is wrong. The sentence is referring to only one party of tourists and so the verb is singular. The sentence should read *The party of tourists is late.*

One of the rules to remember is that company titles, and those of books and films etc., are singular because they refer to one item. Therefore when you are writing use the singular verb. Look at the examples below:

McDonald's is a company that sells fast food.
The Rolling Stones is a group that was popular in the sixties.
Marks & Spencer is one of Britain's most popular shops.

However, if you were referring to more than one person then you would use the plural verb. Look at the examples below:

John and Kulvinder are planning a trip to Florence.
Dan and Ben were members of a band in the seventies.

There may well be an error of agreement in the examination paper for you to correct. It will be circled as an error and you must ensure that you amend it.

Exercise 2.28

Key in the following article, making the amendments as shown. A correct version of this exercise appears in the worked examples on the CD-ROM.

Use double linespacing except where indicated

MUSIC BOX

Music Box ~~are~~ pleased to offer a new shopping service on the Internet. Our website www.musicbox.co.uk is now open for ~~business~~. It offers the same great service and prices as our shops but gives the convenience of shopping from home.

This paragraph in single linespacing

The Internet service can provide you with a wide range of CDs, DVDs, and videos. If we ~~haven't~~ got it we can get it! If we do not have your choice in stock, we ~~is~~ able to get any CD, DVD or video within three days from our suppliers.

Ordering from musicbox.co.uk is easy. Just a few clicks and it's done. You can rest assured that our site is safe and secure. If you don't want to use yr credit card over the Internet, then you may order in the usual way, and send us a cheque. We will hold yr order for up to 5 days.

Music Box ~~are~~ the market leader in entertainment retailing. We feel sure that the opps presented by the Internet can only enhance our service to you. Our confidence is such that if you order by the end of January, you can take advantage of our free packing and postage on all orders.

Extra paragraph here

Postage and packing is charged at a very low rate of £1.50 per item. If your order is for £75 or more then packing and postage is free of charge.   Emphasise this sentence

We feel sure you will enjoy using our website. You can order at yr convenience and be assured that our prices are gntd to be lower than our competitors. Our price promise applies to Internet orders. If you can find the item at a lower price than let us know within 3 days of yr order. We will refund the difference immed.

We (beleive) our delivery service (are) second to none. The majority of items are despatched within 24 hours. If we are out of stock of an item then we will send it to you within 5 working days.

Extra paragraph for Exercise 2.28

Checking details to provide information

In this section you will learn about:

- transferring details from one document to another

You may be asked to check details in one of the following ways:

- Transfer information from one task to another, for example a date or a figure.
- Provide a date for a few weeks ahead – you may use a calendar for this task.
- Check the spelling of a word used in a previous task, for example a name or address.

This sounds easy enough, but you must be sure not to make any errors whilst transferring the information. Given below are some hints on how to ensure you can check details successfully.

- Read the instructions very carefully.
- Do not rush to find the information and pick the wrong material. Look carefully at the examination paper and check that you have chosen the correct information.
- Provide only the correct information, not too much or too little.
- Copy the words exactly, paying particular attention to names, dates, times, etc.
- Check that when you have entered the information the work makes sense. If it doesn't, you may find that you have used the wrong information.

Consolidation practice

The following consolidation exercises will help you prepare for the Text Production examination. Try to complete each set of consolidation pieces in the usual time allowed for this examination, that is 1 hour and 15 minutes.

Remember to check your work carefully, and correct any errors before printing. You should print one copy of each document. The key to these exercises can be found in the worked examples on the CD.

Text production consolidation 1

Our ref LF/HB

Ms Holly Burrows
25 Wood Green Rd
WALSALL
WS6 5BU

Dr Ms Burrows

Thank you for yr completed booking form and cheque for £525.
I am pleased to confirm that yr holiday and accommodation is now booked for the
week commencing (give date for last Saturday in August), at
our Pembrokeshire centre.

If possible, please arrive at the Activity Centre between
3.00pm and 6.00pm. If this is (inconvenient) let us
know yr approx time of arrival one week before the
commencement date.   together with an equipment list
A full itinerary of the activities/will be sent to you when
the programme has been finalised.)

(It would be most helpful if you would choose the
activities in which you would like to participate in
advance. You may, of course, change these during
yr holiday.

I hope you have a very enjoyable ~~vacation~~ holiday and look ✓
forward to meeting you.

Yrs sncly

Louise Fabrice
Manager

To Amanda Wilcox

From Louise Fabrice — (Mark this URGENT)

Ref AW/LF

I have just (received) another booking for the last week in August. The booking form is attached. According to our ~~database~~ records ✓ We now have 15 bookings confirmed for the sports activity week. This means there (is) only five places left for this week. (Please ensure the call centre staff are aware of this. All other weeks in August are fully booked.

As we have had so much interest in the centre, we should look at expanding the business. I (beleive) a centre in the south west would be very popular. [I would like you to work on some projections for the new centre. You may assume that the running costs would be approx 25% higher than the costs for this centre. The number of places and course fees would remain the same. Please let me have the figures by the end of next week.

[In the meantime, please ensure the events arranged for the summer programme are now finalised. In particular, I would like you to contact Rudy Jackson, who is offering an archery course. I note from the files that he has not been contacted since our initial conversation last month. If he is now unavailable we must find another instructor as soon as poss.

Once the programme has been finalised let me have a copy. Include contact numbers and names of all instructors and helpers.

Double linespacing except where indicated

ACTIVITY HOLIDAYS

If you are looking for a holiday with a difference, then consider one of our activity holidays. We run a large activity centre in wonderful P_____. The activities we offer are wide ranging and we gntee you will find something to suit your tastes.

All the activities are organised and supervised by fully trained instructors. Safety is paramount and you can rest assured that you will be able to progress at your own speed. Our instructors are used to people who take little exercise throughout the year. They will ensure that your participation in ~~activity~~ the various activities is suited to your general fitness and ability.

You can choose an active week with sports such as abseiling, archery, tennis, badminton, rock climbing and hill walking. Our water activity week will offer you the opp to try canoeing, white water rafting, diving and surfing.

If you prefer to take things a little easier then you could enjoy one of our craft weeks. Here you can learn new crafts such as model making, pottery, jewellery making, batik and glass painting.

Insert the extra paragraphs here.

All our courses are residential. We own a large hotel in beautiful surroundings. The accommodation is luxurious. All rooms have en-suite facilities and there are a number of lounges, bars and restaurants to ensure you enjoy a superb holiday. The hotel grounds are large and take in formal gardens, woods and countryside for you to wander ~~as you like~~ around. The stunning Pembrokeshire coastline is just two miles away and the coastpath runs through the hotel grounds.

Please use single linespacing for these paragraphs only

Our staff are always pleased to help and as they are usually from the surrounding area, can give you plenty of information on places to visit in your free time.

If you would like to receive our brochure, which gives full details of all our holidays, including costs, please contact us.

We would be delighted to discuss your requirements in detail. Our aim is to ensure you have a relaxing and enjoyable time, what ever your interests.

We hope you visit us soon.

Please emphasise this sentence.

Extra paragraphs for Consolidation 1

An interest in history might lead you to are history holidays. These weeks offer you a chance to visit many castles, ancient ruins and stately homes in and around Pembrokeshire. Guest speakers, all renowned experts in their fields, will enthral you with their knowledge of local history.

We also offer courses in cookery, painting and embroidery) These are only available October to March and are three day breaks. Please ask to be included on our mailing list to ensure you receive a copy of our short course brochure.

Full details of these will be published in July.

Text production consolidation 2

Our ref MS/JD

Miss Katy Powner

129 Royal Cr

STAFFORD

STI 8NP

Mark this PRIVATE

Dr Miss Powner

We ~~is~~ pleased to ~~offer~~ invite you to an interview for the three yr Bachelor of Arts course in Media Studies. The interview will take place on give date for first Friday in February at 10.30am.

Please arrive at reception at 10.00am as you will need to complete some forms before yr interview time.

A map and details of how to reach us is enclosed with this letter. You will see we are within easy reach of the bus and train stations. Also enclosed is a list of guest houses reasonably priced in case you require overnight accomodation.

The interviewing panel will be led by Professor John Davies who is Head of Faculty He will be joined by 3 other members of staff from his team. They will wish to ask you about yr predicted A2 grades, yr interests and yr reasons for taking a Media Studies degree. The interview will last approx 45 minutes.

Please confirm you will be attending this interview by telephoning my ~~secretary~~ assistant Paul Box on the above number. ✓

We look forward to meeting you.

Yrs snely

Peta Sollich
Admissions Officer

To   Paul Box

From   Peta Silloch

Ref   PB/PS

Thank you for yr e-mail. I can confirm that the letters to
applicants (has) been posted today. As (disscus) the dates for
the M — S — course interviews are 17 January and
3, 4, 6 and 7 February. The interviews start at 9.30am
and are scheduled to finish at 4.30pm. The last
interviewee will arrive at 3.45pm. [There are 35 interviews
arranged so far.] Perhaps you could let me know how many
more will be required.   At present over 400 people have
                    a place on
applied for / this course. You may like to give me a few
more interview dates.

I have not (recieved) the location of the interviews from
you.   I have therefore asked interviewees to call at
reception in the first instance.   Please let me have the
~~venue~~
~~location~~ as soon as (poss).   ✓

TAKING A DEGREE

Many people now attend university in order to obtain a degree. <u>Most do this to enhance their career prospects.</u> However, a rising number do so for the enjoyment of studying a subject in which they are interested to an advanced level.

If you have reached the end of yr full time education and you are thinking of taking a degree, how do you know which subject to study? It is easy if you have chosen a (definate) career path, such as medicine, law or architecture. If, however, you have not decided on a final plan then choosing a degree course can be difficult. ~~It will require much time and energy~~

If you are in this position, you need to think about the following points. The first is the type of course you wish to take. Most courses are of three years duration and lead to a Bachelor of Arts (BA) or a Bachelor of Science (BSc) qualification.

However, some courses take longer. This will depend on the subject, for example, medicine and law ,or whether there is a placement involved. Some courses offer the opportunity of studying abroad for a year, thus taking the course duration to 4 years.

Use double linespacing except where indicated.

A placement can be a great opp for you to (experience) the world of work before taking on a job. Many placements actually pay you for being (their) — this will help considerably with the cost of being at university. Studying abroad will give you an opp to try living in a different culture.

The second point to consider, and probably the most important, is the subject. If you have a definite career in mind, then this will be easy. If you do not, then consider carefully the

This paragraph in single linespacing

subjects that interest you and start from there. It is important that you do not take a subject that you find uninteresting. It is unlikely you will find it fascinating when studying it in-depth.

Emphasis this sentence

A broader course will probably be of more use to you if you are unsure of your future career. After all, if by the time you finish your degree you have decided upon a career, then you can always specialise by taking a masters degree.

Insert extra paragraphs here

Finally, ask yourself where you would like to study. Do you want to live in a large town or city? It may be that you would like to leave yr home town and live somewhere new. On the other hand, you may wish to stay close to friends and family. Do not forget to take into a/c the cost of living. London, for example, is extremely expensive in terms of accommodation and living expences.

If you make a considered choice before you start your degree course, you are much more likely to succeed.

Remember to take into account other aspects, such as the reputation of the university, its social and recreational facilities, its resources and the quality of its teaching staff.

You must also consider the subjects you have taken at GCSE and AS or A2 level. Each degree course will state the most suitable subjects required for entry, together with an indication of the necy/grades.

Apply to universities where the entry requirements match yr expectations. If a university is asking for several A grades at A2 level, then it is unreasonable to expect them to accept you if yr predicted grades are several C grades.

Extra paragraphs for Consolidation 2

Taking the examination

This section tells you exactly what the examiner will be looking for when marking your work. It does this by showing you the most common errors in documents submitted for the examination, together with hints on how to resolve these errors.

It also includes two examination practice exercises for you to complete to prepare you for the OCR examination.

Document 1

This document requires you to key in a letter. You may need to add a special mark and indicate an enclosure. The current date must be inserted and you should make the various amendments as indicated in the draft. Remember you must use headed paper or a headed template for the letter.

Exercise 2.29

Look at the two letters shown in Figures 2.13 and 2.14. The first is correct, the second contains 8 errors. Can you spot them?

Our ref MR/GH

27 June 2002

Mrs Martina Huckrak
Rose Cottage
Lavender Drive
STAFFORD
ST1 3NK

Dear Mrs Huckrak

Thank you for your recent letter. We have now investigated your complaint and agree that your dishwasher needs replacing. As your appliance is still under guarantee, the replacement will be made free of charge.

We apologise for the inconvenience you have been caused. Our goods are manufactured to the highest standard. All appliances are tested before they leave the factory. Unfortunately we have been unable to locate the fault in your machine. Upon its return to our factory we shall be testing it thoroughly to see if we can locate the cause of the problems you have been experiencing.

Please contact our customer service team on the above number to arrange for delivery of your new appliance.

Yours sincerely

Margaret Burton
Sales Manager

Figure 2.13
Correct version

Our ref MR/GH

6/27/02

Mrs Martina Huckrak
Rose Cottage
Lavender Dr
Stafford
ST1 3NK

Dear Mrs Martina Huckrak

Thank you for your recent letter. We have now investigated your complaint and agree that your dishwasher needs replacing. As your appliance is still under gntee, the replacement will be made free of charge.

We apologise for the inconvenience you have been caused. Our goods are manufactured to the highest standard. All appliances are tested before they leave the factory.

Unfortunately we have been unable to locate the fault in your machine. Upon its return to our factory we shall be testing it thoroughly to see if we can locate the cause of the problems you have been experiencing.

Please contact our customer service team on the above number to arrange for delivery of your new appliance.

Yours Sincerely
Margaret Burton
Sales Manager

Figure 2.14
Incorrect version

Error 1

The date has been inserted in American style, ie, the month, then the day and then the year. This is not acceptable in OCR examinations. The date must be presented in the following order: day, month, year.

Solution

If you have used the **Insert** function, then you will need to change the format of the date through this menu. Go to **Insert,** choose **Date and Time** and then look at the available formats. Ensure that the highlight is on the correct format. It should look like this:

27 June 2003

Note that there is no punctuation included. Once you have selected the correct format then click OK to close the menu box. You may like to make the English format your default – that means that the date will always be formatted in the chosen style. To do this, after highlighting the correct date, choose **Default** (06/27/2003). A box will appear asking you to confirm your choice. Click on **Yes.** Then click **OK** to leave the menu.

Error 2

The abbreviation Dr has been left in the address block.

Solution

You must check your work to ensure that all abbreviations have been expanded. Make sure you learn all the abbreviations given on page 37.

Error 3

The postal town (Stafford) has been keyed in with an initial capital. All post towns must be keyed in using blocked capitals as in Figure 2.13.

Solution

Ensure you follow draft very carefully. Proof-read before you print your work.

Error 4

The salutation contains the name Martina.

Solution

Key in text exactly as it is shown on the examination paper (apart from abbreviations and spelling errors). Examination papers usually set out the salutation as 'Dear Mrs Huckrak' or 'Dear Mr Cowan' and leave out the first name, although it almost always appears in the address block.

Error 5

The abbreviation gntee has been left in the main text.

Solution

Run the spellchecker to ensure that abbreviations are picked up. This should also help find any spelling or typographical errors that may have been made. You should also ensure that you proof-read your work very carefully.

Error 6

An extra paragraph has been made.

Solution

You must ensure that the paragraphs are exactly the same as the draft. Even if you think the paragraphing of a document is poor or incorrect, at this level you are not expected to insert your own.

Error 7

There is a capital S in sincerely. This is a very common error.

Solution

Again, follow draft for capitalisation. Unless a deliberate error (which will be circled at Level 2) has been made – for example, a lower case letter beginning a sentence – you will not be penalised for following the draft with regard to capital letters.

Error 8

There is no clear space between Yours sincerely and Margaret Burton. This will be penalised in the examination.

Solution

You must ensure that you leave at least one clear line space between the complimentary close and the name. If you haven't enough space left to leave the usual 5 spaces, it is acceptable to leave just one clear line space. If you still haven't got enough room, then you could always adjust the bottom margin of the page to allow one space, or change the size of the font. The best solution is to use a continuation sheet, details of which are given on page 32.

Document 2

This document requires you to key in a memo. A memo template must be used, or you should set out the memo as shown on page 43. You may need to add a special mark and indicate an enclosure. The current date must be inserted and you should make the various amendments as indicated in the draft.

Exercise 2.30

Look at the two memos shown in Figures 2.15 and 2.16. The first is correct, the second contains 6 errors. Can you spot them?

To	John Richburn
From	Terry McDonald
Ref	JR/TM
Date	1 March 2003

URGENT

Please ensure that all staff are aware of the changes to the car parking arrangements. These take effect from the 4 March at 9.30 am.

Staff should apply for their new parking permit by 5 pm tomorrow. Janine will process the permits in time for the new arrangements. I attach an application form for the permits. Please photocopy these as required.

We will allow a few days for the changes to be implemented. From the 10 March, cars parked incorrectly will be clamped.

Enc

Figure 2.15 Correct version

To   John Richburn

From   Terry McDonald

Ref   JR/TM/SS

Date   1 March 2003

Urgent

Please ensure that all staff are aware of the changes to the car parking arrangements. These take effect from the 4 March at 0930 hrs. Staff should apply for their new parking permit by 5 pm tomorrow. Janine will process the permits in time for the new arrangements. I attach an application form for the permits. Please photocopy these as required.

We will allow a few days for the changes to be implemented. From the 10 March, cars parked incorrectly will be clamped.

JR

Figure 2.16 Incorrect version

Error 1

The candidate's initials have been added to the reference. This will incur a penalty in the examination.

Solution

As with all text processing documents, do not add anything to the examination documents, except for the date and an enclosure indicator, if required.

Error 2

The special mark has been keyed in using initial capitals and underscore. This would incur a fault in the examination. This is a very common error.

Solution

You must ensure that you follow the instructions very carefully.

Error 3

Two paragraphs have been merged into one.

Solution

Follow draft carefully to ensure that your paragraphing is exactly the same as the draft.

Error 4

There is an inconsistency of display with the times. One is displayed as the 24 hour clock, the other as the 12 hour clock.

Solution

Check your work very carefully. It is worth spending a few minutes reading through the document before you start, marking on the paper any alterations you need to make and areas of consistency.

Error 5

The candidate has added a closure to the memo (JR). This is not necessary and would incur a penalty in the examination.

Solution

Key in only the text required.

Error 6

The enclosure has not been indicated.

Solution

You must ensure that all enclosures are indicated at the bottom of the text. If you read through the text before you start keying it in, then you will spot that an enclosure needs to be indicated. Write this on the examination paper to remind you.

Document 3

This document requires you to key in an article. You will be expected to keep the layout consistent and to amend the text as indicated. Extra paragraphs of text will be handed to you during the course of the examination and these must be inserted where indicated. A continuation sheet will be required and this must be numbered correctly.

Exercise 2.31

Look at the two articles shown in Figures 2.17 and 2.18. The first is correct, the second has 9 errors. Can you spot them?

STATIONERY OFFERS

Our January Sale has begun and as usual we have reduced hundreds of prices around the store. You will find colour inkjet printers at an amazing price of £55. That's £40 off the recommended retail price. Our own-brand scanners now start at just £35.

Our best-quality laser paper is now a fantastic £3.50 per ream. **Buy 5 reams and get one free!** Premium copy paper is on sale at just £2.20 per ream. But hurry, this price cannot be held for long.

We also have some fantastic deals on office furniture. Our Apollo range has been reduced by 35% on all items. This means a two drawer, under-desk filing cabinet is now £55.00. A 1.8 metre desk is a very low £150. The Apollo range has been extremely popular with our clients and is styled in a beech effect finish.

Office software prices have been slashed. Buy a DTP package and a Webdesign package for only £150. Office organiser programs have been reduced to just £24.99. Software manuals have been reduced by 50%.

Hurry, these offers can't last long!

Figure 2.17 Correct version

STATIONARY OFFERS

Our January Sale has begun and as usual we have reduced hundreds of prices around the store.

You will find colour inkjet printers at an amazing price of £55. That's £40 off the recommended retail price. Our own-brand scanners now start at just £35.

Our best-quality laser paper is now £3.50 per ream. **Buy 5 reams and get one free! Premium copy paper is on sale at just £2.20 per ream.**

We also have some fantastic deals on office furniture. Our Apollo range has been reduced by 35% on all items. This means a under-desk, two drawer, filing cabinet is now £55.00. A 1.8 metre desk is a very low £150. The Apollo range has been extremely popular with our clients and is styled in a maple effect finish.

Hurry, these offers can't last long!

Figure 2.18 Incorrect version

Error 1

The word 'Stationery' has been spelt incorrectly in the title.

Solution

Remember, do not rely on the spellchecker to correct all your errors. The spelling 'stationary' is, of course, a real spelling (if you are talking about stationary vehicles, etc.). The spellchecker will not, therefore, pick this up.

Error 2

The first and second paragraphs should have been run together to form one paragraph.

Solution

Check your work very carefully. If necessary, use a pen or pencil to mark off the corrections as you complete them.

Error 3

Two words 'a fantastic' have been left out of the first sentence of the paragraph beginning 'Our best-quality'. This may be due to a circled insertion.

Solution

You must ensure that all circled instructions are dealt with. Proof-reading and marking off amendments as you go will solve these problems.

Error 4

The emphasis has been extended to the last sentence of the paragraph.

Solution

You must ensure that you emphasise only the necessary parts of an article. Again, you will need to proof-read your work carefully to ensure that the emphasis is as requested. If possible, print your first draft (if your centre allows this) as it is often easier to see errors on the printed copy than on screen. If you need to move any of the text around after you have completed the emphasis then check your text again. Sometimes, you can inadvertently 'hit' a bold or underscore code out of place without realising it.

Error 5

The final sentence of the second paragraph is missing.

Solution

Proof-reading will solve this. You must make sure that any text insertions are correctly placed. Don't forget the instructions can be dotted all over the page. Work through the paper methodically, from top to bottom.

Error 6

The instruction to change a paragraph to single line spacing has been ignored.

Solution

Again, this comes down to checking. Do be aware though, that this is a very common error, as is failure to change back to double line spacing.

Error 7

The transposition of words in the third sentence of the third paragraph has not been completed.

Solution

Ensure that you are completely familiar with the meaning of various correction signs. See page 40. Proof-reading is obviously essential.

Error 8

The last sentence of the third paragraph says the finish is maple and not beech as in Figure 2.17. Did you spot this one?

Solution

Proof-reading, checking amendments have been completed.

Error 9

A whole paragraph is missing. This may have been the extra text that is given out around 15–30 minutes into the examination time.

Solution

You must place the extra piece of the exam paper somewhere you will see it. Your invigilator will probably place the extra sheet on the desk next to you. It is possible that whilst you are moving paper and things around, it could get buried under a pile of paper. The examination paper does ask you to insert the extra paragraphs, but this is easily forgotten. It might be helpful if, when you are given the extra sheet, you place it inside the examination paper at the correct point, ie where document 3 is printed. This should jog your memory.

Examination practice

To help you prepare for the examination, two full examination papers follow. Try to complete these in exam conditions. That is, finish in the 1 hour and 15 minutes allowed, including printing. Do not ask for help or refer to the methods given in this book for information on how to do things. Try not to talk to anyone whilst working on these tasks. If you can do all of these then your work will give you a good indication of whether you are ready to sit the real exam. Once you have completed the tasks, you can check your documents with the worked examples on the CD.

When you are working through these exercises you will need to remember the following:

* Ensure you have corrected any deliberate errors including errors of agreement.
* If you are unsure of a spelling that has been circled as incorrect, use a dictionary

as well as the spellchecker.

- Remember to spellcheck your work after you have finished each document.
- Consistency is very important. Make sure that all your work, including spacing between paragraphs, numbers, etc. shows a consistent display.
- Enclosures must be indicated and continuation sheets numbered.
- When checking details from one document to another, you must ensure the details you key in are absolutely correct.
- Once you have finished keying in the text for a document, check with the exam paper that you have not keyed in the same word or line twice, and that you have not missed a word or line. These are very common errors and can lose you a large number of marks.

If you can complete all the work within the time without too many errors then you should now try working on some old examination papers. These will give you a feel for the type of examination paper you are likely to face. You must not become too complacent, even if you are consistently doing well in practice papers, as the examination itself can make you nervous and this is when it is easy to make mistakes.

The key to success in the examination is proof-reading your work carefully, referring back to the examination paper to check that you have keyed in the correct words, not the ones you think are there or should be there!

Examination practice 1

Our ref EM/LM

Miss Emma Kennedy
Flat 2b
Phoenix Ct
Priorfields Rd
BLACKPOOL
BL6 4AQ

Dr Miss Kennedy

Thank you for yr e-mail enquiry regarding our wedding ~~planner~~ co-ordinator ✓
Services. We enclose an info sheet giving details on how
we can help plan yr special day.

Our buisness has been established for 5 yrs. We has helped
many happy couples organise their wedding to ensure it is a
day to remember.

Whether you know what you want for yr wedding, or you
simply do not know where to start, we can help. Our
services range from planning the entire event or just
providing some of those important extra touches. We are
confident

If you would like to know more then please contact us. We
can then arrange a meeting to discuss the service you
require in more detail.

The cost of our services will obviously depend on the amount of
involvement from are co. As a rough guide, however, if we
was to organise the entire event, the cost would be approx
10% of yr proposed spend.

Yrs sncly
Laura Millard
    Director

To   Marcus Redwood

From   Laura Millard

Ref   LM/MR

Mark this
PRIVATE AND CONFIDENTIAL

I ~~has~~ been looking at our ~~diary's~~ for the next quarter and am concerned at how much work we have taken on. It is good to see the co has plenty of business but we must be able to deliver the highest poss quality / of service to our customers. I wonder whether we will be able to do this with our current level of commitments.

It seems to me that we must employ another member of staff. Emily works extremely hard keeping the office running smoothly. I feel that one solution to our problem is to employ an experienced office administrator to assist with the ~~administration~~ papenwork. // We can then start training Emily to join us in handling alcs. This would also ensure the office still runs efficiently. I am sure Emily would make a very competent wedding co-ordinator.

I would like you to consider this proposal and let me have yr thoughts by (give date for Monday of next week).

Typist/operator: this is the memorandum

She is also able to handle ~~clents~~ very well.

WEDDING SERVICES **Key in using double linespacing except where indicated.**

Once you have decided to get married the focus then becomes the actual wedding. The org of the day can be tremendous fun, but it can also be stressful and time consuming. After all, you do not want any thing to spoil your special day.

A wedding co-ordinator can help remove some of the anxiety. You still have the excitement of making all the decisions. The hard work is taken out of yr hands. We pride ourselves on our attension to detail. Our experence in organising weddings can help enhance yrs.

Insert extra paragraphs here.

This paragraph in single linespacing →

If you would like a themed wedding then give tell us your ideas. We will often be able to assist you in researching your theme. Our expierence can prove invaluable in tracking down unusual items from clothes to vintage cars. Some of our recent themed weddings include a medieval banquet, a fifties rock and roll wedding and an Edwardian theme.

We do not have to plan yr entire wedding for you. It may be that you would just like some help with hiring a good photographer or finding unusual wedding stationery. This is fine with us. We can help with some or all of the arrangements.

One of the first and most important things we help you with is setting yr budget. You do not need to spend a vast amount of money in order to be able to afford our Services. We can save you money in several ways.

Firstly, by helping you keep to your budget. Secondly, our experience means we have built up a great many useful contacts over the years. These are often trade only or wholesale outlets which can mean great savings to you on items such as sta4tionery and table decorations.

We may be able to save you money on items such as flowers and hired cars. As we often recomend carefully selected suppliers, they often give extra discounts to our customer's. The savings on these items alone can run into hundreds of pounds.

Your dream wedding is only a phone call away. Call us on 01308 182882 and let us help you make your dreams come true.

As a rough guide, if we ⬭was⬭ to plan the entire event on yr behalf, we anticipate the cost would be approx ——— % of yr proposed spend.

It can be surprisingly inexpensive to hire our services. The cost of hiring a wedding co- ✓
ordinator ~~should~~ will easily be offset against the savings and discounts you will receive. ⬭Dont⬭
forget the savings in time and stress. It can take many hours to book all the various
components of your wedding. Add on several days for looking through cats and shopping,
trying to find exactly what you want. We have access to a whole range of ↗specialist⬃suppliers, saving
you time and money.

At our first consultation we will ~~find out~~ ^ascertain^ the type of Wedding you would like. If you are unsure we will ⬭discuss⬭ yr likes + dislikes. Once we know a little more about you, we can give you some ideas to build upon.

If you have a firm idea of how yr day should be then we can begin making the arrangements. We will do everything, including booking the ceremony.

Emphasis this sentence

Extra paragraphs for Exam Practice

Examination practice 2

Our ref AC/CC/ST

Mrs Alison Carter
Crystal Co Ltd
Avon Park Rd
BRISTOL
BS19 6JG

Please mark this
CONFIDENTIAL

Dr Mrs Carter

Thank you for meeting with us last week. I am sure you will agree it (were) a very productive meeting.

We have now looked at the figures and we feel that we can produce a website within the budget you mentioned.

The website will be fully interactive with an on-line shopping facility. It will have an initial capacity of 150 products.

approach

You will need to ~~speak to~~ yr credit card co in order to ✓ arrange for cards to be accepted over the Internet. There may be a (Seperate) charge for this service.

As discussed, more can be added at a later date.

If you would like to go ahead with the website please contact us by (give date for 1st Monday of next month.) We will then arrange another meeting with you and yr IT staff.

This will be to (discuse) the final content of the site. It should be (possable) to have the website on-line in time for the Christmas season. We (beleive) this is yr preferred launch date.

If you would like to discuss this proposal further, please do not hesitate to contact us.

We look forward to hearing from you.

Yrs sncly

Simon Taylor
Sales Manager

From   Simon Taylor
To   Martha Cross
Ref   CC/ST

Typist/Operator: this is
the memorandum

Please find attached a copy of a letter I (has) sent to Mrs C___ of the Crystal Co Ltd. We met at her offices last week.

I very much hope that the co will accept our ~~terms~~ proposal as this would be an interesting site to design. You will remember that the co plans to start the site with approx 150 products.

As we have a number of/new projects beginning at the end of the month, I feel we should make a start on the design of this website. // I (beleeve) that yr workload is not (to) heavy at the moment. I would be grateful if you could let me have 2 or 3 draft pages that we could use as a starting point.

Obviously, you will not be able to produce detailed pages. As the customer has a firm deadline for the launch of the site, it would be helpful if we could at least have an outline drafted. This would then speed up the process of building the site once we have the product info.

Let me know if there are any problems or if this request causes you any (inconveneince).

Web Design ← ⟨Emphasise this heading⟩

⟨Use double linespacing except where indicated⟩

The Internet is fast becoming an important medium for all businesses, small or large. The wealth of opp to promote your buisiness and sell products and services to people all over the world should not be missed.

⟨Insert extra paragraphs here⟩

If you are thinking of having yr own website, there (is) a few things to be considered. The first is the type of site yr (busness) requires. Do you want to sell goods over the Internet? If so, you will need to build an e-commerce site. That is, one which allows (Customers') to order on-line and pay by credit card. There is no personal interaction between the customer and the co. The transaction is |electronically| |completed.|

more expensive

Although this is an efficient way to run a business, the start up costs are obviously greater. The order processing section of the site requires more complex programming.

⟨This paragraph in single linespacing⟩

However, as long as the design is fairly simple, it should be affordable by the majority of (company's.) If you do not need this facility then the cost of the website should be very reasonable.

A presence on the web will almost gntee you an increase in business and a large number of new customers. It is probably the most cost-effective method of advertising around today.

The site should also allow you to update it quickly and easily on yr own pc. There is no point in having a site that is static for yrs on end. You should treat it in the same way as other advert methods. Frequent visitors to yr site will expect to see changes on a regular basis. If you cannot update yr site yourself, then you will incur a lot of unnecessary expense.

You should update yr site as regularly as poss.

When discussing your new site, remember that it should be compatible with the rest of your company image. Use your corp22orate colours and logo wherever posseble. Ask your designer to produce a number of different designs before you make your final choice selection.

People of all ages enjoy surfing the net. It has taken the drudgery out of shopping.

A few minutes spent looking for the best buy on the Internet can save literally pounds. As well as saving money, the Internet is an ideal market place for those looking for something different. People who live in rural areas can now shop with the same enthusiasm + opp as those who live in major cities.

difficult

Having a website built is not as ~~complicated~~ as you ✓ might think. There are any number of small firms who specialise in developloping web sites for businesses and co's of all types and sizes. The cost of having a bespoke website has fallen dramatically in the passed few yrs. This is because the software used for designing sites has become increasingly simple + user-friendly.

Extra paragraphs for
Exam Practie 2

Word processing

The Level 2 Word Processing (Intermediate) examination consists of four documents, three of which you recall from the computer or disk. The four documents are:

1 An article or report
2 A notice for display
3 A four column table with subdivisions and multi-line headings
4 A standard document, either a letter or memo, which requires stored phrases to be inserted.

One or more of the documents will contain lists of information which will need to be sorted either alphabetically, numerically or chronologically.

You are allowed 1 hour and 45 minutes in which to complete the examination.

You will be asked to demonstrate a number of skills, by using the keyboard and your knowledge and application of English. Each of the three tasks will contain one or more of the following:

- Emphasis of headings
- Amendments using correction signs
- Information to be transferred from one document to another
- Information which must be keyed in using a consistent format
- A continuation sheet
- Changing the alignment of the text, the line spacing and the line length
- Copying and moving information
- Displaying information in tabular format
- Allocating space
- Inserting headers and/or footers.

In this section you will learn about the following:

- Multi-page articles or reports
- Notice for display
- Four column table
- Standard document
- Consolidation practice
- Taking the examination

Multi-page article or report

This is slightly different to the article contained in the Text Production examination as the majority of the text is already keyed in and saved to disk. Your task is to amend the text as indicated on the examination paper, including keying in more text. The type of amendments you will be expected to make are as follows:

- Adjust the line length of the document.
- Change the text alignment. Information on text alignment can be found on page 21.
- Change the line spacing from single to double or vice versa. Instructions for this can be found on page 9.
- Emphasise a sentence or sentences. Information regarding emphasis can be found on page 55.
- Move text from where it is shown on the examination paper to a new location.
- Copy text to a different location.
- Number a continuation sheet. This has been covered on page 57.
- Use the Search/Replace facility.
- Inset text from margins.
- Insert a header and/or footer.

Adjusting the line length

You will be required to recall a document from a disk, file or CD and change the margins to a specified line length. It is very important that you remember to change all the text contained within the document and that text you add to the document is also at the new line length.

Exercise 3.1

Recall the document called Exercise 3.1 from the CD-ROM and change the line length to 16 cm.

Method

1   Check that the measurements for your document are in centimetres (cm). To do this go to **Tools** and choose **Options**. Click on the **General** tab and the following menu will appear (see Figure 3.1).

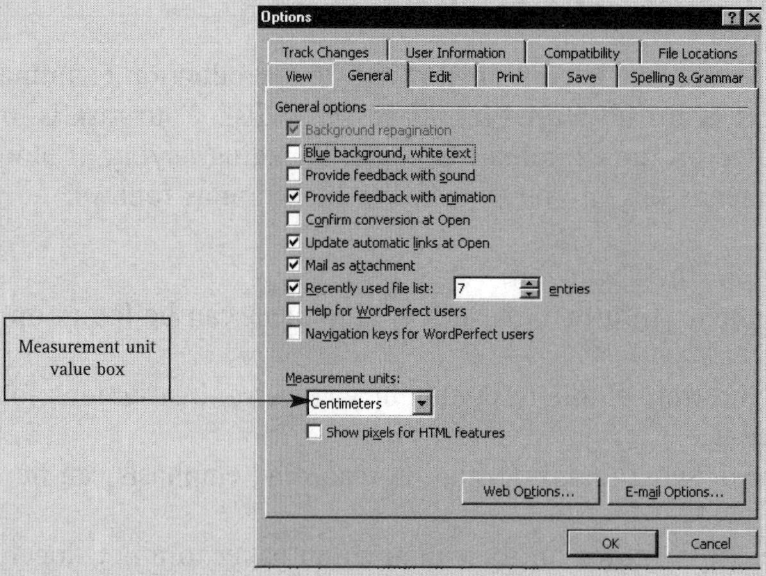

Figure 3.1 Options menu

2   Check that the value in the **Measurement units** box is set to centimetres. If it
    is not, then using the drop down to the right-hand side, change the value.
    Click **OK**.
3   Now go to **File** and choose **Page Setup**. The following menu will appear (see
    Figure 3.2):

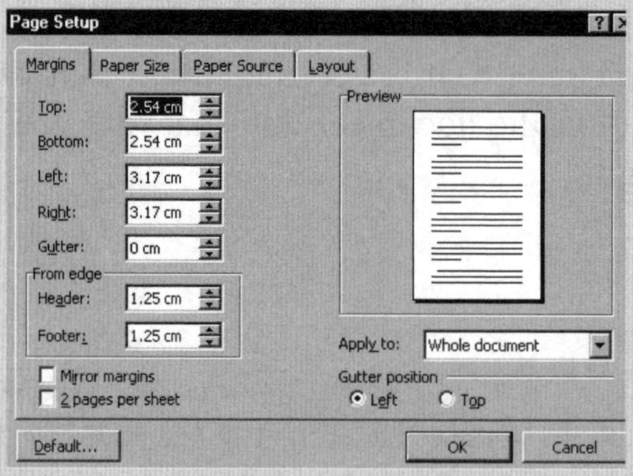

Figure 3.2 Page Setup menu

4   You need to change the Left and Right margins to allow a 16 cm text line. To
    do this, you need to make a calculation.

    The page width for a piece of A4 paper, portrait style is 21 cm. If you forget
    this, then click on the **Paper Size** tab and the size will be displayed. You need
    a 16 cm line so subtract 16 from 21. This gives you 5, so your total left and
    right margins must equal 5 cm. Divide 5 by 2 to get equal margins and you
    are left with 2.5 cm. Key in 2.5 cm in both the **Left** and **Right** margin value
    boxes.

5   When you are sure you have entered the correct figures click **OK**.
6   Save the document as Exercise 3.1 on your disk or hard drive.

NOTE
It is tempting to bypass this method and alter the margins manually on the ruler bar. It is much better in the long run to alter the margins correctly as sometimes the markers move when adjusted manually and you may find that one or more of your paragraphs have reverted to the original size.

Using this method also means that the headers and footers are automatically placed within the new margins and you do not have to move them manually, which can be rather fiddly and time-consuming.

Moving text

The important thing to remember when you are moving text is that the block of text should only appear ONCE in the document. This means that the text should be taken from one location and placed in a different location.

Exercise 3.2

Recall the document you have saved as Exercise 3.1 from the CD-ROM. Move the paragraph that begins 'The harbour itself ...' so that it becomes the third paragraph of the document.

Method 1

1   Highlight the entire paragraph by treble clicking on the text.
2   Hold down the **Ctrl** key and press **X**. The text should disappear.
3   Move to the correct new location and click so that the cursor is flashing.
4   Hold down the **Ctrl** key and press **V**. The text should now appear.
5   Ensure that there is a clear line space above and below the moved paragraph.

OR

Method 2

1   Highlight the entire paragraph by treble clicking on the text.
2   Go to **Edit** and choose **Cut**. The text should disappear.
3   Move to the correct new location and click so that the cursor is flashing.
4   Go to **Edit** and choose **Paste**. The text should now appear.
5   Ensure that there is a clear line space above and below the moved paragraph.

Copying text

The difference between copying and moving text is that the text must appear in two separate places – the original location and the new specified location.

Exercise 3.3

Continue using the document Exercise 3.1. Copy the first paragraph to the end of the document.

Method 1

1   Highlight the entire paragraph by treble clicking on the text.
2   Hold down the **Ctrl** key and press **C**.
3   Move to the correct new location and click so that the cursor is flashing.
4   Hold down the **Ctrl** key and press **V**. The text should now appear.
5   Ensure that there is a clear line space above and below the moved paragraph.

OR

Method 2

1   Highlight the entire paragraph by treble clicking on the text.
2   Go to **Edit** and choose **Copy**.
3   Move to the correct new location and click so that the cursor is flashing.
4   Go to **Edit** and choose **Paste**. The text should now appear.
5   Ensure that there is a clear line space above and below the moved paragraph.

Use the Search/Replace facility

Microsoft Word has a useful search and replace facility which will find a specified word within a document and replace it with another specified word. For example, if you want to replace the word 'teacher' with the word 'lecturer' throughout a document, then you can set up the search and replace facility to do this for you. Although it may seem easier to do this manually, using search and replace will ensure that you do not miss any words that need changing.

Exercise 3.4

Continue using the document Exercise 3.1. Change the word '**city**' to the word '**town**' using the method shown below.

Method

1   Go to **Edit** on the toolbar and choose **Find**. The following menu will appear (see Figure 3.3).

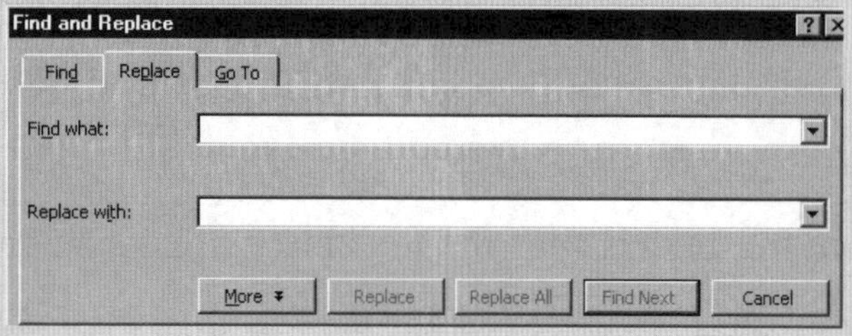

Figure 3.3 Find and Replace menu

2   Click on the **Replace** tab and key in the word you wish to change in the **Find** what box.

3   Now click on the **Replace with** box and key in the new word. Key this in the exact format that it should be seen in the text.
4   Now click on the **Find Next** button. This will take you to the first instance in the document of the word you want to change. If you are sure you wish to change the word highlighted, click on **Replace**. If you do not want to change the word, click **Cancel**. However, if you do this then the menu will close.
5   When you have made your choice, click on **Find Next** again. This will find the next instance. Repeat these steps until the find and replace has finished.

Note: You may use the **Replace All** button that will immediately change all instances of the word to be changed in one go. However, it is recommended that you use the method given above to ensure that only the word(s) you wish to change are replaced.

Inset text from margins

Insetting text from margins means that the text is indented either from the left or both margins. This is often used to make a display feature. Look at Figure 3.4 below.

> This text has been inset 2 cm from both margins and makes a display feature. By insetting the margins correctly the text will remain in neat lines. If you do not use the given method but use the Tab key, you may find there are problems if you have to amend the text at a later stage.

Figure 3.4 Inset text

Exercise 3.5

Continue using the document Exercise 3.1. Inset the paragraph beginning 'Just outside of Brixham .....' by 2 cm from both margins.

Method 1

1   Highlight the text you wish to insert.
2   Go to **Format** and choose **Paragraph**. The following menu will appear.

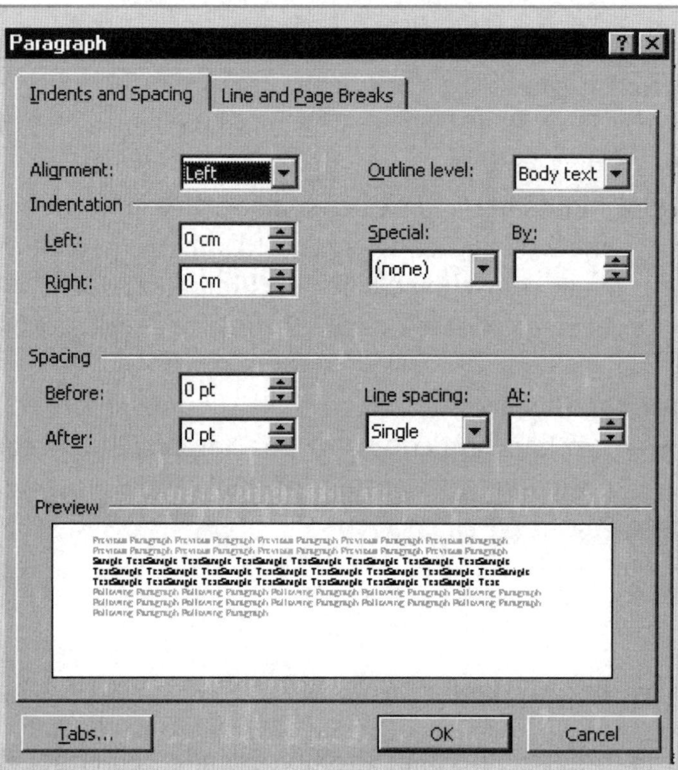

Figure 3.5 Paragraph menu

3   Make sure the **Indents and Spacing** tab is uppermost.
4   In the **Left** value box key in the amount of cm you wish to indent. In this
    instance it will be 2 cm.
5   Repeat this for the **Right** indent.
6   When you are sure you have completed the boxes correctly, click **OK**.

Note: This is the much safer way of indenting text, as if you make any changes or
move paragraphs of text the indent will remain in place.

Method 2

1   Highlight the text you wish to inset.
2   Go to the **ruler bar** at the top of the screen and move the left-hand margin
    markers 2 cm along the scale (see Figure 3.6).

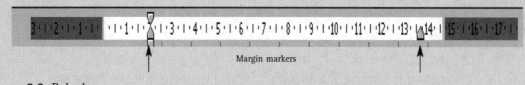

Margin markers

Figure 3.6 Ruler bar

3   Now move the right-hand marker 2 cm across from the current margin. The
    text will now be indented 2 cm from both margins.

Headers and footers

You will be asked to insert a header and/or a footer into the article or report. Headers and footers are items that are printed outside of the top and/or bottom margins and appear on every page. To set up headers and footers you need only key in the text once and they will appear on each page automatically.

Exercise 3.6

Continue using the document Exercise 3.1. Set a header and footer as given below:

Header – to appear at the left-hand margin   Your Name
Footer – to appear in the centre of the page   Page Number

Method

1   Go to **View** and choose **Header and Footer.** The header and footer boxes will appear on screen together with the **Header and Footer** toolbar. The header box will appear at the top of the page, the footer will appear at the bottom of the page (see Figure 3.7).

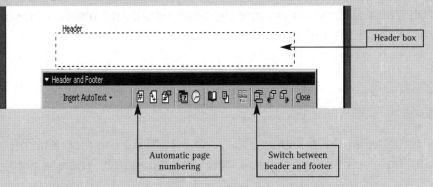

Figure 3.7 Header and Footer menu

2   Key in the text in the position given above. If you need to emphasise the text in any way then use the emphasis icons as usual.
3   When you are sure the header is correct, click on the **Switch between header and footer** icon. You will be taken to the footer box.
4   To get to the centre of the footer, click on the centre alignment icon on the main toolbar.
5   To insert automatic page numbering click on the **Automatic Page Numbering** icon.
6   When you are sure you have entered the header and footer correctly, click on **Close.**

Amending text

You will need to make various amendments to the text. These include: inserting extra text; deleting text; emphasising text and inserting or deleting page.

- When you are inserting text, make sure that you insert it in the correct position, being especially careful to place text within the punctuation if necessary. For example, if you were to add a few words to a sentence, then you must ensure that the full stop is still at the end of the sentence.
- If you are asked to delete text then ensure you only delete the specified text together with any related punctuation. Again, you will need to be very careful when deleting punctuation.
- Be very careful when inserting or deleting paragraph breaks. It can be very easy to insert an extra line space when you are making these changes. Check your work very carefully after you have finished.
- It might be a good idea to tick off the amendments on the examination paper once you have made them. It will be more difficult to forget any changes if you do this.

Inserting and deleting page breaks

The articles you will amend for the examination will have at least one page break inserted. You will have to change the page break and insert a new one. The easiest way to do this is as follows:

Exercise 3.7

Continue using the document Exercise 3.1. Make the amendments as shown, including inserting a page break after the paragraph 'There is plenty to see and do ...'

Method

1 Bring up the 'hidden' codes by pressing the **Show/Hide** icon which should be on your toolbar. ¶
2 Depending on how the file has been constructed you will either see a line space mark ¶ or the words 'page break'. To **Delete**, highlight the mark or words and press **Delete**.
3 To insert a page break, hold down **Ctrl** and press **Return**. A new page break will be inserted.

Make the rest of the amendments as shown and use double line spacing, except where indicated, and a justified right-hand margin. Save as Exercise 3.7 and print one copy. A correct version of this exercise is found in the worked examples on the CD-ROM.

BRIXHAM

Brixham makes an ideal holiday location as there is plenty to see and do. The coastline is spectacular, the climate is mild. You can be assured of a great holiday whatever your age and interests.

This picturesque fishing port is situated on the southern shore of Torbay - regarded by many as Britain's finest sailing waters.

The coastline is spectacular with a number of beautiful ~~day anchorages with~~ coves and beaches. Fishcombe Cove, Elberry Cove and Meadfoot Cove are particularly secluded and well worth a visit. If you prefer, Torquay is directly across the bay. ~~It has its own marina which provides short-stay berths free of charge.~~ Here, you will find plenty of cafes, bars and restaurants, where you can enjoy a delicious meal or snack.

The marina is conveniently located on the harbour quayside of the city. It is particularly sheltered from the south-westerly gales and offers safe access in all weather and tide conditions. The facilities provided at the marina are excellent.

This paragraph in single line spacing

There is plenty to do in and around Brixham. The Berry Head Country Park is a must. With its fabulous views across the bay and out to sea, the rugged coastline provides a fascinating backdrop to the Napoleonic fort. The Country Park also boasts superb woods and countryside and is the home to rare fauna and flora. Britain's smallest lighthouse is also situated in the Country Park.

interesting

The quaint city of Brixham is very ~~relaxing~~. The brightly coloured houses situated around the harbourside provides an interesting contrast to the boats berthed on the marina. There is a replica of the Golden Hind in the harbour and there is always something interesting happening on the quayside. Although the city centre is small, you can spend a few hours wandering around the wide variety of shops. ✓

The harbour itself has a rich history. It was in the early nineteenth century that yachtsmen first discovered the many advantages of this sheltered spot. It was a favourite haunt for smugglers in days gone by.

LLYFRGELL COLEG MENAI LIBRARY

There are several beaches and coves close by. Shoalstone beach, a shingle beach, can be found by the breakwater. A seawater swimming pool is open from July to September. Fishcombe Cove is just a 10 minute walk from the city centre. Sandy beaches such as Goodrington Sands and Broadsands can be found just a few miles from Brixham.

Just outside of Brixham you can find Paignton Zoo and Botanical Gardens. This is well worth a visit. Other attractions in Paignton include the pier, which has traditional seaside amusements and the Paignton to Kingswear steam railway. The railway has authentic steam trains and runs a regular service during the summer months to Kingswear. The trains follow the coastline and the scenery is spectacular.

From Kingswear you can ~~take~~ board a passenger ferry to Dartmouth. The very pretty harbour and shopping centre at Dartmouth makes a great day out for all the family. There are plenty of cafes and restaurants in Dartmouth and you can relax there before taking the train back to Paignton.

Exercise 3.8

Recall the document called Exercise 3.8 from the CD. Make the amendments as shown. Save as Exercise 3.8 and print one copy. A correct version of this exercise is in the worked examples on the CD-ROM.

Recall this document stored under Exercise 3.8. Amend as shown. Change to double linespacing (except where indicated). Adjust the line length to 12 cm. Use a justified right margin. Save as Exercise 3.8 and print one copy.

GAP YEAR ◄ ── *Centre this heading*

Many students decide to have a gap year after finishing their A level studies and before attending university. Universities are usually prepared to offer students a deferred place.

A large number of young people choose to spend some of their year out travelling. Getting together with friends and travelling appeals to many. However this can prove difficult. It is not necessarily safe to travel without having organised a place to stay and something to do in advance. It is very easy to overspend in the early weeks of the trip and be left without sufficient funds to continue with the holiday. ~~This is very dangerous.~~ *around the world with a backpack*

Inset this paragraph 20mm from left margin

Some people think they will easily find work to supplement their savings. Jobs are often difficult to find and can be extremely badly paid, particularly if proper work permits have not been obtained. *Copy this paragraph to point marked ▲*

There are a number of companies that organise trips especially for gap year students. Although the initial outlay ~~might~~ *will* be more expensive, these offer a structured way of travelling. It is possible to combine a trip with learning new skills or following an existing interest.

The New York Film Academy provides students with the opportunity to learn film making skills on their specialist courses. There are a number of courses to choose from in various locations. These include New York, Paris, Mexico City, ~~New York~~, Tokyo and of course the heart of film making, Hollywood. *It is also possible to take a course in London.*

Although the courses ~~can be~~ *are relatively* expensive, a great deal can be gained from them. Students can expect to learn film making skills from experts in the industry. They will also have the opportunity of meeting many other like-minded people from all over the world. If a course abroad is chosen then the experience of discovering a new culture and city adds to the overall value.

This paragraph in single linespacing

If film making doesn't appeal then there are many other options. For example, there are a large number of community projects ~~around the globe~~ in which young people can become involved.

A typical project may be helping natives in Thailand. As a volunteer the activities include teaching English *fresh* or helping the natives install a water system. Placements can last for around 6 - 10 months. *to school children*

These projects are not for those who insist on their creature comforts. Accommodation is usually very basic, often living with the natives in their homes. The rewards, however, are great. They include developing self-confidence, *hands-on experience* ~~an appreciation~~ of coping with different or difficult situations and an understanding of another culture.

Other activities include sailing trips, events organisation and trekking around America. For more information, call one of the specialist agencies that provide gap year adventures.

Emphasise this Sentence

for those who would like to spend time helping others,

Change natives to villagers throughout this document

Insert a footer TRAVEL to appear on every page

Exercise 3.9

Recall the document called Exercise 3.9 from the CD. Make the amendments as shown. Save as Exercise 3.9 and print one copy. A correct version of this exercise is in the worked examples on the CD-ROM.

Recall this document stored under Exercise 3-9. Amend as shown. Change to double linespacing (except where indicated). Adjust the line length to 11 cm. Use a justified right margin. Save as Choc1 and print one copy.

CHOCOLATE ← Centre this heading

Copy this paragraph to point marked Ⓐ

Many people love eating chocolate. To them, it is one of life's greatest pleasures. Chocolate has been around for many hundreds of years.

Chocolate dates back to the ancient people of Mesoamerica who drank chocolate made from cacao seeds as a bitter beverage. They brought back cacao trees from the rainforest and planted them in their settlements.

The seeds from the trees were harvested, fermented, roasted and ground into a paste. The pulp was mixed with water, chilli peppers, cornmeal and other ingredients to make a spicy drink.

It was during the conquest of Mexico in 1521 that the Italians first had contact with chocolate. By this time the Aztec empire dominated Mesoamerica. The precious cacao seeds were used as a form of Aztec money. The beverage was kept for rulers, priests, decorated soldiers and honoured merchants. The Italians recognised the value of cacao seeds and began to ship them back to Europe.

Move this paragraph to point marked Ⓑ.

The Europeans really enjoyed their chocolate and devised all sorts of ways of making the drinking of it more ceremonious. Specially designed porcelain was commissioned together with silver serving cups and pieces. These acted as symbols of wealth and power.

The original method of preparing drinking chocolate was so on improved upon by the Italians. They added sugar, cinnamon and other spices to make it more palatable. They kept this discovery to themselves and it took another 100 years before the rest of Europe discovered the sweetened chocolate drink.

This paragraph in single linespacing

Emphasise this sentence

Obviously cacao seeds and sugar were expensive items to import and so again, chocolate became the preserve of the rich. This remained the case for over 300 years. In France it was decreed that chocolate could only be consumed by members of the royal court.

and people were ordered to use the seeds in order to pay their tributes.

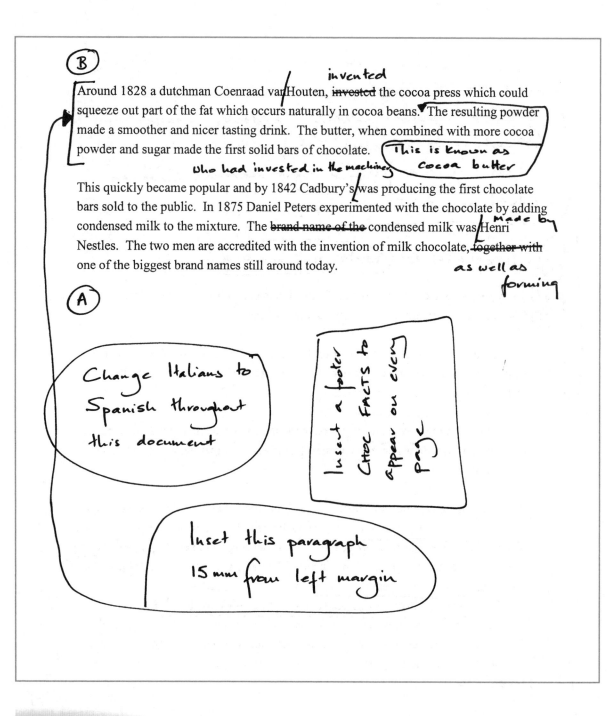

(B)

invented

Around 1828 a dutchman Coenraad van Houten, ~~invested~~ the cocoa press which could squeeze out part of the fat which occurs naturally in cocoa beans. The resulting powder made a smoother and nicer tasting drink. The butter, when combined with more cocoa powder and sugar made the first solid bars of chocolate.

This is known as cocoa butter

who had invested in the machine

This quickly became popular and by 1842 Cadbury's was producing the first chocolate bars sold to the public. In 1875 Daniel Peters experimented with the chocolate by adding condensed milk to the mixture. The ~~brand name of the~~ condensed milk was Henri Nestles. The two men are accredited with the invention of milk chocolate, ~~together with~~ one of the biggest brand names still around today.

Made by

as well as forming

(A)

Change Italians to Spanish throughout this document

Insert a footer Choc Facts to appear on every page

Inset this paragraph 15mm from left margin

Exercise 3.10

Recall the document called Exercise 3.10 from the CD. Make the amendments as shown. Save as Exercise 3.10 and print one copy. A correct version of this exercise is in the worked examples on the CD-ROM.

Recall this document stored under Ex 3.10. Amend as shown. Change to double linespacing (except where indicated). Adjust the line length to 11cm. Use a justified right margin. Save as PAPER1 and print one copy.

Add a header HISTORY NOTES to appear on every page

These were time-consuming and expensive to make.

PAPER MAKING

Paper is one of our ~~Most~~ widely used materials in modern life. Think of the amount of paper you use on a daily basis. The number of trees used to sustain this resource runs into millions each year. The environment cannot keep up with this demand.

The first mention of paper making can be sourced to 104 AD in China. The story is that the Emperor of China loved reading books and constantly needed a new source. At the time books were written on silk scrolls. The Emperor demanded something cheaper and easier to use.

One of her servants, Tsi Lun eventually came up with an alternative. After experimenting with different materials he finally found a solution with a mixture of hemp, mulberry tree bark, silk and old fishing nets. This proved very successful and Tsi Lun was rewarded by the Emperor. ~~He became a favourite courtier.~~

These were ground into a mushy pulp.

Papermaking remained exclusively a Chinese art until around 700 AD when during a war with China, the Arab nations captured an entire town of papermakers. These people were taken back to the middle east as prisoners and forced to work making paper. ~~The secret of paper making was handed over to the Arab nations.~~

During the Crusades, the Western Europeans learned how to make paper from the Arab nations. However, the Church at that time banned the use of paper, calling it a 'pagan art'. It insisted that animal parchment was the only material holy enough to carry the sacred word.

This paragraph in single linespacing

By ~~It wasn't until~~ the seventeenth century Europeans were making paper from linen and cotton rags. The resulting material is extremely durable and long lasting. The name given to this material is rag bond. This proved to be a very successful method and was used for many years. However, as standards of literacy increased during the eighteenth century, there became a shortage of rags and with it the demand for paper, and another method of paper making was sought.

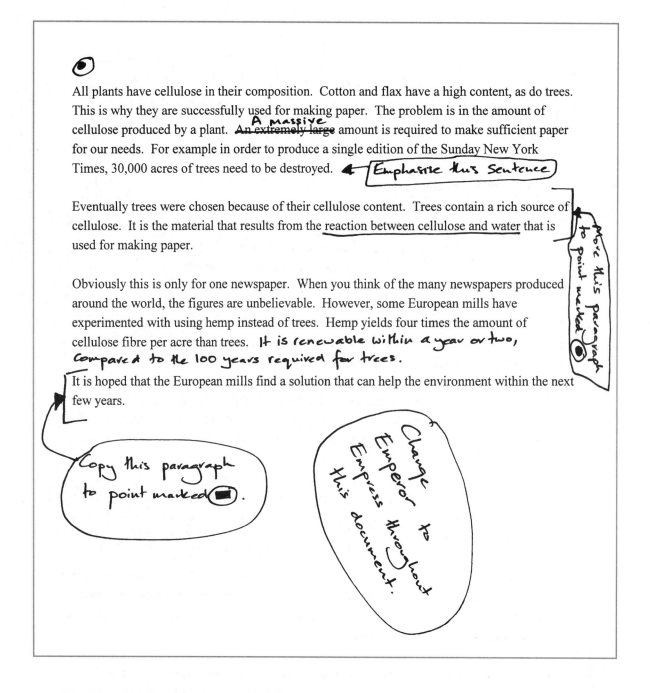

All plants have cellulose in their composition. Cotton and flax have a high content, as do trees. This is why they are successfully used for making paper. The problem is in the amount of cellulose produced by a plant. ~~An extremely large~~ *A massive* amount is required to make sufficient paper for our needs. For example in order to produce a single edition of the Sunday New York Times, 30,000 acres of trees need to be destroyed. ← [Emphasise this sentence]

Eventually trees were chosen because of their cellulose content. Trees contain a rich source of cellulose. It is the material that results from the reaction between cellulose and water that is used for making paper.

Move this paragraph to point marked ⦿

Obviously this is only for one newspaper. When you think of the many newspapers produced around the world, the figures are unbelievable. However, some European mills have experimented with using hemp instead of trees. Hemp yields four times the amount of cellulose fibre per acre than trees. *It is renewable within a year or two, compared to the 100 years required for trees.*

It is hoped that the European mills find a solution that can help the environment within the next few years.

Copy this paragraph to point marked (▣).

Change to Emperor to Empress throughout this document.

Notice for display

The second task of the Word Processing examination is a notice for display. This is a recalled document from disk and you will be expected to do the following:

- Add text to the document
- Inset a section of text
- Sort a list into alphabetical or numerical order
- Leave a specified amount of space in the document.

This is a straightforward task with little new theory except for the list sort and the allocation of space.

Sorting a list

You may be asked to key in the list or it may be part of the recalled text. The list must be sorted into exact alphabetical or numerical order. That means the list must be completely correct.

Exercise 3.11

Recall the document called Exercise 3.11 from the CD-ROM.

Method

1   Ensure you have a clear line space after the final paragraph of text or heading that appears before the start of the list.
2   Key in the list, line by line, using the Enter key to start a new line each time.
3   Once the list is complete, highlight the entire list and go to **Table** on the menu bar. Choose **Sort**. The following menu will appear (see Figure 3.8).

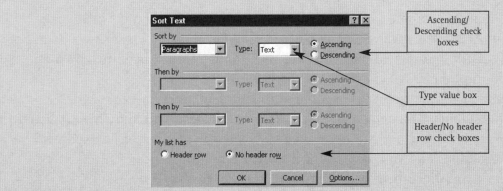

Figure 3.8 Sort Text menu

4   Check that the **Sort by** box is set to **Paragraphs**. Your list has been keyed in in paragraphs because the Enter key was used at the end of each line.
5   Check that the **Type** box is set to **Text**. This is because the list is a text list. If the list was in numbers then you should change the value to **Number** by clicking on the drop down menu at the side.
6   Check that the **Ascending/Descending** check box is set correctly for your sort. In this instance you must sort from A–Z and so the order is ascending. If you had wanted to sort from Z–A then you would need to check the descending box.
7   Check that the **No header row** is selected in the **My List has** dialogue box.
8   Click **OK**. The list should now be sorted into exact alphabetical order.

Allocating space

You will be asked to allocate some space during this task. This means that you must leave a space of a specified size. The specified size must be the minimum amount of space that is left, you can leave more.

Exercise 3.12

Continue using the document from Exercise 3.11 and allocate a space of at least 50 mm between the last two paragraphs.

Method

1   Place the cursor on the clear line space between the two final paragraphs of text.
2   On the bottom toolbar of your screen you will find a measurement bar (see Figure 3.9).

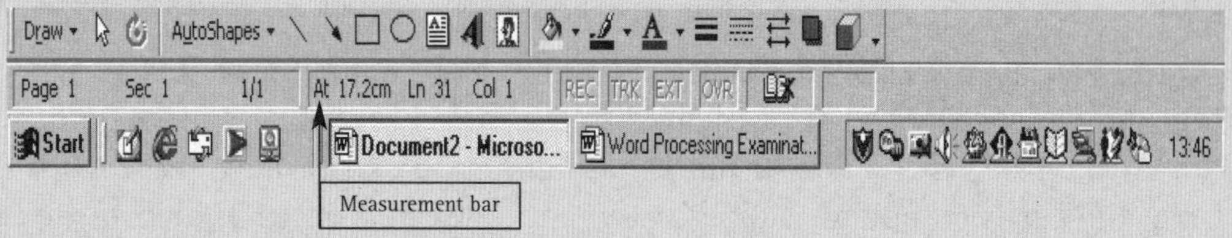

Figure 3.9 Measurement bar

3   The measurement bar will show you exactly where you are on the page. You can see that the measurement bar is showing that the cursor is now at 17.2 cm. In order to leave a space of 50 mm you will need to add 5 cm to the figure of 17.2 cm. This gives a total of 22.2 cm.
4   Now press the Enter key a number of times keeping an eye on the measurement bar. Once you have reached 22.2 cm you know you have left 50 mm of space. It is a good idea to leave one more clear line space to be absolutely sure you have left the correct amount.
5   Save your document as Exercise 3.12 and print one copy.

A worked copy of this exercise can be found in the worked examples on the CD-ROM.

Exercise 3.13

Recall Exercise 3.13 from the CD-ROM. Make the amendments as shown. Save as Exercise 3.13 and print one copy.

Recall this document stored under GAP1. Amend as shown. Use a ragged or justified right margin. Save as GAPYEAR1 and print one copy.

GAP YEAR ADVENTURES   *Centre this heading*

We are a company providing specialist trips for gap year students. Whatever your interests we can find you a trip that will provide all you want from your gap year adventure.

Booking through our agency has many advantages. Your personal safety is assured, you will be travelling to a fixed itinerary and you won't be burdened with any unexpected costs for travel or accommodation.

Trips for the following year include

Film making in New York
Sailing the Seven Seas
Community Projects in Thailand
Trekking through America
Culture tour of Europe
Community Projects in South America
Jungle Trekking
Rainforest Projects

Sort into exact alphabetical order

The duration of these trips range from 3 weeks to 10 months. The cost varies considerably depending on the length and location of the trip. We can assist you in raising the money by suggesting fundraising ideas.

leave at least 40 mm here

We will be visiting schools and colleges in the next few months to promote our adventures. We are sure to be visiting one in your area. Call 01829 8416753 to find out venues and times.

Exercise 3.14

Recall Exercise 3.14 from the CD-ROM. Make the amendments as shown. Save as Exercise 3.14 and print one copy. A correct version of this exercise can be found in the worked examples on the CD-ROM.

Recall this document stored as exercise 3.14. Amend as shown. Use a ragged or justified right margin. Save as RECYCLE and print one copy.

NEWTON COUNCIL RECYCLING PROJECT ← *Centre this heading*

From the beginning of next month, there will be major changes to the way in which Newton Council collects domestic waste.

Within the next week or so all residents will receive a green recycling bin. These will be issued free of charge. From this point, all items listed below must be placed in the new green bin. All other waste should be placed in the existing grey bin.

Tin cans
Plastic bottles
Paper
Newspaper
Cardboard
Shoes
Clothing
Glass bottles and jars

Sort into exact alphabetical order

The way in which your waste is collected will change. The bins will be collected on a two week rotation basis. This means that on the first week the grey bin will be collected. The second week will see the collection of the green recycling bin. You will be sent further details of the new scheme, including the start date, later this month.

Inset this section 30 mm from left margin

Emphasise this sentence

leave a vertical space here of at least 60 mm

We do hope you will help us make this scheme a success. It is important to the conservation of our environment. This is the first of a number of recycling initiatives.

Exercise 3.15

Recall Exercise 3.15 from the CD-ROM. Make the amendments as shown. Save as Exercise 3.15 and print one copy. A correct version of this exercise can be found in the worked examples on the CD-ROM.

> Recall this document stored as Exercise 3.15. Amend as shown. Use a ragged or justified right hand margin. Save as CARS and print one copy.

CARS UNLIMITED

This weekend we have some spectacular offers. We are reducing our entire used car stock.

Massive discounts will be available on over 250 cars. There is a wide range to choose from. From run arounds to people carriers, we have the car for you.

> Leave a vertical space of at least 50 mm

Our current stock includes:

> Centre this line

Hatchbacks
Four wheel drives
MPVs
GTIs
Saloons
Estates
Coupes

> Sort into _exact_ alphabetical order

> Emphasise this sentence

All our used cars have been checked and serviced. They carry a full three year warranty so you can rest assured you are buying a reliable vehicle. We can offer low cost loans and leasing agreements. Your old car can be used towards the deposit payment no matter what condition it is in.

For more details contact our Newton Road showroom. But hurry — these prices cannot last for ever!

Four column table

In this section you will learn about:

- creating a table
- moving columns and rows
- tidying up the table
- sorting the table
- merging header cells
- removing grid lines

One of the documents you will be expected to produce in the examination is a four column table. Look at Figure 3.10 below:

Title	Information and Training Details		Course Cost £
	Lecturer	Length of Course	
Languages			
German	Petra Kennedy	12 weeks	180.00
Spanish	Carmen Baker	12 weeks	180.00
French	Patric Fabrice	12 weeks	190.00
Painting			
Oils	Sirita Khan	10 weeks	140.00
Portrait	Pete Grey	12 weeks	160.00
Watercolours	Jack Hollis	12 weeks	180.00
Sports			
Squash	Stuart Clarke	12 weeks	50.00
Badminton	John Carlisle	10 weeks	75.00

Figure 3.10 Four column table

This table has been set up using the table editor facilities.

Exercise 3.16

Create a four column table with 13 rows.

Method

1 Go to the **Table** icon on the **toolbar** . Click on the icon and the following grid will appear (see Figure 3.11).

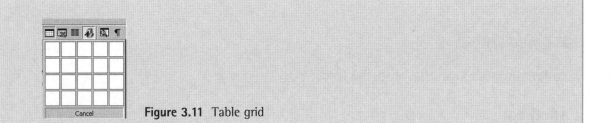

Figure 3.11 Table grid

2   Click on the top left-hand square and drag out the number of columns and down for the number of rows that you will require in your table. For this exercise you will require four columns and thirteen rows. The table grid will change colour and the dimensions of your table will be given at the bottom of the grid. You must keep holding down the mouse button whilst you are doing this. See Figure 3.12 below. To calculate the number of columns and rows you require, just count the number of columns across and then the number of lines down.

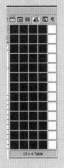

Figure 3.12 The table grid showing a 13 × 4 table

3   Once you are sure you have a correctly sized grid, then release the mouse button. The grid will now appear in your document as shown in Figure 3.13 below.

Figure 3.13 Table grid

You now need to key in the headings of the table as shown in Figure 3.10.

Exercise 3.17

Enter the table headings into the grid.

Method

1 Click in the top left-hand cell of your table and key in the word 'Title'.
2 Press the **Tab** key once to move to the next cell. Key in the words 'Course Cost £'.
3 Press the **Tab** key once to move to the next cell. Here you can see that the title extends across both columns. You will need to merge the two cells so that there is sufficient space to key the title in. You should do this after completing the table so that when you add and delete columns the table remains intact. For now, key the entire heading into the third column. The table should look as Figure 3.14 below.

Title	Course Cost £	Information and Training Details	
		Lecturer	Length of Course

Figure 3.14 Table with column headings

4 Move down to the next row. To do this, use the down arrow key which is situated to the right of the keyboard. Move along the first and second columns using the Tab key and when you reach the third column key in the next heading. Then move to the fourth column and key in the last heading.

Exercise 3.18

Key in the table text.

Method

1 Key in the text as shown in Figure 3.10, using the methods given. When keying in the sums of money, you should use a decimal tab. To do this set a decimal tab in the correct column. Instructions for this are given on page 17.

2 To move to a tab setting when working in a table is a little different as if you press the Tab key you will move to the next column. To overcome this hold down the **Ctrl** key and press the **Tab** key at the same time. This will move you to the tab setting.

The table should look like Figure 3.15 below. Did you remember to underline the sub-headings?

Title	Course Cost £	Information and Training Details	
		Lecturer	Length of Course
Painting			
Portrait	160.00	Pete Grey	12 weeks
Oils	140.00	Sirita Khan	10 weeks
Watercolours	180.00	Jack Hollis	12 weeks
Sports			
Badminton	75.00	John Carlisle	10 weeks
Squash	50.00	Stuart Clarke	12 weeks
Languages			
French	190.00	Patric Fabrice	12 weeks
German	180.00	Petra Kennedy	12 weeks
Spanish	180.00	Carmen Baker	12 weeks

Figure 3.15 Table with text

Moving columns and rows

You will find instructions dotted around the examination paper asking you to move various sections of text around and also to change the order of the columns. You can, of course, make all these amendments as you are keying in the text. However, you may find it easier and more accurate if you key in the text exactly as shown and then move the table around using the table editor facilities.

Exercise 3.19

Move the Languages section so that it becomes the first section of the table.

Method

1   Count how many rows of information you will be moving. In this case it will be four – one heading row and three rows of information.
2   Place the cursor in the cell containing the sub-heading 'Painting' before the first character (P). Go to **Table** and choose **Insert** and then choose **Rows Above**. A new row will be inserted into the table. Do this four times so that you have four blank rows above the Painting section.
3   Highlight the four rows of text you wish to move and hold down the **Ctrl** key. At the same time press **X** to cut the text from the table.
4   Go to the first of the four new rows you have inserted and click so that the cursor is flashing. Hold down **Ctrl** and press **V** to paste in the new text. It should appear in the correct position.
5   Now highlight the four empty rows at the bottom of the table. Go to **Table** and choose **Delete: Delete rows**. The rows should disappear. The table should look like Figure 3.16 below.

Title	Course Cost £	Information and Training Details	
		Lecturer	Length of Course
Languages			
French	190.00	Patric Fabrice	12 weeks
German	180.00	Petra Kennedy	12 weeks
Spanish	180.00	Carmen Baker	12 weeks
Painting			
Portrait	160.00	Pete Grey	12 weeks
Oils	140.00	Sirita Khan	10 weeks
Watercolours	180.00	Jack Hollis	12 weeks
Sports			
Badminton	75.00	John Carlisle	10 weeks
Squash	50.00	Stuart Clarke	12 weeks

Figure 3.16 Changing the order of the text

You will also be expected to move columns around changing the position of all of the text contained within one column.

Exercise 3.20

Change the position of the 'Course Cost £' column so that it becomes the last column.

Method 1

1 First of all, highlight the column you wish to move. You can do this by clicking at the top of the column so that the entire column is selected.
2 Click the **right** mouse button and the following menu will appear (see Figure 3.17).

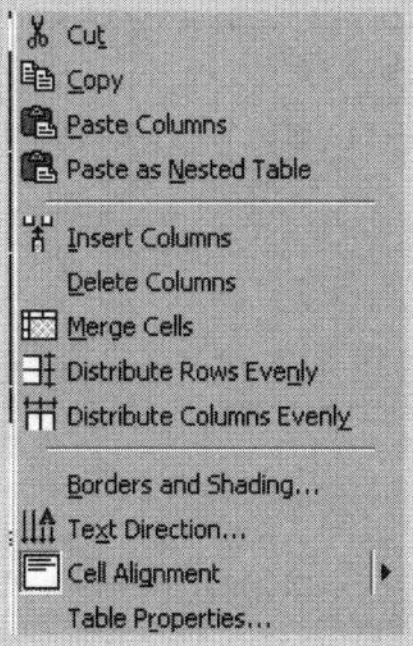

         Figure 3.17   Right click options

3 Choose **Cut**. The column will disappear.
4 Now (left) click in the position in which you want the new column to appear.
5 **Right click** the mouse again and choose **Paste Columns**. The column should now appear in the correct position and the rest of the table should have moved to its new position (see Figure 3.18).

Method 2

1 Highlight the column you wish to move to.
2 Now using the **Cut** and **Paste** facilities on the **Edit** menu, **Cut** the 'Course Cost £' column from its original position and then click so that the cursor is flashing **outside** of the table, immediately by the top right-hand cell of the table, and then **Paste** the new column into position. The table should look like Figure 3.18 below.

Title	Information and Training Details		Course Cost £
	Lecturer	Length of Course	
Languages			
French	Patric Fabrice	12 weeks	190.00
German	Petra Kennedy	12 weeks	180.00
Spanish	Carmen Baker	12 weeks	180.00
Painting			
Portrait	Pete Grey	12 weeks	160.00
Oils	Sirita Khan	10 weeks	140.00
Watercolours	Jack Hollis	12 weeks	180.00
Sports			
Badminton	John Carlisle	10 weeks	75.00
Squash	Stuart Clarke	12 weeks	50.00

Figure 3.18 Moving columns

Note: The reason for clicking **outside** of the table is because you needed to insert a column at the **end** of the table. Columns are always pasted to the right of the column in which the cursor is positioned. Therefore, if you had placed the cursor in the 'Length of Course' column, the 'Course Cost £' column would have appeared between the 'Lecturer and Length of Course' columns.

Tidying up the table

You will need to tidy up the table so that the headings remain on one line.

Exercise 3.21

Ensure that all headers are on one line except for the 'Information and Training Details' heading.

Method

1   Using the mouse, drag over the left-hand line of the 'Length of Course' column to provide more room for the 'Course Cost £' column.
2   Now move the left- and right-hand lines of the 'Course Cost £' column so

that the heading is displayed in full. You must ensure that the 'Length of Course' heading remains on one line only (see Figure 3.19 below).

Title	Information and Training Details		Course Cost £
	Lecturer	Length of Course	
Languages			
French	Patric Fabrice	12 weeks	190.00
German	Petra Kennedy	12 weeks	180.00
Spanish	Carmen Baker	12 weeks	180.00
Painting			
Portrait	Pete Grey	12 weeks	160.00
Oils	Sirita Khan	10 weeks	140.00
Watercolours	Jack Hollis	12 weeks	180.00
Sports			
Badminton	John Carlisle	10 weeks	75.00
Squash	Stuart Clarke	12 weeks	50.00

Figure 3.19 Table tidied up

Sorting the table

The examination requires you to sort the table in some way, either alphabetically, numerically or chronologically. You can, of course, sort the order manually and key in the table in the sorted order, however it is probably safer in terms of accuracy to sort the table using the table editor.

The most important aspect of sorting the table is that you sort ALL the material correctly. This means that all the information is kept together. For example, looking at the table you have created, you need to sort the 'Course Cost' in ascending order within each section. This means that in the 'Painting' section the 'Course Cost' should start with the lowest rising to the highest cost. The 'Oils' section will appear first and the name of the lecturer, the course title and the length of course should all remain on the same line.

Exercise 3.22

Sort the table so that the 'Course Cost' is in ascending order (lowest first) within each section. Ensure that all corresponding details are kept together.

Method

1   Highlight the first three rows of the '**Languages**' section, ensuring you highlight all the information contained in the three rows.
2   Go to **Table** and choose **Sort**. The following sub-menu will appear (see Figure 3.20).

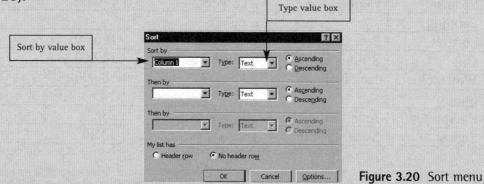

Figure 3.20 Sort menu

3   You need to insert the sort criteria. The first is the column by which the sort is going to work. In this exercise the column will be column 4
4   The **Type** needs to be set. By using the drop down menu to the right you can set a text, number or date search. For this exercise you will be using a **number** search, so change the value to **Number**. When you have completed these two boxes, click OK. The table should now look like Figure 3.21 below.

Title	Information and Training Details		Course Cost £
	Lecturer	Length of Course	
Languages			
German	Petra Kennedy	12 weeks	180.00
Spanish	Carmen Baker	12 weeks	180.00
French	Patric Fabrice	12 weeks	190.00
Painting			
Portrait	Pete Grey	12 weeks	160.00
Oils	Sirita Khan	10 weeks	140.00
Watercolours	Jack Hollis	12 weeks	180.00
Sports			
Badminton	John Carlisle	10 weeks	75.00
Squash	Stuart Clarke	12 weeks	50.00

Figure 3.21 Sorted table

5   Now repeat these steps for the 'Painting' and 'Sports' sections. The table will now look like Figure 3.22 below.

Title	Information and Training Details		Course Cost £
	Lecturer	Length of Course	
Languages			
German	Petra Kennedy	12 weeks	180.00
Spanish	Carmen Baker	12 weeks	180.00
French	Patric Fabrice	12 weeks	190.00
Painting			
Oils	Sirita Khan	10 weeks	140.00
Portrait	Pete Grey	12 weeks	160.00
Watercolours	Jack Hollis	12 weeks	180.00
Sports			
Squash	Stuart Clarke	12 weeks	50.00
Badminton	John Carlisle	10 weeks	75.00

Figure 3.22 Sort completed

Note: You must ensure that you highlight the entire rows when using the sort as you must place all the corresponding details into order.

Merging the header cells

The examination paper will show a heading that spans two columns. It is recommended that you do not merge any cells until you have completed all the text entry and manipulation. This is because it can make it rather difficult to move columns and rows if two cells have been merged, as Word may place columns incorrectly and even mix two columns.

Exercise 3.23

Merge the two header cells so that the 'Information and Training Details' header spans two columns.

Method

1 Highlight the cell containing the heading and the blank cell to the right.
2 Go to **Table** and choose **Merge Cells**.
3 The cells will be merged.
4 You can now reduce some of the space between the 'Lecturer', 'Length of Course' and 'Course Cost £' columns, using the methods given in the **Tidying up Your Table** exercise. Your table should look like Figure 3.23 below.

Title	Information and Training Details		Course Cost £
	Lecturer	Length of Course	
Languages			
German	Petra Kennedy	12 weeks	180.00
Spanish	Carmen Baker	12 weeks	180.00
French	Patric Fabrice	12 weeks	190.00
Painting			
Oils	Sirita Khan	10 weeks	140.00
Portrait	Pete Grey	12 weeks	160.00
Watercolours	Jack Hollis	12 weeks	180.00
Sports			
Squash	Stuart Clarke	12 weeks	50.00
Badminton	John Carlisle	10 weeks	75.00

Figure 3.23 Table completed

Inserting spaces

You now need to insert some clear line spaces so that there is a space between the headings and the text. Look at Figure 3.10 to see how the table should look.

Method

1 Insert the cursor after the words **Course Cost £**. Now press the **Return** key to insert a line space.
2 Insert the cursor at the end of the words **Length of Course**. Press the **Return** key to insert a line space.
3 Insert the cursor at the end of the word **Languages**. Press the **Return** key to insert a line space.
4 Insert the cursor at the end of the word **Spanish**. Press the **Return** key to insert a line space.

5 Insert the cursor at the end of the word **Painting.** Press the **Return** key to insert a line space.

6 Insert the cursor at the end of the word **Watercolours.** Press the **Return** key to insert a line space.

7 Insert the cursor at the end of the word **Sports.** Press the **Return** key to insert a line space.

Your table should now look like this:

Title	Information and Training Details		Course Cost £
	Lecturer	Length of Course	
Languages			
German	Petra Kennedy	12 weeks	180.00
Spanish	Carmen Baker	12 weeks	180.00
French	Patric Fabrice	12 weeks	190.00
Painting			
Oils	Sirita Khan	10 weeks	140.00
Portrait	Pete Grey	12 weeks	160.00
Watercolours	Jack Hollis	12 weeks	180.00
Sports			
Squash	Stuart Clarke	12 weeks	50.00
Badminton	John Carlisle	10 weeks	75.00

Figure 3.24 Table completed

Removing the grid lines

The gridlines, the black border lines of the table, must *not* be printed in the examination. These are quite simple to remove.

Exercise 3.24

Remove all gridlines from the table.

Method

1 Select the entire table, by clicking on the top of the table and dragging the mouse from left to right. The entire table should now be highlighted.

2 Go to the **Border** icon on the toolbar and click on the drop down menu. The following options will appear on screen (see Figure 3.25).

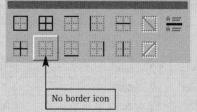

No border icon

Figure 3.25 Border options

3 Choose the **No Border** icon as shown in Figure 3.25. The gridlines should now be removed and your table will look like Figure 3.26 below

Title	Information and Training Details		Course Cost £
	Lecturer	Length of Course	
Languages			
German	Petra Kennedy	12 weeks	180.00
Spanish	Carmen Baker	12 weeks	180.00
French	Patric Fabrice	12 weeks	190.00
Painting			
Oils	Sirita Khan	10 weeks	140.00
Portrait	Pete Grey	12 weeks	160.00
Watercolours	Jack Hollis	12 weeks	180.00
Sports			
Squash	Stuart Clarke	12 weeks	50.00
Badminton	John Carlisle	10 weeks	75.00

Figure 3.26 Completed table

It has probably taken you quite some time to work through this table using the methods given above. It is a very accurate method to ensure that the text remains in the same columns, and with a little practice will become much quicker once you are used to moving lines around and entering text into the table editor.

Exercise 3.25

Now try keying in the following table, working through the instructions given above. A correct version of this table can be found in the worked examples on the CD-ROM.

Key in the following table. Save as SALE and print one copy. Do not rule the table.

Modify the layout so that the Home Accessories Dept comes before the Toy Dept

SUMMER SALE

Our summer sale will begin shortly. It will last for a period of of 2 weeks. We hope to be able to clear some old stock that has been stored in the warehouse for quite some time. The list below shows the various items that will be reduced by 50% or more. Please note that quantities are limited and items cannot be reordered.

Please sort REDUCED £ column into numerical order starting with the lowest figure. Ensure corresponding details are also rearranged.

ITEM	QUANTITY	RETAIL PRICE	DETAILS
		CURRENT £	REDUCED £

Toy Department

		150.00	70.00
Dolls house	6	650.00	300.00
Rocking horse	3	25.00	12.00
Baby doll	2	35.00	17.00
Fortress	29		

Kitchenware Department

		28.00	10.00
Neon coloured kettle	100	175.00	85.00
Steel knife set	5	55.00	24.00
Copper saucepan	18	18.00	9.00
Bread bin	32		

Garden Department

		295.00	140.00
Teak bench	8	140.00	70.00
Teak chair	22	100.00	50.00
Blue parasol	15		

Home Accessories Department

		48.00	15.00
Zebra print	22	25.00	10.00
Magazine rack	10	18.00	5.00
Scarlet throw	5	50.00	15.00
Floor cushion	2	20.00	10.00
Steel vase	25		

Modify layout so that the QUANTITY column becomes the last column

Exercise 3.26

Key in the following table. A correct version of this table can be found in the worked examples on the CD-ROM.

Key in the following table. Save as CATALOGUE and print one copy. Do not rule the table.

CHRISTMAS CATALOGUE

Our buying trips have been very successful and we have found a number of new items for the Christmas catalogue. Sample items will be arriving during the next few weeks.

The table below shows these items and the section in which they will be displayed.

Please sort CATALOGUE CODE into numerical order within each section starting with the lowest figure. Ensure corresponding details are also rearranged

ITEM	PRICE DETAILS		CATALOGUE CODE
	COST £	RETAIL £	
Pages 1–10, Gifts for Men			
Novelty cuff links	7.50	12.50	M 1398
Leather briefcase	58.00	125.00	M 1388
Mouse mat	2.00	6.50	M 1375
Executive toy	1.80	4.50	M 1379
Shoe cleaning kit	3.20	9.50	M 1381
Pages 33–40, Gifts for the Home			
Suede cushions	10.00	35.00	H 1782
Wicker storage basket	3.00	8.00	H 1773
Seaside picture	10.00	22.00	H 1778
Pages 11–25, Gifts for Women			
Velvet scarf	8.00	16.00	W 1550
Cashmere gloves	7.50	22.00	W 1562
Aromatherapy gift set	5.00	12.50	W 1553
Scented soap set	2.00	6.00	W 1569
Luxury writing paper	4.00	10.00	W 1551
Pages 41–50 Gifts for the Kitchen			
Rocket egg cup	3.00	7.50	K 1826
Cat mug	4.00	8.00	K 1841
Tea towel	1.50	4.00	K 1823

Modify layout so that the Gifts for Women Section appears before the Gifts for the Home Section

Modify layout so that CATALOGUE CODE becomes the second column

Exercise 3.27

Key in the following table. A correct version of this table can be found in the worked examples on the CD-ROM.

key in the following table. Save as MAG and print one copy. Do not rule the table.

MAGAZINE CIRCULATION

This year has been very successful. We have achieved circulation growth for most of our titles. There are however issues concerning one or two of the titles and these will be discussed at our next meeting. The figures in this table have been rounded to the nearest 5,000. *Modify layout so that the General Interest section becomes the final section.*

TITLE	COVER PRICE	CIRCULATION JAN – DEC	
		2001	2002
General Interest			
Photography	£2.90	320,000	340,000
Water Sports	£3.20	180,000	185,000
Cycling	£3.10	275,000	260,000
Vintage Cars	£3.20	190,000	195,000
Steam Trains	£3.40	160,000	165,000
Computing			
Web Design	£3.25	220,000	250,000
Home Publishing	£3.10	140,000	130,000
Computing Times	£2.80	345,000	360,000
Games Review	£3.40	385,000	400,000
Crafts			
Tapestry Monthly	£2.65	185,000	185,000
Woodworking	£3.20	75,000	80,000
Machine Knitting	£2.80	165,000	150,000
Quilting	£3.10	130,000	135,000
Female Interest			
Life Style	£3.20	455,000	465,000
Cookery Today	£2.90	225,000	225,000
Home Style	£3.50	285,000	310,000
Beautiful You	£3.60	230,000	230,000

Please sort COVER PRICE into numerical order within each section starting with the lowest figure. Ensure corresponding details are also rearranged.

Modify the layout so the COVER PRICE becomes the last column.

Standard document

> **In this section you will learn about:**
> - inserting phrases
> - taking copies
> - routing copies

The final task of the examination is a standard document (either a letter or a memo) that requires phrases to be inserted. The phrases will be stored on a disk or the hard drive of your computer. You will be given more phrases than are required to be inserted and you must ensure that you insert the correct files.

The insertion of phrases is a very simple task in Word. However there are several things to watch out for when inserting phrases:

- You must ensure you choose the correct phrase.
- You must ensure that the text is spaced correctly. For example, if you were inserting a phrase in the middle of a sentence then there should be the usual space before the inserted text. If you are inserting a completely new sentence then you must ensure that you have left either one or two spaces after the previous full stop (depending on your usual method).
- If the phrase has been keyed in a different font or font size, then you must ensure that it is correctly formatted to match the rest of your text.

Letter and memo layouts have been covered in the Text Production section and the rules for these are exactly the same. One of the most important things to remember is that the date will not be given on the examination paper, but it must be keyed in to the document.

Exercise 3.28

Key in the following draft letter and insert phrases from the CD-ROM where specified. A correct version of this table can be found in the worked examples on the CD-ROM.

Our ref KL/CAT

Ms Kerry Latham
76 Perry Close
DERBY
D23 1NP

(Top + 2 copies please. One for Tasbir Patel and one for our files. Indicate routing.)

Dear Ms Latham

Thank you for your enquiry regarding our mail order service. A catalogue has been sent to you today under separate cover. We are sure you will be delighted with the selection of kitchenware we have found for our catalogue this season. There are many new and interesting items ranging from novelty timers through to sets of professional grade stainless steel pans and roasters.

(Insert phrase 1 - Exercise 3.28 here)

New for this season is our Internet store. This gives full details of all our products together with clearance and end of line items. You can order goods online 24 hours a day from our secure site. The website is simple to use and quick to download. Ordering is easy and secure.

(Insert phrase 2 - Exercise 3.28 here)

If you would like any further information, please do not hesitate to contact one of our helpful call centre staff.

Yours sincerely
Samantha Morrison
Director

Method

1 Ensure the cursor is flashing at the exact point where the phrase is to be inserted.
2 Go to Insert and choose File ... . You will be taken to the main directory. Depending on where the phrase is stored you may have to move around the drives and directories until you find the correct location.
3 When you have found the name of the correct file, click on the filename and then click Insert. The file will be inserted into your document.
4 Ensure that the inserted text is correctly spaced and consistent with the rest of your document.

Taking copies

You may be asked to send a copy of a document to another person and of course you should keep a copy for your files. Do the following:

- Leave a clear line space after the enclosure(s), if there are any, and key in the word 'Copy' or 'Copies' (if there are two or more to be taken).
- Then leave at least one character space and key in the name of the person who will be receiving the copy.
- On the line directly underneath, key in the word 'File'. It is much neater if you can line this up with the name of the person below (see Figure 3.27). Although it is not essential to key in the word 'File', it does prompt you to print two extra copies in the examination.

Copies   Tasbir Patel
           File

Figure 3.27 Copies

Exercise 3.29

Indicate copies to Tasbir Patel and File at the end of the standard letter.

Method

1 Ensure you leave a clear line space after the complimentary close.
2 Key in the word 'Copies' and then set a left-hand tab a few spaces away to ensure that there is a space after the word. Key in the name Tasbir Patel. Press return.
3 On the next line press the Tab key to move to the correct position. Key in the word 'File'.

A correct version of this table can be found in the worked examples on the CD-ROM.

Routing copies

This means to indicate which copy must go to the named person and which must be kept for the file.

- You can use a pen to tick the names, or a highlighter, or underscore on the word processor.
- Remember to indicate the routing of both the extra copies.
- Do not route the original copy.

Look at Figure 3.28 below to see the routing for a letter that has two extra copies.

Original		**Copy 1**		**Copy 2**	
Copies	N Maddock	Copies	N Maddock ✓	Copies	N Maddock
	File		File		File ✓

Figure 3.28 Routing copies

Exercise 3.30

Print out three copies of the standard document you completed in Exercise 3.29 and route the two copies as shown above.

A worked example of Exercises 3.28–3.30 can be found on the CD-ROM.

Exercise 3.31

Key in the following standard letter and take copies as indicated. A correct version of this exercise can be found in the worked examples on the CD-ROM.

Please key in the following document using a ragged or justified right margin. Insert the phrases as indicated. Save as HOLIDAY and print one copy.

Our ref RJ/EN
Mrs Molly Sinclair
42 Victoria Terrace
YORK
YO6 3QT

Top + 2 copies please. One copy to Robert Jay and one for our files. Indicate routing.

Dear Mrs Sinclair

Thank you for your completed booking form and deposit payment. We are pleased to confirm that two places on our Culture Tour of Italy have been reserved.

Your holiday will commence on Saturday 2 August. The return date is Saturday 9 August. Accommodation will be provided on a half-board basis.

Insert Phrase 2 - Ex 3.31

I note from the booking form that you have requested coach travel to the airport. This has been booked on your behalf. The coach pick up point is York coach station. The coach will be leaving at 8.30am on the 2 August. Please ensure you arrive at the pick up point in good time. The cost of the return coach travel is £25 per person. Please send a cheque for this amount to our Accounts Department as soon as possible.

Insert Phrase 1 - Ex 3.31

You will be sent further information closer to your holiday date. In the meantime, if you have any queries, please do not hesitate to contact me.

Yours sincerely

Elliott Neale

Manager

Exercise 3.32

Key in the following standard letter and take copies as indicated. A correct version of this exercise can be found in the worked examples on the CD-ROM.

Please key in the following document using aragged or justified right margin. Insert the phrases as indicated. Save as SERVICE and print.

Our ref IS/JI

Mr J Lovesley
12 Shelley Avenue
ST AUSTELL
TR32 8TX

Dear Mr Lovesley

Top + 2 copies please. One copy to John Inness and one for our files. Indicate routing

According to our records your central heating system is due for its annual service. The payment for this is covered under your maintenance contract.

Our engineer, John Inness, will call on the 22 September at 8.30 am. He will carry out a full service of the system including the boiler.

Insert Phrase 1 – Ex 3.32

If there are any problems with your system John will try to fix them at the same time. However, if any non-standard parts are required then a second visit may be necessary.

Insert Phrase 3 – Ex 332

We hope that this date will be convenient for you. If you are unable to keep this appointment please contact me as soon as possible. Your reference number is YS235 and it would be helpful if you could quote this when speaking to our staff.

Yours sincerely

Ivan Smith
Contract Manager

Exercise 3.33

Key in the following standard letter and take copies as indicated. A correct version of this exercise can be found in the worked examples on the CD-ROM.

Please key in the following document using a ragged or justified right margin. Insert the phrases as indicated. Save as PRINTING and print.

MEMORANDUM

To   Maxine MacDonald
From   Lewis Barnes
Ref   CC/LB/mm

Top + 2 copies please
One copy to Eleanor Spencer
and one for our files.
Indicate routing.

I have arranged a print date for our Christmas catalogue with the printing firm. It has been booked in for the first week in August. The process will take approximately three weeks.

Insert Phrase 2 - Ex 3.33

I suggest you draw up a schedule so that we do not forget anything. We will also be able to use it to ensure we are on track. // The photographic studio has been booked for the whole of the last week in May. Please liaise with Eleanor regarding the arrangements for photographing new items.

Insert Phrase 3 - Ex 3.33

I have also asked Eleanor to set aside some time to help you write the copy. She will contact you in the next few days to discuss this matter.

Any problems, let me know.

Consolidation practice

The following consolidation exercises will help you prepare for the Word Processing examination. Try to complete each set of consolidation pieces in the usual time allowed for this exam, that is 1 hour and 45 minutes.

Remember to check your work carefully, and correct any errors before printing. You should print one copy of each document. Correct versions of these exercises can be found in the worked examples on the CD-ROM.

Word processing consolidation 1

Recall this document stored under WORKPLACE. Amend as shown. Change to double linespacing (except where indicated). Adjust the line length to 10.5 cm. Use a justified right margin. Save as WORK1 and print one copy.

SURVIVING IN THE WORK PLACE

Copy this paragraph to point marked

It used to be the case that once in a job, people would stay for as long as possible. Often people would remain in the same employment from the time they left full-time education until retirement.

Certain jobs were considered to be 'a job for life'. These included any public service employment, such as police and ambulance workers, ~~and care workers~~ civil servants, teachers. Jobs in banking, insurance and other financial sectors were also considered as safe.

Insert this paragraph at least 20mm from the left margin

This concept has changed dramatically over the past fifteen years or so. Employment is not as secure and it is widely accepted that a career change may be necessary more than once during your working life. ~~You are almost bound to be made redundant at least once during your career.~~

How can you prepare for a changing work role

~~What is the best way to cope with this prospect?~~ One way is to accumulate as many talents as possible. Learn to drive, under take health and safety training, make sure you can keyboard at a reasonable rate. These talents will make you much more employable in almost any career you choose.

Once you are in employment

~~If you are lucky enough to have a job,~~ you should continue to improve your talents and qualifications. If you are offered the chance to attend training courses then take it.

Employers and prospective employers are always pleased to see people who are keen to learn and continue a programme of self-development.

If your employment does not offer these opportunities then ~~Do not wait around for your employer to train you,~~ train yourself. Think about evening classes, correspondence courses, the Open University and even self-study packs.

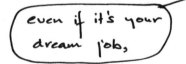
even if it's your dream job,

Move this paragraph to point marked ✱

If you are planning to attend university, it is worth discussing your choice of career with a professional advisor. A broader course may be more useful than a highly specialised course if you are not completely sure of the career path you wish to follow.

Another way to ensure you stay one step ahead is to look for other opportunities. It may be that you have an interest or hobby that could develop into an income earner. You may find when you are looking for employment that you can use your talents in other areas.

▲

Having to change your employment half way through your working life may not be the disaster it first appears. If you have some transferable talents, then you may find the change challenging ~~invigorating~~. It may be that the change gives you a whole new lease of life and the chance to do something you have always dreamed of doing.

This paragraph in single linespacing

Change talents to skills throughout this document

Insert a header CAREERS INFO on every page

Recall this document stored under WORKPLACE2. Amend as shown. Use a ragged or justified right margin. Save as WORK2 and print one copy.

BUSINESS SERVICES ← (Centre this heading)

Choices Ltd are pleased to announce their new service. From next month we will be assisting young people to start their own business.

↕ leave at least 50 mm vertical space here

Our three-day seminars give an intensive overview to starting your own business. They will cover all you need to know, from how to research your new business to employing staff. They are also suitable for people who are currently running a small business.

The courses include:

Researching your idea
Producing a business plan
How to attract funding
Approaching your bank
Finding premises
Employment law
PAYE
Advertising
Marketing Strategies
Cashflow projections
Budget setting
Insurance regulations
Health and safety regulations
Customer service
Starting a limited company

Sort into exact alphabetical order

The first of a series of seminars will be held at the King William Hotel in Farnborough on 20 March. Places are limited to 15 and cost £285. If you would like to reserve one of these places please call 01879 4291752 and speak to Indiva Wilson.

→ Alternatively for further information, email us at info@choices.co.uk. (Emphasise this sentence)

We look forward to meeting you.

Key in the following table. Save as WORK3 and print one copy. Do not rule the table.

Please sort the DATE column into exact chronological order. Ensure corresponding details are rearranged.

CHOICES LTD   Modify layout so that PLACES becomes the last column.

The following table shows the seminars we will be holding during the next three months. If you are interested in attending one or more of these events please e-mail us at info@choices.co.uk.

COURSE TITLE	NO OF PLACES	COURSE DETAILS	
		DATE	COST

King William Hotel, Farnborough

Marketing Secrets	20	23 March	£185
IT Update	18	28 March	£175
Customer Service	25	27 March	£190
Starting Your Own Business	18	20 March	£285

Check this detail from document 2 and amend if necessary.

Norton Hotel, Birmingham

Starting Your Own Business	15	1 April	£285
Health and Safety In The Work Place	18	15 April	£240
Health and Safety Risk Assessment	18	16 April	£240
Communication Skills	20	8 April	£320
Staff Management	10	2 April	£420

Modify layout so that the Manchester section appears before the Farnborough section.

Lansdowne Hotel, Manchester

Marketing Secrets	20	15 April	£185
Communication Skills	20	19 April	£320
IT Update	18	7 April	£175
Staff Management	10	10 April	£420

King's Hotel, Bristol

Developing Strategies	10	4 May	£375
Senior Management Skills	10	1 May	£320
Policy Making	10	3 May	£420

The prices shown above are per person and include lunch and refreshments. All courses begin with registration at 9.30am and finish at 4.30 pm.

Please key in the following document using a ragged or justified right margin. Insert the phrases as indicated. Save as WORK4 and print.

MEMORANDUM

To   Blanche Jackson

From   Tony Romero

Ref   FW|TR|BJ

Training Course – Farnborough

Top + 2 copies please.
One for Joseph Brown
One for files. Indicate routing

The date for the Starting your own Business seminar has now been confirmed as 20 March., A programme will be sent to you shortly.

Please confirm you are able to deliver this seminar. As this event is not in your current contract you will be paid separately for it. The fee will be at the agreed rate for a one-day course. Travel and subsistence expenses will also be paid. Please note that payment will not be made until a completed claim form has been submitted.

Insert Phrase 3 stored as Phrase 3 Work here

I would also like you to run the seminars in Manchester during April. Please let me know as soon as possible if this is convenient for you. These will also be in addition to your contracted hours, and again, a separate payment will be made for each.

The courses will follow the usual format. Each event will commence at 9.30 am and finish at 4.30 pm. Morning coffee, afternoon tea and a buffet lunch will be provided. The delegates will be given a comprehensive information pack. These will be sent to the venue in advance.

Insert Phrase 1 stored as Phrase 1 Work here.

Word processing consolidation 2

Recall this document stored under GARDEN1. Amend as shown. Change to double linespacing (except where indicated). Adjust the line length to 11 cm. Use a justified right margin. Save as GARDEN CENTRE and print one copy.

Copy this paragraph to point marked ②

KNOWLES GARDEN CENTRE

The Knowles Garden Centre is conveniently situated on the western outskirts of Newton. We are open 7 days a week from ~~8.30~~ 8.00 am to ~~6.30~~ 7.00 pm.

We stock a wide range of plants, furniture, garden accessories, and tools. In addition, we have recently introduced a garden water centre. This contains everything you need to install a water feature in your garden, including the fish!

Our range of shrubs and hedging is second to none. If you are looking for an instant garden, then visit us. We stock mature shrubs and hedges and will advise you on planting and care. If you are looking for something larger then we can order trees and fully grown ~~plants.~~ shrubs. ✓

② The garden centre also has a cafe where you can relax over a cup of ~~coffee~~ tea. Our light lunches and ~~snacks~~ Sandwiches are expertly prepared by our chef, And provide excellent value for money. ✓

If you wish, Richard can visit your home and prepare a detailed plan. He will listen to your ideas and advise you on the planting and colour schemes that will suit your garden. The design will also include any structural or water features. There is a small charge for this service.

Whether you are a novice gardener or an expert with many years' experience, we are sure we can help you plan your garden so that you can make the most of it. ~~We have lots of design ideas that you can view on our website.~~ We have a resident garden designer Richard, who will give you plenty of hints and tips on how to make beautiful displays.

Once you have decided on your garden design we can arrange for the work to be undertaken. We have a team of expert builders and gardeners who can help Richard translate your design into the real thing, without you having to lift a finger.

Inset this paragraph 20 mm from left margin

Move this paragraph to point marked ⓧ.

As garden experts we are obviously very aware of the changing seasons. We are constantly changing our range to suit each season. Our Christmas displays are magnificent. We stock Christmas trees and decorations from early December.

For special occasions at any time of the year, visit us. Our in-house florist can prepare wonderful bouquets and floral arrangements. We would be delighted to provide your wedding flowers. We guarantee you will be delighted with the quality and the price.

This paragraph in single Wrappacks

If you would like to learn more about gardening techniques we run a range of courses and workshops. These can take the form of a twelve- week part time course or a specialist one day workshop. Please ask at reception for further information. ~~These courses cost from £25 per day~~

including the bridal bouquets and table arrangements for the reception.

Change Richard to Matt throughout this document

Insert a header Information Sheet to appear on every page

> Recall this document stored under GARDEN2. Amend as shown. Use a ragged or justified right margin. Save as Garden Courses and print one copy.

KNOWLES GARDEN CENTRE

> Check this detail from Document 1 and amend if necessary

Would you like to know more about gardening techniques? Why not enrol on one of our 10 week part time courses?

> leave at least 40 mm vertical space here

These are held every Tuesday + Thursday afternoons between 2.00pm – 4.00pm. The course content includes:

Hints and tips
Growing vegetables
Organic gardening
Water features
Feeding your garden
Dealing with garden pests
Attracting wildlife
Lawn maintenance
Hedging and fencing
Planning a colour scheme

All our lecturers are expert gardeners with many years' experience. There will be an opportunity for students to discuss their particular interests with their lecturer.

We also offer one-day workshops. These include Making Christmas Decorations, Building a Patio or Planning a Garden Pond. Please call us for further information including course fees.

> Key in the following table. Save as BOUQUETS and print one copy. Do not rule the table.

> Modify layout so that the <u>Valentine</u> section comes before the <u>Mothering Sunday</u> section.

> Modify layout so that the REF NO becomes the 2nd column

KNOWLE BOUQUETS

We can provide bouquets for any occasion and deliver to your door. You may order your bouquet any time up to 5.30 pm for next-day delivery. A charge of £2.50 is made for this service to include delivery within a 10 mile radius of the Garden Centre. You can also combine your bouquet with a box of luxury chocolates to make a truly special occasions.

> Please sort the BOUQUET column into ascending price order. Ensure corresponding details are also rearranged.

FLOWERS	PRICE DETAILS (INCLUDING DELIVERY)		REF NO
	BOUQUET	BOUQUET AND CHOCS	
Mothering Sunday Specials			
Freesias	£18.00	£25.00	MS 12
Carnations	£10.00	£16.00	MS 10
Tiger lilies	£15.00	£22.00	MS 06
Mixed flowers	£18.00	£25.00	MS 09
Valentine Day Specials			
One dozen red roses	£35.00	£45.00	VS 22
Six red roses	£20.00	£28.00	VS 20
Large mixed bouquet	£25.00	£32.00	VS 17
Medium mixed bouquet	£18.00	£25.00	VS 15
Seasonal Flowers			
Spring posy	£12.00	£17.00	SF 14
Autumnal colours	£18.00	£24.00	SF 21
Christmas colours	£20.00	£25.00	SF 12
Summer flame posy	£18.00	£24.00	SF 19
Miscellaneous			
Chrysanthemum pot	£10.00	£15.00	MC 05
Outdoor container	£18.00	N/A	MC 11
Hanging basket	£19.00	N/A	MC 07
Window box	£25.00	N/A	MS 14

Please key in the following document using a ragged or justified right margin. Insert phrases as indicated. Save as Interviews and print.

MEMORANDUM

To   Matt Davis
From   Peter Knowles
Ref   PK/MD/TG

Top + 2 copies please. One copy to Pam Jordon and one copy for our files. Indicate routing.

We have received a large number of applications for the position of Assistant Garden Designer. I am very pleased with the response. We are sure to find a suitable person for this position.

A shortlist for interviews will need to be drawn up. I would be grateful if you could help me with this. I have set aside Thursday afternoon for this task. Perhaps we could meet at my office at 2.30 pm.

The advertisement for the position stated the following:

(Insert Phrase 3 - Gardens)

However, we have not had many applicants with this particular combination of qualifications. Do you think we need to find someone with proven design skills, or would an interest in gardening with some sort of artistic ability be sufficient? Please put some thought to this.

The starting salary and hours of work were advertised as:

(Insert Phrase 2 - Gardens)

If you would like to look at the application forms before Thursday please ask Pam. She will let you have them if I am not available.

Taking the examination

This section tells you exactly what the examiner will be looking for when marking your work. It does this by showing you the most common errors in documents submitted for the examination, together with hints on how to resolve these errors.

It also includes two examination practice exercises for you to complete to prepare you for the OCR examination.

Document 1

This task requires you to recall an existing document, usually an article or report, and make the necessary amendments. You may be asked to change line spacing, adjust the line length, use a specified text alignment and inset a paragraph from the margin. You will also be asked to insert headers and footers, find and replace a word or phrase and make proof corrections.

Look at Figures 3.29 and 3.30 below. The first document is correct, the second has 5 errors. Can you spot them?

HARTCLIFFE COMMUNITY COLLEGE

The Governing Body of Hartcliffe Community College is pleased to present this report to parents and interested parties of the school.

We would be interested to receive your comments regarding the inspection process, or the panel's finding. Please let us have these by the beginning of next term.

We were delighted to receive such a positive OFSTED report following our inspection in May of this year. It was felt that the experience was positive overall. It helped us to focus on the needs of the school, the students and of course the staff. Our pre-inspection preparation was well rewarded as the inspection panel found many strengths in our school. We are justifiably proud of the findings of the panel.

Generally, the panel found there were many more strengths than weaknesses at the school. Overall, the teaching was regarded as 'excellent' in over 75% of the lessons observed. This came as no surprise to us, but it is good to know our hard work has paid off.

Our position in the league tables is, as you are aware, very high. It is anticipated that our excellent examination results will continue. The panel found that our students were hard-working, keen and enthusiastic. They performed well in class and generally the coursework and homework were well prepared and of a good standard.

The pupils' behaviour was commented upon as being 'generally well-behaved and disciplined'. The panel did

not find any evidence of bullying in the school. The level of absence generally is low and unauthorised

absence much lower than county and national average.

The teaching staff were obviously commended for their excellence in teaching. However, praise was also given for their dedication and commitment. The school has a number of thriving after-school activities. It was felt by the inspection panel that these added considerable breadth and enrichment to student life. The Governing Body would like to thank the staff for their hard work throughout the inspection process.

There were, however, some weaknesses found. These all relate to the fabric of the school buildings. As you are aware, these are issues that are dealt with by the local authority. We are pleased they have been brought to the attention of the local authority in such a formal way. These particular issues have, of course, been reported to the local authority on a number of occasions.

We would be interested to receive your comments regarding the inspection process, or the panel's finding. Please let us have these by the beginning of next term.

SCHOOL REPORT

Figure 3.29 Correct version

HARTCLIFFE COMMUNITY COLLEGE

The Governing Body of Hartcliffe Community College is pleased to present this report to parents and interested parties of the school.

We would be interested to receive your comments regarding the inspection process, or the panel's finding. Please let us have these by the beginning of next term.

We were delighted to receive such a positive OFSTED report following our inspection in May of this year. It was felt that the experience was positive overall. It helped us to focus on the needs of the school, the students and of course the staff. Our pre-inspection preparation was well rewarded as the inspection panel found many strengths in our school. We are justifiably proud of the findings of the panel.

Generally, the panel found there were many more strengths than weaknesses at the school. Overall, the teaching was regarded as 'excellent' in over 75% of the lessons observed. This came as no surprise to us, but it is good to know our hard work has paid off.

The teaching staff were obviously commended for their excellence in teaching. However, praise was also given for their dedication and commitment. The school has a number of thriving after-school activities. It was felt by the inspection panel that these added considerable breadth and enrichment to student life. The Governing Body would like to thank the staff for their hard work throughout the inspection process.

Our position in the league tables is, as you are aware, very high. It is anticipated that our excellent examination results will continue. The panel found that our students were hard-working, keen and enthusiastic. They performed well in class and generally the coursework and homework were well prepared and of a good standard.

The pupils' behaviour was commented upon as being 'generally well-behaved and disciplined'. The panel did not find any evidence of bullying in the school. The level of absence generally is low and unauthorised absence much lower than county and national average.

There were, however, some weaknesses found. These all relate to the fabric of the school buildings. As you are aware, these are issues that are dealt with by the local authority. We are pleased they have been brought to the attention of the local authority in such a formal way. These particular issues have, of course, been reported to the local authority on a number of occasions.

Figure 3.30 Incorrect version

Error 1
The line length has not been adjusted.

Solution
Remember to alter the line length. The size of the line length will be contained in the instruction box at the top of the page. You may wish to highlight the instructions in this box as quite a number are placed here.

If you have an uneven line length then maybe you have just pulled in the margins using the ruler bar at the top of the page. This method is not reliable if you are moving text around. Follow the instructions given on page 95.

Error 2
The text is not justified.

Solution

The instructions for justifying text can be found on page 21. Again, the instruction for this will be in the large box at the top of the page. Remember to tick off the amendments as you make them.

Error 3

The paragraph beginning 'The pupils' behaviour ...' has not been changed to double line spacing.

Solution

Instructions for changing line spacing can be found on page 9. Don't forget to proof-read your work carefully to ensure that all amendments have been made. It can be difficult to follow all the amendments, particularly if you move around the page. Try to follow the amendments logically. Start at the top and work down. If you have to make amendments to a paragraph that is going to be moved or copied, make them BEFORE you move or copy it. That way, you will not become distracted.

Error 4

The paragraph of text beginning 'The teaching staff ...' has been moved incorrectly.

Solution

Be very careful when moving or copying text. Once you have made the move, read the instructions again to ensure you have done so correctly. This is a very common error.

Error 5

The paragraph 'We would be interested ...' is missing from the bottom of the document.

Solution

This is the paragraph that has to be copied. Do make sure you read the instructions carefully and **move** a paragraph that is to be **moved** and **copy** a paragraph that is to be **copied.** For a move the paragraph of text should only be seen once in the document. When you are copying text it should obviously be present in at least two places. It is surprising how many students fail to do this correctly. If the problem is that you are unsure of how to carry out moving and copying text, the instructions are on page 98.

Error 6

The footer is missing.

Solution

You must ensure that there is a footer (or header) on every page of your document. If you have not got a footer or header on the first page, but one appears on all the other pages, then you may have set your footer incorrectly. Go back and look at the instructions on page 101.

LLYFRGELL COLEG MENAI LIBRA

Document 2

This document requires you to sort a list into alphabetical order and allocate some space between two paragraphs. You may also be required to use emphasis, check a detail and inset a paragraph of text.

Look at Figures 3.31 and 3.32 below. The first document is correct, the second has 5 errors. Can you spot them?

JEWELLERY SALE

The Jewellery Store is offering amazing reductions on all jewellery items. This clearance is to allow for our wonderful new designs which will be arriving next month.

There is up to 50% on the following items

        Bracelets
        Broaches
        Cuff links
        Diamond rings
        Earrings
        Engagment rings
        Eternity rings
        Necklaces
        Signet rings
        Tie pins
        Watches
        Wedding bands

Many of our wedding and engagement ring sets are also included in the sale. With up to 50% off **these are excellent value**.

All our jewellery is of a very high quality. We use small independent designers so you can be sure you are purchasing a highly crafted, original piece of jewellery.

The sale will finish on the 30 April.

Figure 3.31 Correct version

JEWELLERY SALE

The Jewellery Store is offering amazing reductions on all jewellery items. This clearance is to allow for our wonderful new designs which will be arriving next month.

There is up to 50% on the following items

Bracelets
Broaches
Cuff links
Diamond rings
Engagment rings
Earrings
Eternity rings
Necklaces
Signet rings
Tie pins
Watches
Wedding bands

Many of our wedding and engagement ring sets are also included in the sale. With up to 50% off **these are excellent value**.

All our jewellery is of a very high quality. We use small independent designers so you can be sure you are purchasing a highly crafted, original piece of jewellery.

The sale will finish on the 30 April.

Figure 3.32 Incorrect version

Error 1
The heading has not been centred.

Solution
Careful proof-reading will solve these types of problems. Information on how to centre text can be found on page 21.

Error 2
The list has not been sorted into exact alphabetical order.

Solution
You must use the automatic sort facility in Word to do this accurately. If you decide to drag the pieces of text around then you may well end up with something in the wrong place. Instructions on how to use the sort facility can be found on page 111.

Error 3
The list has not been inset.

Solution
You must ensure that you make all the amendments given on the examination paper. In order to do this, tick off each amendment as you make it. Once you think you have finished, go back over the paper, reading it carefully to ensure you have not missed any instructions. If you do not know how to inset text, see page 99 for further information.

Error 4
The emphasis continues onto another line.

Solution
This is a very common error. You should check the screen and, if you have time and your centre allows, your printed copy. It can be that when you are moving text or adding line spaces, etc., the 'turn off bold' code is erased. If you are making this kind of amendment, go back and check that enhancements, such as embolding, line spacing, insetting, etc., are as they should be.

Error 5
The allocation of space is insufficient.

Solution
Do be careful with this. It is easy to move the space and then, when altering and amending text, accidentally move paragraphs up and remove the clear lines. If you have just guessed the amount of space required, this is not accurate enough to use in an examination. Follow the instructions on page 112.

Document 3

It is so easy to make errors on the table that you must allow sufficient time to proof-read this document very carefully. You are expected to key in a table, move a column, rearrange lines of text within the table and sort as specified.

Look at Figures 3.33 and 3.34. Figure 3.33 is correct, Figure 3.34 has a number of errors. Can you spot them?

CHOICES LTD

The following table shows the seminars we will be holding during the next three months. If you are interested in attending one or more of these events please e-mail us at info@choices.co.uk.

COURSE TITLE	COURSE DETAILS		NO OF PLACES
	DATE	COST	
King William Hotel, Farnborough			
Starting your own business	20 March	£285	15
Marketing secrets	23 March	£185	20
Customer service	27 March	£190	25
IT Update	28 March	£175	18
Norton Hotel, Birmingham			
Starting your own business	1 April	£285	15
Staff Management	2 April	£420	10
Health and Safety in the workplace	5April	£240	18
Communication skills	8 April	£320	20
Health and Safety risk assessment	16 April	£240	18
Lansdowne Hotel, Manchester			
IT Update	7 April	£175	18
Staff management	10 April	£420	10
Marketing secrets	15 April	£185	20
Communication skills	19 April	£320	20
King's Hotel, Bristol			
Senior management skills	1 May	£395	10
Policy making	3 May	£420	10
Developing strategies	4 May	£375	10

The prices above are per person and include lunch and refreshments. All courses begin with registration at 9.30 am and finish at 4.30 pm.

Figure 3.33 Correct version

CHOICES LTD

The following table shows the seminars we will be holding during the next three months. If you are interested in attending one or more of these events please e-mail us at info@choices.co.uk.

COURSE TITLE	NO OF PLACES	COURSE DETAILS	
		DATE	COST
Norton Hotel, Birmingham			
Health and Safety in the workplace	18	5April	£240
Health and Safety risk assessment	18	16 April	£240
Starting your own business	15	1 April	£285
Communication skills	20	8 April	£320
Staff Management	10	2 April	£420
Lansdowne Hotel, Manchester			
IT Update	18	7 April	£175
Staff management	10	10 April	£420
Marketing secrets	20	15 April	£185
Communication skills	20	19 April	£320
King William Hotel, Farnborough			
Starting your own business	15	20 March	£285
Marketing secrets	20	23 March	£185
Customer service	25	27 March	£190
IT Update	18	28 March	£175
King's Hotel, Bristol			
Senior management skills	10	1 May	£395
Policy making	10	3 May	£420
Developing strategies	10	4 May	£375

The prices above are per person and include lunch and refreshments. All courses begin with registration at 9.30 am and finish at 4.30 pm.

Figure 3.34 Incorrect version

Error 1

The section 'King William Hotel, Farnborough' has been moved incorrectly.

Solution

This might be because the rows were not placed correctly when moving. The other cause of this problem might be because the student worked out the table before keying in.

It is much better to use the instructions given on page 120. This will ensure that the rows are moved correctly. However, when using these instructions, you must ensure that the move is accurate. You will need to proof-read your table very carefully once you think you have made all the amendments.

Error 2

The 'Course Details' for the 'Norton Hotel, Birmingham' section are in the wrong order.

Solution

If you decide to work out the amendments and then key in the table using your annotated copy then you must check your copy very carefully before keying in. It is much better to follow the instructions given on page 123. However, when using this method you must ensure that all the rows are highlighted before you make the sort.

Error 3

The 'No of Places' column appears in the wrong place.

Solution

You must check very carefully where you are placing the new column when moving it. Again, it is much better to follow the instructions given on page 121 than trying to work out where to put the columns before you start keying in.

Document 4

This is a standard letter or memo with phrases inserted. You may have to check a detail from another document, inset a paragraph or emphasise some text.

Look at Figures 3.35 and 3.36. Figure 3.35 is correct, Figure 3.36 has several errors. Can you spot them?

MEMORANDUM

To

From   Andy Pearson

Ref   JC/AP/12/SLS

Date   28 January 2003

The company that provides the health and safety risk assessment will be arriving on the 23rd of next month. This is for a preliminary inspection before the Health and Safety Executive sends one of its officers for our annual inspection in March.

Please ensure that all staff are aware of the health and safety regulations. They must comply with instructions and report any hazards. Failure to do so can lead to dismissal.

I will be holding a meeting for senior management next week to discuss our health and safety strategy. Please ensure that you have carried out all the health and safety checks before that date. You can then report your findings to the meeting.

Figure 3.35 Correct version

MEMORANDUM
To

From   Andy Pearson

Ref   JC/AP/12

Date   28 January 2003

The company that provides the health and safety risk assessment will be arriving on the 23rd of next month. This is for a preliminary inspection before the Health and Safety Executive sends one of its officers for our annual inspection in March.

Accident books and hazard reporting books are kept in each department manager's office.

I will be holding a meeting for senior management next week to discuss our health and safety strategy. Please ensure that you have carried out all the health and safety checks before that date. You can then report your findings to the meeting.

Figure 3.36 Incorrect version

Error 1

The student has added his or her initials to the reference.

Solution

Key in only the text that is written on the examination paper (with the exception of the current date which must be added). Do not add any of your own details.

Error 2

The student has inserted the incorrect phrase for paragraph 2.

Solution

You must ensure that you insert the correct phrase. Check the examination paper very carefully against your worked copy. Open each of the phrase files to ensure that you have inserted the correct text. If you read the examination paper carefully you will see which of the phrases makes the most sense in the correct position. Although the sentence shown above does make sense and relates to the same topic, it is hard to see why you would want to insert that particular sentence in the memo.

Examination practice

To help you prepare for the examination, two full examination papers follow. Try to complete these in exam conditions. That is, finish in the 1 hour and 45 minutes allowed, including printing. Do not ask for help or refer to this book for information on how to do things. Try not to talk to anyone whilst working on these tasks. If you can do all of these then your work will give you a good indication of whether you are ready to sit the real exam. Once you have completed the tasks, you can check your documents with the worked examples on the CD-ROM.

When you are working through these exercises you will need to remember the following:

- If you are unsure of a spelling, use a dictionary as well as the spellchecker.
- Remember to spellcheck your work after you have finished each document.
- Consistency is very important. Make sure that all your work, including spacing between paragraphs, numbers, etc. shows a consistent display.
- Continuation sheets numbered.
- Ensure that any vertical space you allocate is correct by measuring with a ruler.
- Make sure that you make all the amendments in a document. It can be helpful to tick these off as you go along.
- When checking details from one document to another, you must ensure the details you key in are absolutely correct.
- Once you have finished keying in the text for a document, check with the exam paper that you have not keyed in the same word or line twice, or that you have not missed a word or line. These are very common errors and can lose you a large number of marks.

If you can complete all the work within the time without too many errors then you should now try working on some old examination papers. These will give you a feel for the type of examination paper you are likely to face. You must not become too complacent, even if you are consistently doing well in practice papers, as the examination itself can make you nervous and this is when it is easy to make mistakes.

The key to success in the examination is proof-reading your work carefully, referring back to the examination paper to check that you have keyed in the correct words, not the ones you think are there or should be there!

Examination practice 1

> *Recall this document stored under KNITTING. Amend as shown. Change to double linespacing (except where indicated). Adjust the line length to 12 cm. Use a justified right margin. Save as KNITS and print one copy.*

KNITTING – A BRIEF HISTORY   ← *Centre this heading*

It is believed that knitting began as a cottage industry in the Yorkshire Dales at the end of the sixteenth century. The industry lasted until the beginning of the twentieth century.

(A)   *profitable income.*

Handknitting as a ~~money earner~~ was only undertaken where there was little opportunity to earn a living from other trades. This was because hand knitting is rarely profitable in terms of pay per hour.

Move this paragraph to point marked (B).

Although knitting as a cottage industry died out during the early nineteenth century it remained a popular hobby for many. It was also a much cheaper way of clothing your family than buying ready-made garments. *The cost of wool was relatively inexpensive at the time.*

We do know that in 1590 a school was set up in York to teach the children of the poor to knit. However, the project was not successful and was moved to the Richmond area of the Dales. ~~Where~~ *Here* there was less chance of gaining any other type of employment.

During the seventeenth century the handknitting trade spread rapidly throughout the Yorkshire Dales. The business ~~operators~~ *owners* would travel around the remote areas of the Dales and collect completed garments, usually stockings, and drop off more wool.

Often whole families knitted, men, women and children. When the natural light faded they would knit in the dark or under their blankets. The knitting was often undertaken in groups and ~~group~~ singing was one way of relieving the monotony. ~~It is believed that many choirs began in this way.~~

During the nineteenth century schools were set up in some of the larger farmhouses. Children were taught how to knit stockings, gloves, caps, petticoats and waistcoats. Conditions were often hard and the slowest children were punished.

This was to help them earn a small income.

This paragraph in single linespacing

(B)

During the 1970_s the hobby became much less popular with the advent of /cheap/ ready-made garments becoming available. Women did not have so much time available for hobbies and this, combined with the large increase in the cost of wool, meant that the craft almost died out.

There is however an interest in reviving old crafts today. It is well worth finding out if any of your friends or relations could teach you this fascinating skill.

Copy this paragraph to point marked (A).

Change wool to yarn throughout this document.

Add a footer CRAFTS 2003 on every page.

Recall this document stored under KNITTING 2. Amend as shown. Use a ragged or justified right margin. Save as PATTERN and print one copy.

Emphasise this sentence

Pattern.com

We are a new Internet only company that specialises in knitting patterns and yarns. We can supply everything you need to produce beautiful and unique hand-made knitted garments for yourself, your family and friends.

We stock:

Knitting patterns by the latest designers
Yarns of all types and colours
Knitting needles
Buttons
Tape measures
Pattern holders
Row counters
Sewing needles
Circular needles
Overlockers
Stitch holders
Cable needles

Sort into exact alphabetical order and inset 20mm from the left margin.

leave at least 40 vertical space here

For full details of our range visit our website at www.pattern.com. All items have a full description and colour photograph.

It is easy to order from us, just follow the step-by-step instructions on our online form. We accept all types of major credit card. If you prefer, you can print out your order and post it to us with a cheque payment.

We are sure you will find all you need for this fascinating craft. However, if you are looking for something unusual then e-mail us your requirements and we will do our best to assist.

Key in the following table. Save as YARN and print one copy. Do not rule the table.

KNITTING YARNS

> modify layout so that COST PER BALL becomes the second column

The following yarns can be purchased by mail order from Pattern.co.uk. You can place your order by phone, fax or email. There is a £2.50 charge for packing and postage. Orders are normally despatched within 2 – 3 working days.

> Check this detail from Doc 2 and amend if necessary.

YARN TYPE	WEIGHT KNITTING	INFORMATION PER BALL	COST PER BALL
Baby Wool			
Pure wool	Double	80 grm	£1.85
Baby soft	4 ply	60 grm	£1.90
Acrylic	Double	100 grm	£1.70
Washable wool	4 ply	50 grm	£1.75
Aran Wool			
Pure wool	Aran	100 grm	£3.60
Wool / acrylic mix	Aran	80 grm	£2.20
Acrylic	Aran	70 grm	£1.90
Washable wool	Aran	100 grm	£4.50
Cotton			
Cotton denim	Aran	100 grm	£2.60
Cotton soft	4 ply	50 grm	£1.90
Cotton/linen mix	4 ply	70 grm	£2.90
Cotton/silk mix	4 ply	70 grm	£2.80
Cotton soft	Double	50 grm	£1.90
Miscellaneous			
Angora	4 ply	50 grm	£5.25
Chenille	Double	100 grm	£3.80
Silk slub	Double	100 grm	£4.25

> modify layout so that the Aran section appears before the Baby Wool section.

> Please sort the Yarn Type into exact alphabetical order within each section. Ensure corresponding details are also rearranged.

Please key in the following document using a ragged or justified right margin. Insert the phrases as indicated. Save as YARN ORDER and print.

Our ref PL/DY

Miss L Kovicz

98 Penn Lea Road

MILTON KEYNES

MK64 7RZ

Top + 2 copies please. One for Jasmine Bowan and one for our files. Indicate routing.

Dear Miss Kovicz

Thank you for your order. We can confirm that your yarn has been despatched to you today under separate cover.

Insert Phrase 3 - knitting

The denim yarn you have purchased is a very high quality yarn. It knits well and produces a hard-wearing garment that will last for many years. There are, however, a few points that should be kept in mind whilst using this type of material.

Insert Phrase 1 - Knitting

You should wash your knitted pieces before sewing up. Include sufficient yarn to complete the sewing in your wash. This is to ensure the yarn is pre-shrunk before completion.

When you are knitting with denim yarn, small amounts of dye will be released. This can result in some staining of your hands and clothes. You may wish to protect your clothes when knitting.

The dye will fade with each washing. As with denim jeans the colour will lighten with repeated washing. Over a long period the colour will turn from dark to pale blue. Please ensure you wash the garment separately to avoid staining other garments.

We are sure that if you follow these simple care instructions you will be delighted with the completed garment.

Yrs sncly   Peter Lester

Examination practice 2

Recall this document stored under Labradors. Amend as shown. Change to double linespacing (except where indicated). Adjust the line length to 11 cm. Use a justified right margin. Save as Rescue and print one copy.

Labrador Rescue Centre

This paragraph in single linespacing

, as its name suggests,

The Labrador Rescue Centre is/a centre that looks after unwanted and abandoned labrador dogs. It was founded 10 years ago by Jack and Emma Bowen, who had always been keen labrador and retriever owners.

The Centre has 45 purpose built kennels and can house up to 70 dogs. The Centre is a registered company and relies wholly upon donations for financial support.

Copy this paragraph to point marked

(✳)

If you would like to take on one of our rescued dogs, please contact us. In order to help find the dogs suitable homes we do ask prospective owners to attend an interview. This is to ensure that people are aware of the commitment they must make when taking on a pet dog. A charge of £80 is made for each of our animals. This helps to cover the cost of looking after the animal, including veterinary fees, whilst they have stayed at the Centre.

Obedience

We strongly encourage owners to attend our dog training and ~~agility~~ classes. These make the experience of looking after a pet more enjoyable and trouble-free. The classes are held between 7 and 9 pm, ~~Tuesdays~~ Mondays and Thursdays.

You do not have to have a rescue dog to join the classes as they are open to any dog owner. This is an enjoyable way to meet new people and the dogs ~~have a great time~~ really enjoy themselves. For those that are interested we compete in regional/competitions in obedience and agility.

and national

funds

⊘ In order to help raise ~~money~~ the Centre has a company shop. This sells second hand goods plus a small range of gift items for both animal lovers and pets.

This is located in the Centre of Cambridge.

LLYFRGELL COLEG MENAI LIBRARY

Insert **INFORMATION SHEET** as a header on every page

As we rely entirely on donations we really need your help to keep the Centre running.   By donating good quality items for us to sell or spending a few hours each week as a volunteer shop assistant you will help us raise vital funds.   Alternatively, we would be delighted if you would like to help at the kennels.   Here we need people to walk the dogs. *or assist with feeding*

Move this paragraph to point marked (✱)

If you cannot help, please consider sponsoring a dog or just simply making a donation. Information can be obtained from the company.   Call Jack or ~~Amelia~~ *Emma* on 01372 299107. They will be sent photographs and information of their adopted pet and if they wish they can visit it on a regular basis.

a minimum of

Sponsorship lasts for one year and is ideal for those who would like to own a pet, but do not have a suitable lifestyle or time to take on the commitment.

(▲)

Unwanted or abandoned animals are always given shelter for as long as necessary, however the Centre aims to rehome dogs wherever possible.

Sponsoring a dog makes a great gift for family and friends.

Change Company to charity throughout this document.

Recall this document stored as Open Day. Amend as shown. Use a ragged or justified right margin. Save as Open Day1 and print one copy.

OPEN DAY ← Centre this heading

The Labrador Rescue Centre Open Day is always held on the first Sunday in September. We invite the public to look around the Centre and meet some of our residents.

Special events are held during the day and these are enjoyed by animals and owners alike.
These include:

Obedience competition
Prize raffle
Teas and refreshments
Prettiest dog competition
Most like their owner competition
Agility display
Gun dog display
Children's games
Tombola
Bouncy castle
Coconut shy
Tours of the kennels

Sort into exact alphabetical order

There will also be a number of trade stands. These include pet accessory suppliers, gift stands, training accessories and representatives from various dog clubs and societies.

Leave at least 50 mm vertical space here

Admission is just £1 per person. Please support the Open Day. It is a great day out for all the family, including the dog!

Emphasise this sentence

Key in the following table. Save as Dogs and print one copy. Do not rule the table.

Modify layout so that the Golden labrador section appears after the chocolate labrador section.

DOGS REQUIRING RE-HOMING

We currently have the following dogs who are desperate to find a new home. If you think you can help please contact us. There is a small charge of £60 made for homing an animal. This helps us recover the costs of veterinary care, feeding and caring for the dog.

Check fee from Document 1 and change it necessary.

The Family Suitability Column shows how the dog copes with other dogs and children. It is important that the animal fits into your home as quickly and as easily as possible. Unfortunately, some dogs are not happy in homes where there are other pets and/or children.

Modify layout so that AGE becomes the last column.

NAME	AGE	FAMILY SUITABILITY	
		DOGS	CHILDREN
GOLDEN LABRADOR			
Holly	6	No	Yes, all ages
Buster	9	Yes	No
Red	3	Yes	Yes, over 5 years
Felix	2	No	Yes, over 10 years
BLACK LABRADOR			
Gemma	5	Yes	Yes, all ages
Billy	2	Yes	No
Bruno	7	No	Yes, over 5 years
Archie	4	Yes	Yes, all ages
Fido	10	No	Yes, over 10 years
CHOCOLATE LABRADOR			
Millie	3	Yes	Yes, all ages
Pavlov	8	Yes	No
Max	4	Yes	Yes, over 5 years
Marilyn	7	Yes	Yes, all ages
Jake	6	No	No
Hamish	3	Yes	Yes, over 10 years
Daisy	1	Yes	Yes, all ages

Please sort AGE into exact numerical order within each section starting with the lowest number first. Ensure corresponding details are also rearranged.

Please key in the following document using a ragged or justified right hand margin. Insert the phrases as indicated. Save as [blank] and print.

Our ref KN/LH

Top + 2 copies please. One for Jayne Hayward and one for our files. Indicate routing.

Mrs K Norris
4 Lime Gardens
York
YO6 9BY

Check this detail from Doc 3 and amend if necessary

Dear Mrs Norris

Thank you for your interest in re-homing Daisy our (black) labrador. As you know, Daisy is a lovely dog and has a very even temperament. She is happy to be with other animals and children of all ages. We are sure she will make a super family pet.

In order to ensure that you appreciate the commitment of owning a pet such as Daisy, we would ask you to attend a short interview.

Insert Phrase 2 – Rescue

Insert Phrase 1 – Rescue

We have made a provisional appointment for Saturday 1 February at 11.30 am. If this is inconvenient please let us know as soon as possible. The interview will be conducted by Jayne Hayward. Please ask for her at reception.

We are sure you will appreciate the need for us to assess your suitability to take one of our dogs. This process will help ensure that both you and the animal are suited and that your expectations are met.

We look forward to meeting you.

Yours sincerely

Martin Huchvak
Centre Manager

Mailmerge

The Level 2 Mailmerge (Intermediate) examination offered by OCR consists of four tasks:

1   Amend an existing datafile
2   Create a new datafile
3   Setting up and merging a letter or memo to use with the amended datafile
4   Setting up and merging a letter or memo to use with the newly created datafile

You will need to be familiar with the layout of standard letters and memos and be able to use various types of emphasis.

You are allowed 1 hour and 30 minutes to complete the examination.

> **NOTE**
> In this section of the book, the instructions and exercises have not been presented in the same order as in the examination paper. This is because it is easier to understand using mailmerge if you are familiar with datafile. The consolidation and exam practice sections are, however, in the same order as the examination paper.

You will be asked to demonstrate a number of skills, by using the keyboard and your knowledge and application of English. Each of the four tasks will contain one or more of the following:

*   Emphasis of headings
*   Amendments using correction signs
*   Information which must be keyed in using a consistent format
*   Setting up datafiles and standard documents

In this section you will cover the following topics:

*   Mailmerge
*   Consolidation practice
*   Taking the examination

Mailmerge

> **In this section you will learn about:**
>
> *   setting up a datafile
> *   creating records
> *   setting up queries
> *   amending existing datafiles
> *   sorting a datafile
> *   creating a datafile
> *   creating a main document
> *   complex queries
> *   adding new records
> *   printing a datafile

Mailmerge is a very useful tool that can be used to merge information into letters, memos and other documents. For example, if you were secretary of a sports club or something similar you may wish to send a letter to each of your members reminding them to pay their membership fees. You would only need to key in one letter with special codes for items such as the name and address, and amount of fees, and then you could merge it with your datafile to produce personalised letters. This would save lots of time and effort.

The OCR examination expects you to be able to set up a small datafile, amend an existing datafile (which will be provided on disk or on your hard drive) and print various letters using queries. Queries are used when you need just some of the information contained in the datafile to make up your standard letters. For example, if you only wanted to send letters to members of the sports club whose membership is due to run out within a week or two, you could set up a query to do just that.

The examination always asks you to amend the existing datafile first, then print out some letters using the amended datafile. The third and fourth tasks relate to setting up your own datafile.

This section will look at setting up your own datafile first. This is because by doing this, you will become much more familiar with the structure of datafiles. You will then be able to amend the existing datafile very easily.

In order to understand the process of using mailmerge, you need to be familiar with the following terms.

Datafile

In order to be able to merge documents you will need a datafile that stores all the relevant information such as names and addresses, etc. Using the example of a sports club, the following information shows you how a datafile could be set up.

Fields

The main structure of the datafile is made up of different fields. These are the various items of information that you require, for example membership number, date fees are due, name and address of member. You can have as many or as few fields as you need in each datafile. All information stored about each member would be kept as a **record**.

Records

The information you hold on each member of the club is stored in a separate record. Each record contains all the fields in the datafile. For each new member that joins the sports club, a new record is entered into the datafile.

Merge document

This is the letter or report into which you place your fields. For example, the sports club would write to members whose membership is about to run out asking them for the next year's fees. Once a merge document has been created it can be stored so that at the beginning of each month, the club secretary could open the document and produce letters for all members who need to renew their membership during the coming month.

In order to start the mailmerge process you will need to have the relevant information stored in a datafile.

Setting up a datafile

Obviously, before you can start entering data into a datafile you have to set up the various fields for each piece of information required. Look at the example data form in Figure 4.1.

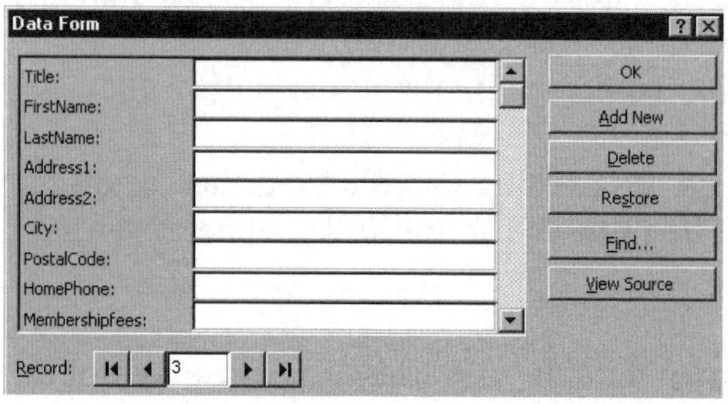

Figure 4.1 Data form

This data form contains all the information required for the sports club datafile. You can only see the first 9 fields of this data form – to see the rest you need to scroll down using the arrows at the side of the form.

The fields that have been used for the sports club datafile are shown in Figure 4.2.

Field

Title	For Mr, Mrs, Ms, Miss, etc.
FirstName	It is better to split these into different categories so that it is easy to do labels, etc.
LastName	
Address1	Again, it is better to split the address into different sections
Address2	
City	
PostalCode	
HomePhone	
Membershipfees	
Datedue	
DateofBirth	

Figure 4.2 Datafile fields

Creating a datafile

You will now set up a datafile to use when merging documents.

Exercise 4.1

Method

1 Open a new blank document. Go to **Tools**, click on **Mail Merge**. The following box will appear (see Figure 4.3).

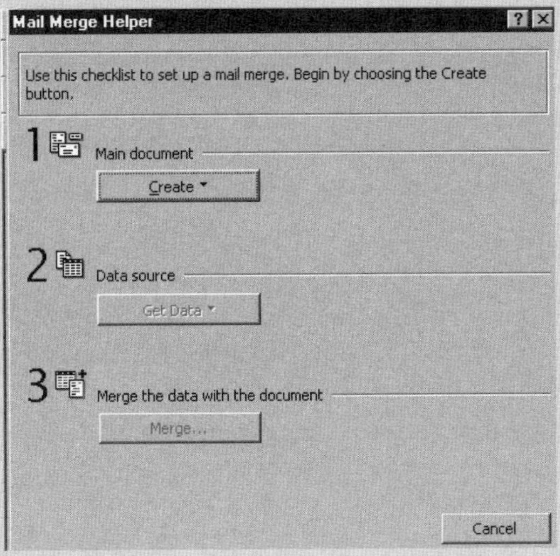

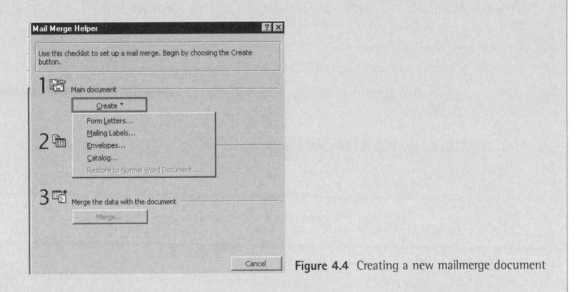

Figure 4.3 Mail Merge Helper

You will note that the only available option is to create a main document. The main document is the document into which you will merge the information.

2 Click on **Create**. The following box will appear (see Figure 4.4).

Figure 4.4 Creating a new mailmerge document

3 Click on **Form Letters** ... The following box will appear (see Figure 4.5).

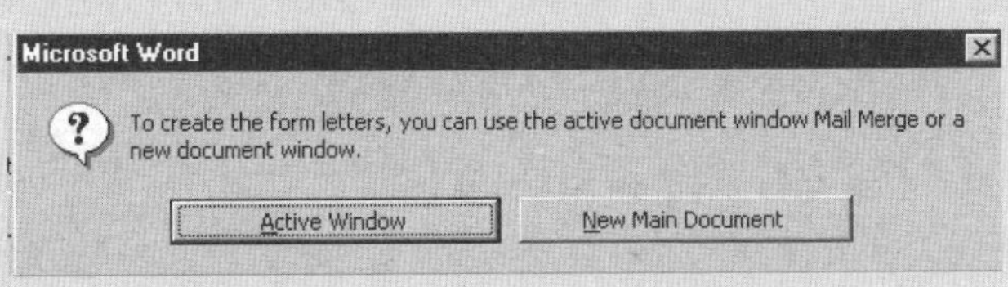

Figure 4.5 Creating a main document

You are given a choice of using the 'Active Window' or a 'New Main Document' in which to create your main document. If you choose 'Active Window' then the document that you have opened (and should still be blank) will become the main document. If you choose 'New Main Document' then Word will open another blank document for you to use.

4 Choose <u>A</u>ctive Window.

5 The Mail Merge Helper box will now change as follows (see Figure 4.6).

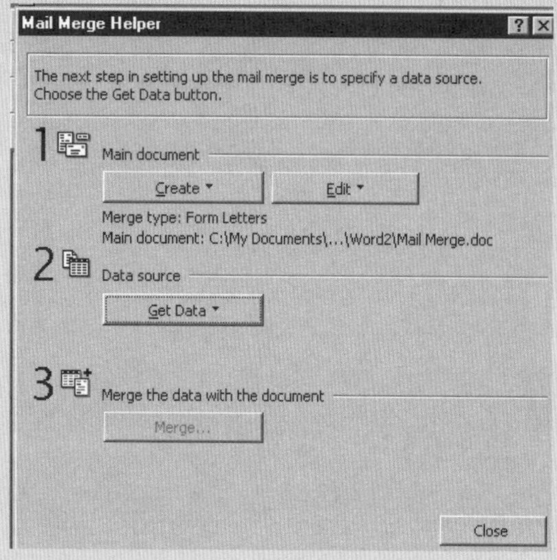

Figure 4.6 Mail Merge Helper

6 At this point it is a good idea to save the document. To do this, click on **Close** and then save your document in the usual way. For more information on saving documents see page 13. Call the document **Membership Letter**.

7 You will now have to reopen the Mail Merge Helper. To do this, go to **Tools** and choose **Mail Merge**.

8 Because you have created a main document, more choices are available. To start setting up the datafile click on **Get Data**. The following menu will appear (see Figure 4.7).

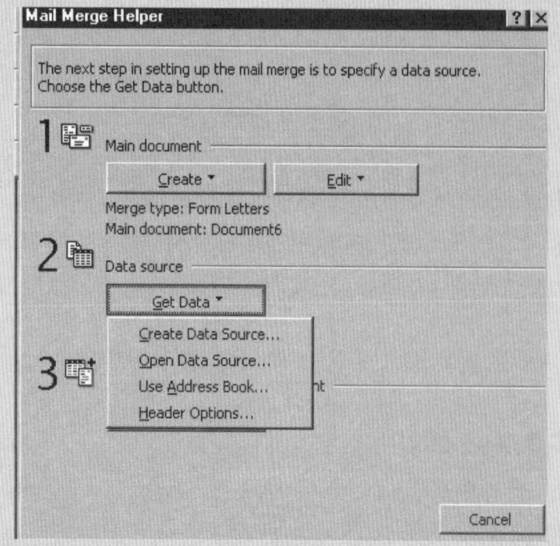

Figure 4.7 Get data

9 You will need to choose the **Create Data Source ...** option as you are starting a new datafile. The following menu will appear (see Figure 4.8).

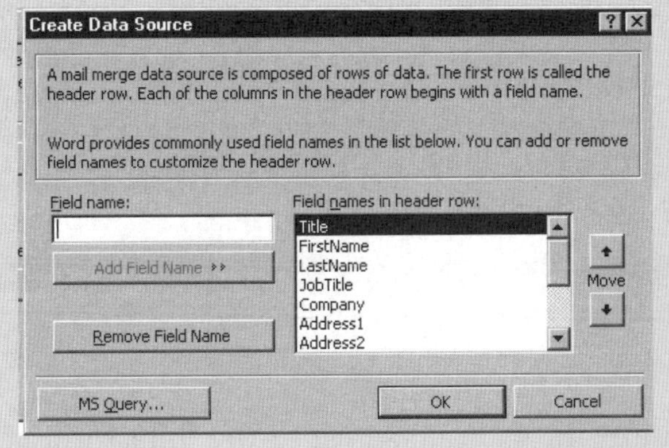

Figure 4.8 Create Data Source

10 This box gives the default field names. You should look at each one, scrolling down the list when necessary, and decide if you need the field in your datafile. For example, the first three fields listed, Title, FirstName and LastName, will all be required in the datafile. However, the next two, JobTitle and Company, will not. It is best to delete these so that the datafile is easy to manage. To do this click on 'JobTitle' and then click on Remove Field Name. Repeat this for the field 'Company'.

11 Continue scrolling through the list and delete 'State', 'Country' and 'WorkPhone' using the instructions given above.

12 You will also need to add some field names. To do this, click in the Field name box. Key in the words Membershipfees exactly as shown. Click on the Add Field Name box which will now be active.

13 Using the instructions given in 8 above, add the following field names:
    Feesdue
    DateofBirth

14 When you have completed adding the field names, click OK. You will then be taken to the save menu. You must save your datafile somewhere sensible at this point. Call your datafile Membership.

15 As soon as you have saved the datafile the following dialogue box will appear (see Figure 4.9).

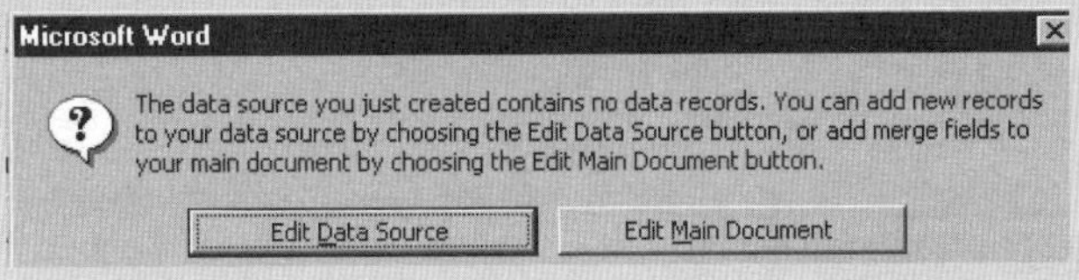

Figure 4.9 Edit Data Source or Edit Main Document

16 As you need to enter records into the datafile choose Edit Data Source. The following will appear on screen (see Figure 4.10).

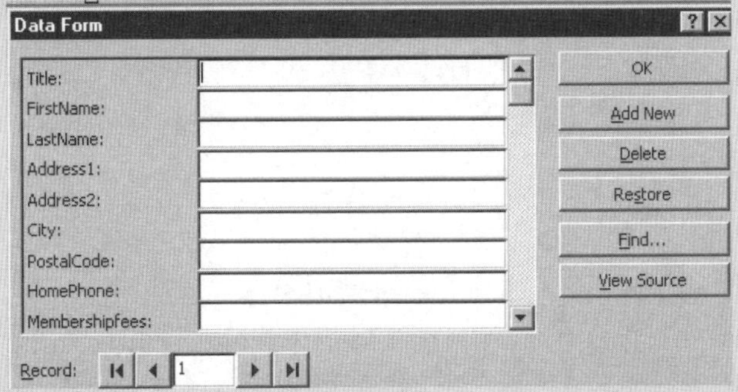

Figure 4.10 Data Form

> 17 The form that appears on screen contains all the fields that are in your datafile. You can use this for entering records. At the bottom of the form you have a record counter. This shows that you are viewing the first record of your datafile. You can key in your information directly into the data form to create records. Use a separate record for each person.

Creating records

To create records, key in the information for each person into the data form created in Exercise 4.1. Use the **Tab** key to move from field to field.

Exercise 4.2

Enter 8 records into the datafile membership.

Method

1 Enter the following information into the first record:

Title	Mrs
FirstName	Jennifer
LastName	Lewis
Address1	12 Fellowes Lane
Address2	Weston
City	BATH
PostalCode	BA3 8NQ
HomePhone	01225 721930
Membershipfees	£120
FeesDue	1/10/03
DateofBirth	26/4/65

Your data form will now look like Figure 4.11.

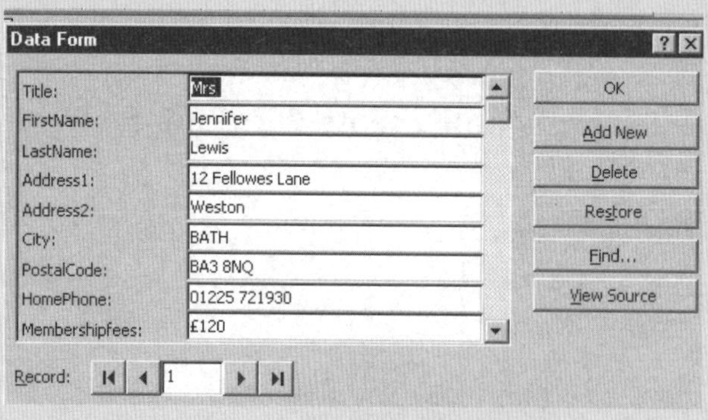

Figure 4.11 Complete data form

2 Once you have finished keying in the record, click on **Add** New. Another blank record will appear on screen and the number in the **Record** box will change to 2.

3 Key in the following records (2–8) using the methods given above.

	Record 2	Record 3	Record 4	Record 5	Record 6	Record 7	Record 8
Title	Mr	Mrs	Mr	Ms	Miss	Mr	Mrs
FirstName	John	Greta	Kevin	Sally	Anna	Hans	Lily
LastName	Pike	Tauber	Davis	Garrett	Rose	Tauber	Castle
Address1	10 Meadow Walk	47 Perfect View	15B Prospect Flats	54 Station Road	6 Manor Way	47 Perfect View	Rose Cottage
Address2	Weston	Lansdown	Highland Way	Newbridge	Larkhall	Lansdown	Saltford
City	BATH	BATH	BATH	BATH	BATH	BATH	BATH
PostalCode	BA2 4BE	BA1 5TU	BA3 9QM	BA1 8YW	BA3 1NP	BA1 5TU	BA2 8KL
HomePhone	01225 981270	01225 289344	01225 283911	01225 583187	01225 472917	01225 289344	01225 471920
Membershipfees	£150	£120	£180	£110	£150	£120	£180
Feesdue	1/10/03	14/10/03	5/11/03	2/11/03	25/10/03	14/10/03	7/11/03
DateofBirth	2/6/56	27/12/59	5/4/68	29/8/68	17/8/73	30/7/55	2/1/60

4 When you have finished entering the records, check your work very carefully. When you are sure that it is all correct, click **OK**. The data form will disappear. Your records for this datafile are now complete.

Creating a main document

You now need to complete your main document in order to print the merged document.

Exercise 4.3

Create a letter to send to all members whose fees are due.

Method

1 Go to **Tools**, click on **Mail Merge**. The following box will appear (see Figure 4.12) – note that the options have changed.

Mail Merge Helper

The main document and data source are ready to merge. Choose the Merge button to complete the merge.

1 Main document

   [Create ▾] [Edit ▾]

   Merge type: Form Letters
   Main document: C:\...\Membership letter.doc

2 Data source

   [Get Data ▾] [Edit ▾]

   Data: C:\...\Membership.doc

3 Merge the data with the document

   [Merge...] [Query Options...]

   Options in effect:
      Suppress Blank Lines in Addresses
      Merge to new document

   [Cancel]

Figure 4.12 Mail Merge Helper

2 In the **Data Source** section, click on **Get Data**. Choose **Open Data Source** from the list of options. You will be taken to the main directory. Choose the data source file you created called Membership. The following box will appear (see Figure 4.13):

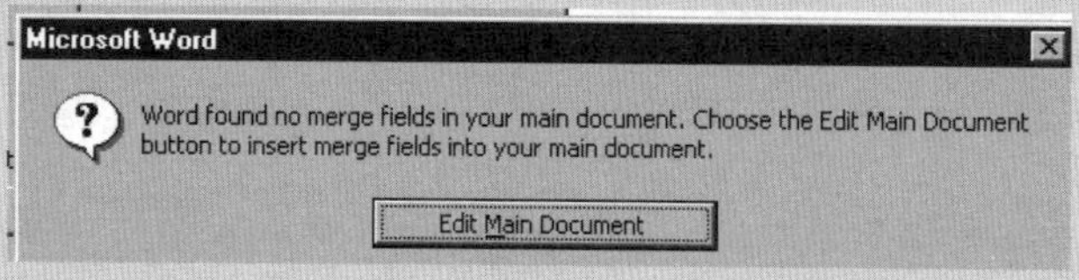

Figure 4.13 Edit Main Document

3 Because the main document is blank there are no merge fields available. This box prompts you to insert merge fields into the main document. Click on **Edit Main Document**.

4 All boxes will now disappear and you will be left with a blank page. Note that on the toolbar these two buttons have appeared (see Figure 4.14).

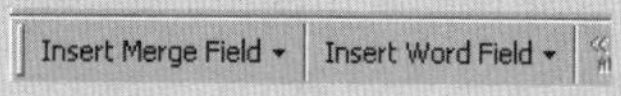

Figure 4.14 Insert field buttons

5 You will start your merge letter with the name and address of the members. To do this click on **Insert Merge Field**. A list of fields will appear as in Figure 4.15 below.

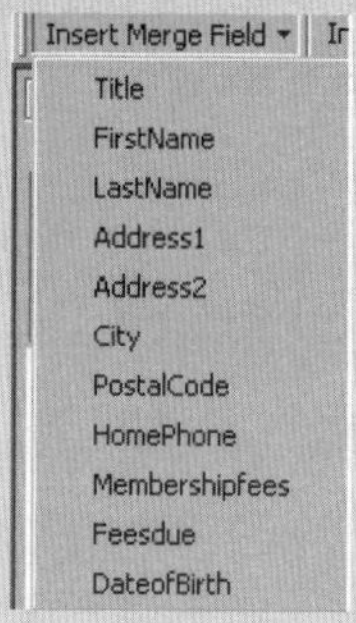

Figure 4.15 Available merge fields

6 Click on 'Title'. The merge code for title should now appear in your document as in Figure 4.16 below.

Figure 4.16
Example of merge field

7 Now, before you add the 'FirstName' field, you **must** press the space bar once, in order to leave a clear space between the Title and the First Name. If you do not then the words will run together. Remember that when you are setting out the merge fields you should treat each as an ordinary word and use spacing and punctuation as usual.

8 Choose the 'FirstName' field from the **Insert Merge Fields** menu and then, remembering to leave a space between, add the 'LastName' field. Press the Enter key to move to a new line and add the 'Address1' field. Repeat this for 'Address2', 'City' and 'PostalCode' fields. Your page should now look like this (see Figure 4.17):

Figure 4.17 Merge fields for name and address block

9   Now press **Enter** twice to leave a clear line space and insert the automatic date field. To do this, go to **Insert** and choose **Date and Time**. The following menu will appear (see Figure 4.18):

Date and Time	? X
Available formats:	**Language:**
13/09/2002	English (U.K.)
Friday, 13 September 2002	
13 September 2002	
13/09/02	
2002-09-13	
13-Sep-02	
13.09.2002	
13 Sep. 02	
September 02	
Sep-02	
13/09/2002 16:18	
13/09/2002 16:18:01	
4:18 PM	
4:18:01 PM	
16:18	
16:18:01	

Check this box for automatic update of the date

☑ Update automatically

Default...   OK   Cancel

Figure 4.18 Automatic date menu

Choose the format that gives the day, month and year in full by clicking on it. Remember that American dates (month, day, year) are always penalised in the examination. If you would like the date to be updated each time you open the document, check the **Update automatically** box. Once you have chosen the date, click **OK**.

10 Now leave a clear line space and key in the salutation as shown below. Don't forget to use the merge fields for the title and last name.

Dear <<Title>> <<LastName>>

11 Now key in the rest of the letter as shown below, using merge fields where appropriate.

> Membership Fees
>
> I hope you have enjoyed your membership of the Bath and District Sports Club. The fees for the year 2002/2003 will be due on «Feesdue». For your current level of membership the amount payable will be «Membershipfees».
>
> I do hope that you will renew your membership and look forward to seeing you soon.
>
> Yours sincerely

12

Once you have finished keying in the text, go back to the **Mail Merge** option on the <u>T</u>ools menu and the following menu will appear (see Figure 4.19):

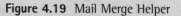

Figure 4.19 Mail Merge Helper

13 Choose the <u>Merge</u> … option. Note that under the <u>Merge</u> button, the menu shows you the default options. These are **Suppress Blank Lines in Addresses** and **Merge to new document**. The **Suppress Blank Lines in Addresses** option means that if a record does not use all of the available address lines in the merge fields, then it will automatically close up the gap. The **Merge to new document** option means that the merged documents will appear separately and your main document, which contains the merge fields, will remain unchanged.

Once you have clicked on <u>Merge</u> … the following menu will appear (see Figure 4.20):

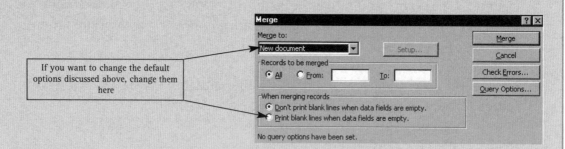

Figure 4.20 Merge menu

14 For this exercise you will merge all the records. Later on you will learn how to set up queries so that you can choose the people who require a letter. Once you are sure your box looks like Figure 4.20 above, click <u>Merge</u>.

15 You can now either print your documents or save them to file. For this exercise, you should print the documents.

Worked examples of the documents can be found on the CD-ROM.

Note: You may wish to print your merged letters onto headed letter paper or memo form. In order to do this, you will need to open the headed paper template or memo template and then start the mailmerge process. As you will be choosing Active Window in which to create your mailmerge document, it will be printed with the headed paper (or memo).

Setting up queries

When you completed the mailmerge you merged documents for all the records contained in the datafile. However if you want to mail only those members whose membership fees are due in October you can set up your mailmerge to do just that. You will, however, need to set up a query, which is a series of comparisons or sums so that the computer can run through the datafile records and select the correct records to merge.

Exercise 4.4

Set up a query to select all members whose fees are due in October.

Method

1   Open the main document called **Membership Letter.** Your merge document containing merge fields should be on screen.
2   Go to **Tools** and choose **Mail Merge.** The **Mail Merge Helper** will appear and should look like Figure 4.20.

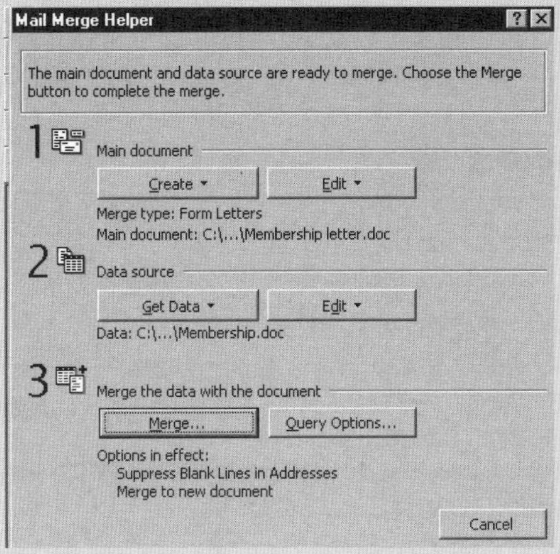

Figure 4.20 Mail Merge Helper

3   You are going to set up a query so click on the **Query Options ...** button. The following menu will appear (see Figure 4.21).

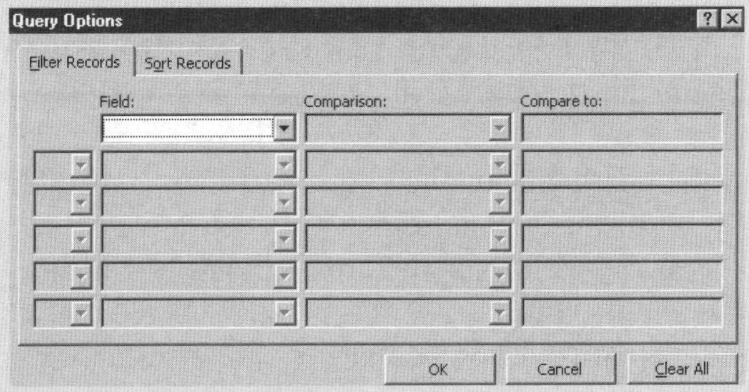

Figure 4.21 Query Options menu

If there is any text in the boxes then click on **Clear All.**

4 You are going to filter records rather than sort them. If you were to sort your records then it would put them in some kind of order, for example in alphabetical order by last name. You are going to print letters to only those members whose membership fees are due during October. Ensure that the **Filter Records** tab is to the front and that the menu looks like the one in Figure 4.21 above.

5 In the **Field** box click on the arrow to the right-hand side and you will see a list of all the fields contained in your datafile (see Figure 4.22).

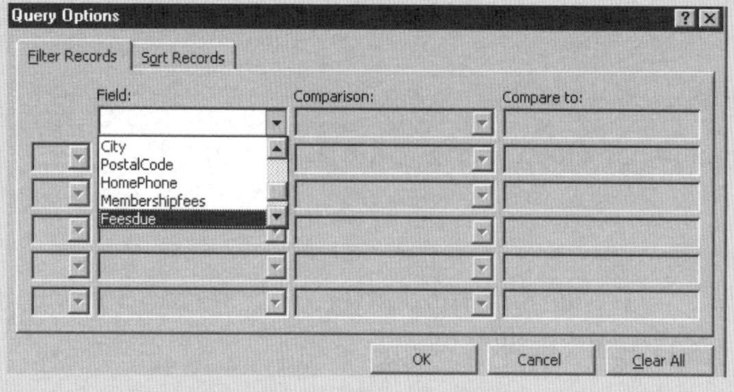

Figure 4.22 Fields

6 Click on the field 'Feesdue' so that it appears in the **Field** box.

7 The **Comparison** box should now be highlighted. Again, click on the arrow to the right-hand side to see a list of comparisons that can be made. It should look like Figure 4.23 below.

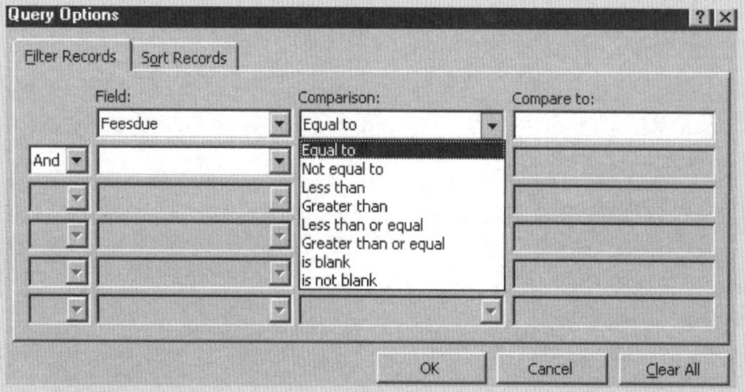

Figure 4.23 Comparisons

8 The comparison that you will need is '**Greater than or equal to**', so find this comparison and click on it. It will be displayed in the **Comparison** box.

9 In order to test the comparison against the datafile you will need to give further information. You have already set the '**Greater than or equal to**' comparison and next you need to tell mailmerge that you want the date to be 1 October 2003 or later (ie greater than or equal to 1 October 2003). Key in 01/10/03 in the **Compare to...** box.

10 You will also need to set the upper limit for the end of October as merging the letters now would print all of the records from 1 October onwards. To do this, click in the second line of the **Field** box and choose 'Feesdue' again.

11 In the **Comparison** box you will need to choose '**Less than**'. (Note that you do not choose '**Less than or equal to**' when you key in the 1 November as your 'less than' figure, because you do not want to print letters for those whose membership fees are due on 1 November.)

12 In the **Compare to ...** box you should key in 01/11/03. Your table should now look like Figure 4.24 below.

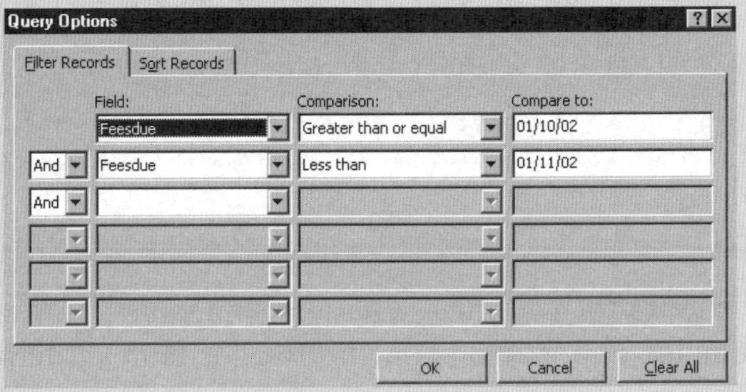

Figure 4.24 Query options set

13 When you are sure you have completed the boxes correctly click **OK**. You will return to the **Mail Merge** main menu. Click on **Merge** ... . The following menu will appear (see Figure 4.25):

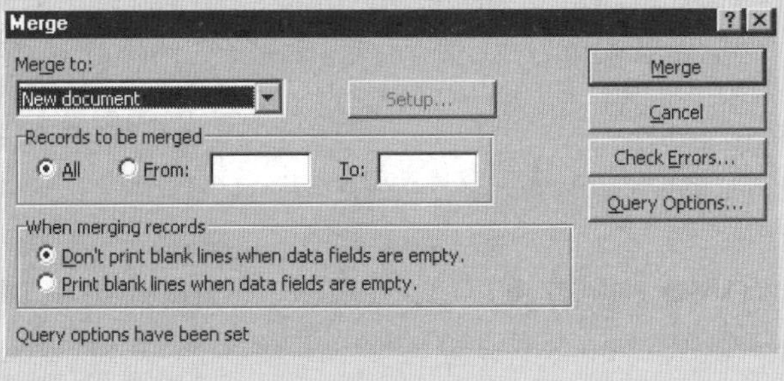

Figure 4.25 Merge options

Check that the **Merge to** box shows **New Document** and that the **Records to be merged** button is set to **All**. When you are sure that everything is correct, click **Merge**. Your members' new letters should now appear on screen. There should be five letters in total to the following: Jennifer Lewis, John Pike, Greta Tauber, Anna Rose, Hans Tauber.

Exercise 4.5

You can now try another merge, this time sending letters to all those whose membership fees are £120.

Method

1 Follow steps 1–3 of Exercise 4.4. Make sure that at step 3, when you call up the **Query Option** box, you click on **Clear All** to delete the query options you set above.

2 You will need to complete the **Query Option** box as follows:

Field	Comparison	Compare to
Membershipfees	Equal to	120

Make sure that you do not key in the £ sign. If you do, then Mail Merge will not recognise it and an error message will be given telling you the query is not valid. The £ sign will be printed in your document however.

3 Follow the rest of the steps in Exercise 4.4.

4 There should be three merge letters to Jennifer Lewis, Greta Tauber and Hans Tauber.

More complex queries

You have set up two separate queries for your merge letters. Sometimes, however, the query needs to be more complex and may be done on two (or more) criteria.

Exercise 4.6

Using the datafile **Membership** and the main document **Membership Letter**, set up a query so that letters are produced for members whose fees are due during October and whose membership fees are £150.

Method

1 Ensure you have opened **Membership Letter** as the main document and the **Membership datafile** as the data source.

2 Go to the **Query Option** box and set the following criteria:

Field	Comparison	Compare to
Feesdue	Greater than or equal to	1/10/02
Feesdue	Less than	1/11/02
Membershipfees	Equal to	150

The **Query Option** box should look like Figure 4.26.

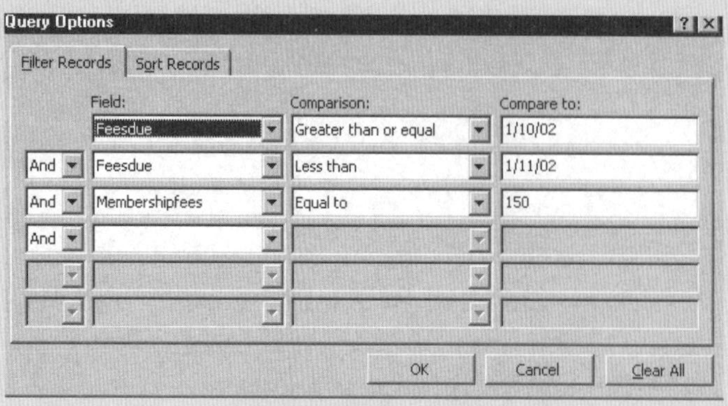

Figure 4.26 Completed Query Option box

3 Click **OK**.

4 Click **Merge** and then set the **Merge** box to 'New Document'.

5 Your merged letters should appear on screen. These should be to Anna Rose and John Pike. Worked examples of these letters can be found on the CD-ROM.

NOTE

If you are asked to use a time such as 2 pm in the query, the same rule applies as with amounts of money. In the Query box, you will need to key in just the figure, for example 2. Do not key in the am or pm. The document will print with the full time, including am or pm extension.

Exercise 4.7

Create the following datafile and standard letter. Set up the query options as given in the instructions. Correct versions are in the worked examples on the CD-ROM.

Please key in the following records as a datafile suitable for use with the following standard letter. Save as COURSES and print one copy.

Peter Marsden
Production Manager
IT Basic
21 March
9.30 am
B124

Laura Broome
Admin Assistant
Database
21 May
9.30 am
D169

Peta Gruber
Sales Assistant
Database
28 April
10.00 am
D167

Maxine Clarke
Design Assistant
Web Design
29 May
10.00 am
W149

Lucy Cartwright
Design Manager
Web Design
29 May
10.00 am
W149

Carole Hollingdale
Human Resources Assistant
Database
28 April
10.00 am
D167

Joseph Francis
Operations Manager
Spreadsheets
1 June
9.00 am
S162

Samantha Jones
Sales Assistant
Database
21 May
9.30 am
D169

Charles Passmore
Accounts Assistant
Spreadsheets
1 June
9.00 am
S162

Chris Moore
Operations Assistant
Database
28 April
10.00 am
D167

Please key in the following standard document to merge with the Datafile COURSES. Insert merge codes where indicated by * and use a ragged right margin. Print one copy of the standard document and also print documents to all those who are going to attend a database course on 28 April.

MEMORANDUM

To   * name   * job

From   Keith Richards   Human Resources Manager

Ref   IT/KR

IT Training

According to our records you requested IT training at your last appraisal. We have now been able to arrange some intensive one-day courses. These will be held at Newtown College.

You have been enrolled on a * course course. This is to be held on * date. The start time will be * time.   . . Please report to room * room. All courses are due to finish at 4.30pm.

If for any reason you cannot attend please let me know as soon as possible. We may be able to offer training at a later date.   (Please emphasise this words)

Exercise 4.8

Create the following datafile and standard letter. Set up the query options as given in the instructions. Correct versions are in the worked examples on the CD-ROM.

Please key in the following records as a datafile suitable for use with . Save as COLLEGE and print one copy

Kirsty
Daniels
Business Administration
Lisa Murray
1 May
9.00 am
Room 63

John
Mackenzie
Advanced Programming
Lisa Murray
30 April
2.00 pm
Room 4

Paul
Hopkins
Business Management
Jack Cates
1 May
9.30 am
Room 101

George
Masters
Operational Management
Lisa Murray
1 May
11.00 am
Room 65

Lesley
James
Marketing
Lisa Murray
30 April
11.45 am
Room 19

Ying
Hsiao
Statistics
Jack Cates
29 April
10.00 am
Room 24

Emily
Dixon
Customer Service
Lisa Murray
1 May
2.00 pm
Room 10

Sandra
Neale
Call Handling
Jack Cates
1 May
11.30 am
Room 20

Marcus
Bennetto
Systems and Control
Lisa Murray
30 April
6.00 pm
Room 92

Derek
Haslow
Human Resources Management
Lisa Murray
28 April
9.30 am
Room 42

Please key in the following standard document to merge with the datafile COLLEGE. Insert merge codes where indicated by * and use a ragged right margin. Print one copy of the standard document and also print documents to all those who will be inspected by Lisa Murrey on 1 May.

Memorandum

To   * FIRSTNAME   * SURNAME

From Declan Loughlin   Ref IT/03

In order to maintain high standards, the senior management team observes lessons on a regular basis. This is purely to ensure good practice in the classroom and should be viewed as a part of your on-going training.

Your * SUBJECT class   will be inspected on * DATE at   * TIME .   The observer will be * INSPECTOR. Please ensure you send him/her a copy of your lesson plan and scheme of work for the course one week before the inspection date.

If this causes any problems, please let me know.

Please emphasise this sentence.

Exercise 4.9

Create the following datafile and standard letter. Set up the query options as given in the instructions. Correct versions are in the worked examples on the CD-ROM.

Please key in the following records as a datafile suitable for use with exercise 4.9. Save as Details and print one copy.

Mr John Crook
7 King Street
BATH
BA1 3LJ
Castle Cottage
pets accepted
no smoking allowed

Ms Carole Hall
64 Cumber Close
BIRMINGHAM
B2 9 PD
Harbour Lights
pets accepted
smoking allowed

Mrs Phyllis Greene
21 Coronation Road
LIVERPOOL
L31 6QT
Mermaid Cottage
no pets accepted
smoking allowed

Mr Chris Smith
22 Chaucer Road
GUILDFORD
GU3 7AP
Torfrey
no pets accepted
smoking allowed

Mrs Patricia Wright
91 Haverland Way
PERTH
PH3 2AB
Lantern Cottage
no pets accepted
no smoking allowed

Mr Adrian Brown
3 Rose Cottages
EXMOUTH
EX21 6JG
Drimmin
no pets accepted
no smoking allowed

Mrs Mercedes Zarrabi
44 West Avenue
SALISBURY
Sundial
no pets accepted
no smoking allowed

Mr Steve Ross
14 Mount Road
IPSWICH
IP2 3BY
Samphire House
pets accepted
no smoking allowed

Mrs Anita Garner
16 Sharpe's Hill
ROMFORD
RM1 3JJ
Compass Cottage
pets accepted
no smoking allowed

Mr Declan Sullivan
6 Ballantyne Avenue
LEEDS
LS3 5AK
Park Court
no pets accepted
smoking allowed

Please key in the following standard document to merge with the datafile Details. Insert merge codes, where indicated, by * and use a ragged right margin. Print one copy of the standard document and also print documents to those who do not allow pets or smoking.

Our ref IL/Owners

* Name
* Street
* Town
* Post Code

Dear * Name

Holiday Property * Cottage

We are currently preparing the brochure for next season. As usual, we would like to check a few details with you. This will help ensure the brochure is accurate.

Your current listing states the following *pets and * smoking. Please confirm these details are correct.

We would be grateful if you could let us have this information within the next few days. The brochure is going to print at the end of the month. Any remaining inaccuracies after that point cannot be corrected.

Yours sincerely
Ian Lynott
Manager

Amending an existing datafile

In this section you will learn to amend existing datafiles, including adding a new field to each record.

In order to follow the examples given you will need to access the datafile called HOLIDAYS on the CD-ROM.

Exercise 4.10

Open the existing datafile called HOLIDAYS.

Method

1 First of all you will need to find out where the datafile is being stored. It may be on a floppy disk, the CD that accompanies this book or the hard drive of your computer. Once you know its location, go to **File**, choose **Open** and move around the directories until you are in the correct place.

2 Click on the file named HOLIDAYS and the datafile will appear. As you can see, this is set out in table format. The file will act as a table and it is not possible to view the file as individual records. This is because you do not have an open main document in which to merge fields. You can, however, alter records, add new records or delete fields within this format.

   Depending on the page orientation (Portrait or Landscape) you may not be able to see all of the fields in your table. If this is the case, then do the following:

3 Go to **File**, choose **Page Setup** and on the **Paper Size** tab, you will find the orientation buttons. Choose **Landscape**. Your data source file should now look like Figure 4.27 below.

Title	Initials	Surname	Street	Town	Postcode	Property	Start Date	Finish Date
Mrs	H	Wilkins	42 Linthorpe Way	BRISTOL	BS2 4NK	Drimmin	1/10/02	8/10/02
Ms	N	Viner	10 Charnouth Road	CAMBRIDGE	CB2 9NP	Park Court	23/08/03	06/09/03
Mr	P	Pascal	65 Copsthorne Road	ROMFORD	RM7 3WA	Sea View Cottage	23/08/03	30/08/03
Ms	W	Tyrell	73 Oakhill Drive	OXFORD	OX8 2NP	Torfrey	5/07/03	12/07/03
Miss	B	McWilliams	Rose Cottage	HAVERFORDWEST	DF3 0LS	Castle Cottage	2/06/03	9/06/03
Mr	D	Gardner	21 Russell Square	NOTTINGHAM	NG3 4UB	Lantern Cottage	02/11/02	09/11/02
Dr	M	Ashley	80 Harlow Drive	KESWICK	CA12 3VB	Compass	2/08/03	09/08/02
Mrs	J	Howich	121 Rosslyn Road	BATH	BA2 3NO	Fortune Cottage	2/08/03	09/08/03
Mr	Q	Wrench	22 Ashley Avenue	MANCHESTER	M21 4NR	Fortune Cottage	23/08/03	30/08/03
Mrs	C	Zarrabi	94 Longfellow Avenue	HULL	HU1 7CH	Mizzen	03/01/03	10/01/03
Mr	P	Singh	47 Lake Close	KESWICK	CA12 7PY	Mermaid Cottage	26/04/03	3/05/03
Mrs	A F	Pointen	7 Mount Pleasant	SCARBOROUGH	YO12 6GV	Harbour Lights	24/05/03	31/05/03
Dr	K B	Ridgley	7B Parkham Crescent	PORTSMOUTH	PO2 8BN	Sundial	15/07/02	22/07/02
Mr	C D	Ballantyne	38 Centry Drive	WINCHESTER	SO21 7NP	Sea Holme	02/06/03	09/06/03
Mrs	N P	Wing	30 Liversham Close	SOLIHULL	B90 2LS	Coastguard Cottage	26/04/03	03/05/03
Mrs	J	Capstan	58 Holywell Road	IPSWICH	IP29 5NL	Mizzen	19/07/03	26/07/03
Mrs	G S	Shaftesbury	8 North Burnham Road	GUILDFORD	GU3 7AP	Sapphire House	15/06/03	22/06/03
Mr	I A	Spencer	121 Oldway Road	TRURO	TR3 9JL	Sea Holme	27/07/03	03/07/03
Mrs	E K	Latham	62 Acer Drive	BELFAST	BT16 3NA	Drimmin	16/03/03	23/03/03
Mr	S I	Thomas	76 Prospect Road	PETERBOROUGH	PE1 6SF	Mermaid Cottage	17/05/03	24/05/03
Miss	A Y	Greenslade	46 Newlands Road	LIVERPOOL	L21 8BY	Drimmin	6/09/03	13/09/03

Figure 4.27 Data source file HOLIDAYS

Method 2

1 Open a blank new document. Go to <u>T</u>ools and click on **Mail Me<u>r</u>ge**.
2 Create a **form letter** using the **active window** as shown in the instructions for setting up a datafile on page 172.
3 Now go to **Data Source** and choose <u>O</u>pen data source. You will need to open the data source file entitled HOLIDAYS. The menu will prompt you to insert Word Fields into the document. Just click on the **Edit Main Document** button and the prompt will disappear, taking you back to a blank document.
4 The toolbars will now have changed and you will see a new toolbar that relates only to mailmerge features. If you choose the following **Edit Data Source icon** , then the records will be displayed individually as shown in Figure 4.1 on page 172.
5 You can now move backwards and forwards changing the records as appropriate. If you wish to delete a record in its entirety then click on **Delete**.
6 When you have finished making your amendments click on OK. The records will disappear from your screen leaving you with the blank document.

Note: If you choose to use this method then you must ensure that you have opened the mailmerge facility or you will not be able to find the correct icon. Remember, it only appears when the Mail Merge Helper has been opened.

The following exercises will show you how to alter the existing datafile HOLIDAYS. You will make the following amendments to the data source using either the table format method or the record method as shown in Exercise 4.10.

Existing Text	Amendment
Capstan (Surname Column)	Change to Captain
Scarborough (Town column)	Change to SALCOMBE
YO12 6GV (Postcode column	Change to EX32 8AN
Mrs W Cruikshank	Delete record
Mrs O'Sullivan	Change Property to Drimmin
Mrs F R Whitmarsh	Change initials to F B
Mrs J Godrey	Change 45 Acorn Avenue to 56 Acorn Avenue

Amending single cells

Exercise 4.11

Method

1 To amend a single entry such as the 'Surname', click in the cell you wish to amend. For example, using the amendments given above, you will click in the 'Surname' cell containing 'Capstan'. Highlight the entire contents of the cell.
2 Key in the new text.
3 Save the datafile on your own disk or hard drive as HOLS.

Deleting records

Exercise 4.12

Method

1 Open the datafile stored on your disk or hard drive called HOLS.
2 To delete an entire record, highlight all the cells contained in the record – you will in fact highlight the entire row.
3 Go to **Table** and choose **Delete.** The following menu will appear (see Figure 4.28).

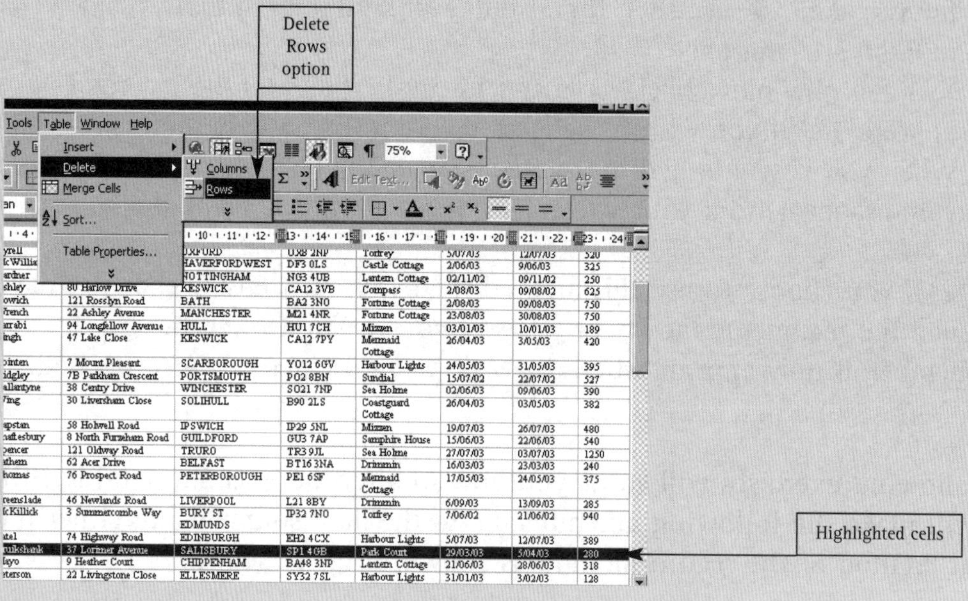

Figure 4.28 Deleting records

4 Choose **Rows.** The row will disappear from the table. If you accidentally delete the wrong row, immediately click on **Undo.** It will then be reinstated.
5 Save your datafile.

Inserting new fields

Exercise 4.13

You will be asked to insert a new field into your records. You will need to enter the information for all of the records contained in your datafile.

Method 1

1 Open the datafile called HOLS. Click just outside the last column in the datafile. Make sure that the cursor is in line with the top of your table, next to the header row. This will ensure that the correct number of rows is inserted.

2   Go to **T**a**ble** and choose **Insert** and **Columns to the right**.
3   A new column will appear as in Figure 4.29 below.

Title	Initials	Surname	Street	Town	Postcode	Property	Start Date	Finish Date	
Mrs	H	Wilkins	42 Linthorpe Way	BRISTOL	BS2 4NK	Drizmin	1/10/02	8/10/02	
Ms	N	Viner	10 Charmouth Road	CAMBRIDGE	CB2 9NP	Park Court	23/08/03	06/09/03	
Mr	P	Pascal	65 Copothorne Road	ROMFORD	RM7 3WA	Sea View Cottage	23/08/03	30/08/03	
Ms	W	Tyrell	73 Oakhill Drive	OXFORD	OX8 2NP	Torrey	5/07/03	12/07/03	
Miss	B	McWilliams	Rose Cottage	HAVERFORDWEST	DF3 0LS	Castle Cottage	2/06/03	9/06/03	
Mr	D	Gardner	21 Russell Square	NOTTINGHAM	NG3 4UB	Lantern Cottage	02/11/02	09/11/02	
Dr	M	Ashley	80 Harlow Drive	KESWICK	CA12 3VB	Compass	2/08/03	09/08/02	
Mrs	J	Howich	121 Rosslyn Road	BATH	BA2 3NO	Fortune Cottage	2/08/03	09/08/03	
Mr	Q	Wrench	22 Ashley Avenue	MANCHESTER	M21 4NR	Fortune Cottage	23/08/03	30/08/03	
Mrs	C	Zorrabi	94 Longfellow Avenue	HULL	HU1 7CH	Mizzen	03/01/03	10/01/03	
Mr	P	Singh	47 Lake Close	KESWICK	CA12 7PY	Mermaid Cottage	26/04/03	3/05/03	
Mrs	A F	Pointon	7 Mount Pleasant	SCARBOROUGH	YO12 6GV	Harbour Lights	24/05/03	31/05/03	
Dr	K B	Ridgley	7B Parkham Crescent	PORTSMOUTH	PO2 8BN	Sundial	15/07/02	22/07/02	
Mr	C D	Ballantyne	38 Centry Drive	WINCHESTER	SO21 7NP	Sea Holme	02/06/03	09/06/03	
Mrs	N P	Wing	30 Liversham Close	SOLIHULL	B90 2LS	Coastguard Cottage	26/04/03	03/05/03	
Mrs	J	Capstan	58 Holwell Road	IPSWICH	IP29 5NL	Mizzen	19/07/03	26/07/03	
Mrs	G S	Shaftesbury	8 North Furnehan Road	GUILDFORD	GU3 7AP	Sapphire House	15/06/03	22/06/03	
Mr	I A	Spencer	121 Oldway Road	TRURO	TR3 9JL	Sea Holme	27/07/03	03/07/03	
Mrs	E K	Latham	62 Acer Drive	BELFAST	BT16 3NA	Drizmin	16/03/03	23/03/03	
Mr	S I	Thomas	76 Prospect Road	PETERBOROUGH	PE1 6SF	Mermaid Cottage	17/05/03	24/05/03	

Figure 4.29 New column added

4   You can now key in the text. In the header key in 'Contract issued'. For each record key in the word 'Yes'.

To move easily down the column, use the arrow keys. If you press tab you will jump across the cells which can be annoying and time-consuming.

5   Save your datafile.

Method 2

1   Using the instructions given in Exercise 4.10, ensure that you have opened the Mail Merge Helper and the mailmerge toolbar is on screen. Choose the **Edit Data Source** icon as before. The individual records will appear on screen.
2   Now choose the **View Source** button. The table as shown in Figure 4.27 above will appear.
3   The toolbars will have changed again. Choose the following **Manage Fields** icon [icon]. The following menu will appear (see Figure 4.30).

Manage Fields

Field name:

| |

Field names in header row:

Title
Initials
Surname
Street
Town
Postcode
Credit_Check
Card_Limit_

Add »
Remove
Rename...

OK   Cancel

Figure 4.30 Manage Fields menu

4   You can now add a field by keying in the correct name in the **F**ield **name** box and then clicking **OK**.
5   The new column will now appear on the table. You can either follow the method given above to enter the information in the new field in table format or you can click on the **Edit Data Source** icon to get back to the record format where you can enter the information record by record.

Exercise 4.14

Finish making the amendments as shown on page 193. Save your datafile.

Adding new records

You can also add new records whilst viewing the data source as a table.

Exercise 4.15

Add the following records to your table.

Title	Initials	Surname	Street	Town	Postcode	Property	Start Date	Finish Date	Contract Issued
Mr	P S	Delaney	1 Fairway Close	LEEDS	LS1 3DW	Castle Cottage	08/11/03	15/11/03	Yes
Mrs	B	Parker	38 West Avenue	WHITBY	YO22 1NP	Drimmin	20/12/03	27/12/03	Yes
Ms	K	Lewis	7 Windy Hill	GLASGOW	G3 4NU	Lantern Cottage	19/07/03	26/07/03	Yes

Method 1

1 Open the datafile HOLS. Click in the last record of the table.
2 Go to **Table** and click **Insert**. The following menu will appear (see Figure 4.31).

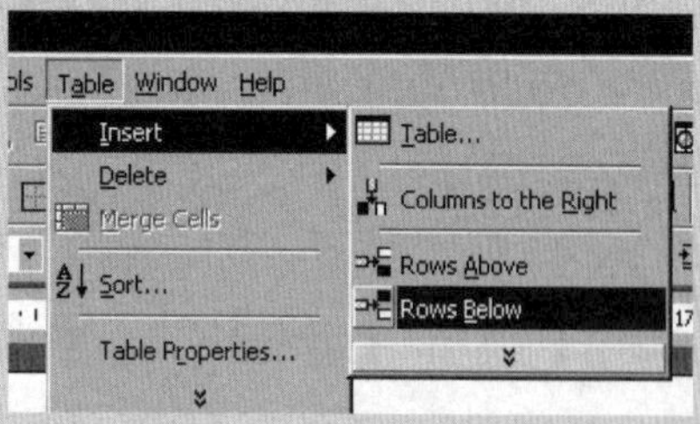

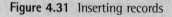

Figure 4.31 Inserting records

3 Choose **Rows Below**. A new row will appear below the last record in your table. When you have chosen this option a new set of icons will appear on the toolbar. If you need to add more than one row (which in this example, you do), then choose the icon shown in Figure 4.32. Note that it only appears on the toolbar immediately after you have inserted the new row. The moment you click the mouse these options disappear. If this happens then you will have to go back through the Table, Insert, Rows Below options as described above.

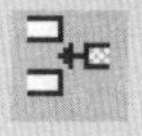

Figure 4.32 Insert New Row icon

4 Save the datafile.

Method 2

1 Using the instructions given in Exercise 4.10, ensure that you have opened the Mail Merge Helper and the mailmerge toolbar is on screen. Choose the **Edit Data Source** icon as before. The individual records will appear on screen.

2 Now choose the **Add New** button. You will be presented with a clean record. Fill this in and repeat until you have added all new records.

Sorting your datafile

You will be required to sort the datafile in some way, for example by date or surname.

Exercise 4.16

Sort the your HOLS datafile by alphabetical order of surname.

Method

1 Open the datafile. Go to **Table** and **Sort**. The following menu will appear (see Figure 4.33).

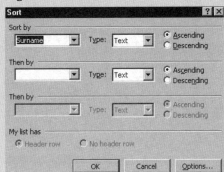

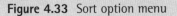

Figure 4.33 Sort option menu

2 You can see from Figure 4.33 that the 'Surname' field has been selected in the **Sort by** value box. When you click on the arrow to the right of this box, a list of your fields will appear. Choose the 'Surname' field.

3 The **Type** box has automatically selected 'Text' as it recognises this field as a text box. You do not need to do anything to this. You do, however, need to check this is correct, because if, for example, you keep the 'Text' value when it should be 'Number' or 'Date' then it will not work correctly.

4 The **Ascending** box has already been checked as this is the default setting. If you want to change this, just click the button.

5 Click **OK**. The table will sort itself by surname. All the corresponding fields will automatically change so you don't need to worry about this.

6 When you are sure you have made all the amendments correctly, save your work.

Printing your datafile

You will need to print the datafile with at least three records showing on the page.

Exercise 4.17

Print the datafile HOLS.

Method

1 Make sure you have all the text displayed on the page and that there are no columns 'falling off' at either end. If you wish, you can reduce the text size so that the text fits neatly on the page.
2 To change the text size, select the entire table by going to **Edit** and choosing **Select All**. The entire table should now be highlighted. Whilst you have the highlight on, go to the **Font size** box and using the **drop down** arrow at the side of the box, choose a smaller size, perhaps 10 or 9.
3 When you are sure that all the text is on the page, print your document in the usual way.

See worked example on the CD-ROM.

4 Now save your work and close the file.

Exercise 4.18

Recall the datafile stored under HOLIDAYS and follow the instructions given. A worked example of this exercise can be found in the worked examples on the CD-ROM.

Handwritten instruction: Recall this datafile stored under HOLIDAYS. Amend as shown. Sort the amended datafile by chronological order of Start date. Save as HOLIDAY BALANCE. Print one copy ensuring that at least three records are printed on each page.

Handwritten note (with arrow pointing to the Date Due column): Please add this field to each record

Title	Initials	Surname	Street	Town	Postcode	Property	Start Date	Balance	Date Due
Mrs	H	Wilkins	42 Linthorpe Way	BRISTOL	BS2 4NK	Drimmin	01/10/02	480	01/09/02
Ms	N	Viner	10 Charmouth Road	CAMBRIDGE	CB2 9NP	Park Court	23/08/03	1240	23/07/03
Mr	P	Pascal	65 Copythorne Road	ROMFORD	RM7 3WA	Sea View Cottage	23/08/03	650	23/07/03
Ms	W	~~Tyrell~~ *Driver*	73 Oakhill Drive	OXFORD	OX8 2NP	Torfrey	05/07/03	520	05/06/03
~~Miss~~	~~B~~	~~McWilliams~~	~~Rose Cottage~~	~~EXETER~~	~~EX2 1KS~~	~~Castle Cottage~~	~~02/06/03~~	~~325~~	~~02/05/03~~
Mr	D	Gardner	21 Russell Square	NOTTINGHAM	NG3 4UB	Lantern Cottage	02/11/02	250	02/10/02
Dr	M	Ashley	80 Harlow ~~Drive~~ *Close*	KESWICK	CA12 3VB *BA1 3LJ / BA2 3NQ*	Compass	02/08/03	625	02/07/03
Mrs	J	Howich	121 Rosslyn Road	BATH		Drimmin	02/08/03	750	02/07/03
Mr	Q	Wrench	22 Ashley Avenue	MANCHESTER	M21 4NR	Fortune Cottage	23/08/03	750	23/07/03
Mrs	C	Zarrabi	94 Longfellow Road	HULL	HU1 7CH	*Sundial* ~~Mizzen~~	03/01/03	189	03/12/02
Mr	P	~~Singh~~ ~~Pointon~~ *Jones*	47 Lake Close	KESWICK	CA12 7PY	Mermaid Cottage	26/04/03	420	26/03/03
Mrs	AF		7 Mount Pleasant	SCARBOROUGH	YO12 6GV	Harbour Lights	24/05/03	395	24/04/03
Dr *Mrs*	KB	Ridgley	7B Parkham ~~Crescent~~ *Mews*	PORTSMOUTH	PO2 8BN	Sundial	15/07/02	527	12/05/03
Mr	CD	Ballantyne	38 Centry Drive	WINCHESTER *MOSELEY* ~~SOLIHULL~~	S021 7NP	Sea Holme	02/06/03	390	02/05/03
Mrs	NP	Wing	30 Liversham Close		B90 2LS	Coastguard	26/04/03	382	26/03/03
Mrs	J	Captain	58 Holwell Road	IPSWICH	IP29 5NL	Mizzen	19/07/03	480	19/06/03
Mrs	GS	Shaftesbury	6 Greenbank Place	GUILDFORD	GU3 7AP *TR1 3KY / TR19JL*	Samphire House	15/06/03	540	15/05/03
Mr	IA	Spencer	121 Oldway Road	TRURO		Sea Holme	27/08/03	1250	27/06/03
Mrs	EK	Lathem	62 Acer Drive	BELFAST	BT16 3NA	Drimmin	16/03/03	240	16/02/03

Title	Initials	Surname	Street	Town	Postcode	Property	Start Date	Balance	Date Due
Mr	S I	Thomas	76 Prospect Road	~~PETERBOROUGH~~ *ELY*	~~PE1 6SF~~ *CM6 9BP*	~~Mermaid~~ *Sundial* Cottage	17/05/03	375	17/04/03
Miss	A Y	Greenslade	46 Newlands Road	LIVERPOOL	L21 8BY	Drimmin	06/09/03	385	06/08/03
Ms	V	McKillick	3 Summer ~~Way~~ *Lane*	IPSWICH	IP32 7NO	Torfrey	07/06/03	940	07/05/03
Mrs	R	Patel	74 Highway Road	EDINBURGH	EH1 6LM	Harbour Lights	05/07/03	389	05/06/03
Ms	L	Mayo	9 Heather Drive	CHIPPENHAM	BA48 3NP	~~Lantern~~ *Mermaid* Cottage	21/06/03	318	21/05/03
~~Mr~~	~~S~~	~~Peterson~~	~~22 Livingstone Close~~	~~ELLESMERE~~	~~SY32 7SL~~	~~Harbour Lights~~	~~31/01/03~~	~~128~~	~~31/12/02~~
Ms	T	Wright	84 Ringwood Road	PERTH	PH3 2AB	Compass Cottage	17/05/03	328	17/04/03
Mrs	M	Elkins	44 Temperance Steps	SALISBURY	SP3 4GJ	Castle Cottage	19/07/03	486	19/06/03
Mr	I L	Wilson	7 King Street	PAIGNTON *YARMOUTH*	TQ3 8BN	Compass	06/09/03	295	06/08/03
Mr	T	Hedley	43 ~~York~~ Street	LOWESTOFT	NR32 3NQ	Sundial	20/09/03	420	20/08/03
Mrs	*S C*	O'Sullivan	388 Woodford Drive	LONDON	E12 3NO	Drimmin	06/09/03	280	06/08/03
Ms	J	Norris	51 Southdown Rise	LIVERPOOL	L32 1NE	Lantern Cottage	04/10/03	189	04/09/03
Mrs	D	Fisher	29 Bennetts Lane	LEICESTER	LE2 1NQ	Harbour Lights	15/02/03	210	15/01/03
Mr	A K	Jackson	17 Ragland Lane	~~COVENTRY~~ ~~Bristo-~~ *BRIGHTON*	~~CV3 7WR~~ ~~BS2 7SJ~~ *BN3 1SJ*	Compass Cottage	08/03/03	195	08/02/03
Mrs	F R	Whitmarsh	39 Perrymead *Close*	BRIGHTON		Castle Cottage	24/05/03	429	24/04/03
Ms	M	Saunders	52 Lincoln Hill	WINCHESTER	SO21 4FH	Park Court	09/08/03	780	09/08/03
Mr	X	Jones	138 Newhall Drive	LEICESTER	LE4 5BJ	Harbour Lights	24/05/03	650	24/04/03
~~Mrs~~	~~J~~	~~Godfrey~~	~~45 Acorn Avenue~~	~~BATH~~	~~BA1 5LA~~	~~Harbour Lights~~	~~09/08/03~~	~~530~~	~~09/07/03~~
Mr	S	Reese	4 Oldfield Road	TORQUAY	TQ1 1PX	Compass Cottage	01/08/03	420	09/07/03
Mrs	L	Baston	26 Aston Road	YEOVIL	BS22 9FS	Seaspite House	27/08/03	620	27/6/03
Mrs	K	Long	17 High Street	BIRMINGHAM	B12 6DS	Torfrey	15/02/03	230	15/01/03

Please add these records to the datafile

Please key in the following standard document to merge with the datafile HOLIDAY BALANCE. Insert merge codes where indicated by * and use a ragged right margin. Print one copy of the standard document and also print documents to all those whose balance is due during July.

Our ref BD/JE
* Title * Initials * Surname
* Street
* Town
* Post code

Dear * Title * Surname

* Property

Further to your booking of the above holiday property for week commencing * Start date. We would respectfully remind you that the balance payment of £* balance is due on * Due date.

You may pay by cheque, debit or credit card. Unfortunately because of the high charges we incur we charge a 1.5% fee for using a credit card. Debit cards may be used free of this charge.

Please note, if your balance payment is not received by the due date, the provisional booking will be cancelled.

We look forward to hearing from you.

Yours sincerely

Joseph Elliott

Manager

Please emphasise this sentence

Exercise 4.19

Recall the datafile stored under HOLIDAYS and follow the instructions given. A worked example of this exercise can be found in the worked examples on the CD-ROM.

Recall this datafile stored under HOLIDAYS. Amend as shown. Sort the amended datafile by ascending order of BALANCE. Save as KEYS. Print one copy ensuring at least three records are printed on each page

Please add this field to each record

Title	Initials	Surname	Street	Town	Postcode	Property	Start Date	Balance	Finish Date
Mrs	H	~~Wilkins~~ Wilson	42 Linthorpe Way	BRISTOL	BS2 4NK	Drimmin	01/10/02	480	08/10/02
Ms	N	Viner	10 Charmouth Road	CAMBRIDGE	CB2 9NP	Park Court	23/08/03	1240	06/09/03
~~Mr~~	~~P~~	~~Pascal~~	~~65 Copythorne Road~~	~~ROMFORD~~	~~RM7 3WA~~	~~Sea View Cottage~~	~~23/08/03~~	~~650~~	~~30/08/03~~
Ms	W	Tyrell	73 Oakhill Drive	OXFORD	OX8 2NP	Torfrey	05/07/03	520	12/07/03
Miss	B	McWilliams	Rose Cottage	EXETER	EX2 1KS	Castle Cottage	02/06/03	325	09/06/03
Mr	D	Gardner	21 Russell Square	NOTTINGHAM	NG3 4UB	Lantern Cottage	02/11/02	250	09/11/02
Dr	M	~~Ashley~~ Ashwood	80 Harlow Drive	KESWICK	CA12 3VB	Compass	02/08/03	625	09/08/03
Mrs	J	Howich	121 Rosslyn Road	BATH	BA2 3NO	Drimmin	02/08/03	750	09/08/03
Mr	Q	Wrench	22 Ashley Avenue	MANCHESTER	M21 4NR	Fortune Cottage	23/08/03	750	30/08/03
Mrs	C	Zarrabi	94 Longfellow Road	~~HULL~~ YEOVIL	~~HU1 7CH~~ BS22 6KH	Mizzen	03/01/03	189	10/01/03
Mr	P	Singh	47 Lake Close	KESWICK	CA12 7PY	Mermaid Cottage	26/04/03	420	03/05/03
Mrs	A F	Pointen	7 Mount Pleasant	SCARBOROUGH	YO12 6GV	Harbour Lights	24/05/03	395	31/05/03
Dr	K B	Ridgley	~~7B~~ 7 Parkham Crescent	PORTSMOUTH	PO2 8BN	~~Sundial~~ Mizzen	15/07/02	527	22/07/03
Mr	C D	Ballantyne	38 Centry Drive	WINCHESTER	S021 7NP	Sea Holme	02/06/03	390	22/06/03
Mrs	N P	Wing	30 Liversham Close	SOLIHULL	B90 2LS	Coastguard	26/04/03	382	03/05/03
~~Mrs~~ Dr	J	Captain	58 Holwell Road	IPSWICH	IP29 5NL	Mizzen	19/07/03	480	26/07/03
Mrs	G S	Shaftesbury	6 Greenbank Place	GUILDFORD	GU3 7AP	Samphire House	15/06/03	540	22/06/03
Mr	I A	Spencer	121 Oldway Road	TRURO	TR3 9JL	Sea Holme	27/08/03	1250	03/09/03
Mrs	E K	Lathem	62 Acer Drive	BELFAST	BT16 3NA	Drimmin	16/03/03	240	23/03/03

Title	Initials	Surname	Street	Town	Postcode	Property	Start Date	Balance	Finish Date
Mr	S I	Thomas	76 Prospect Road	PETERBOROUGH	PE1 6SF	Mermaid Cottage	17/05/03	375	24/05/03
Miss~~Mr~~Ms	A Y	~~Greenslade~~	46 Newlands Road	LIVERPOOL	L21 8BY	Drimmin	06/09/03	385	12/09/03
Mrs	V	McKillick	3 Summer Way	IPSWICH	IP32 7NO	Torfrey	07/06/03	940	28/06/03
Mrs	R	Patel	74 Highway Road	EDINBURGH	EH1 6LM	Harbour Lights	05/07/03	389	12/07/03
Ms	L	Mayo	9 Heather Drive	CHIPPENHAM	BA48 3NP	Lantern Cottage	21/06/03	318	28/06/03
Mr	S	Peterson	22 Livingstone Close / mews	ELLESMERE	SY32 7SL	Harbour Lights	31/01/03	128	07/02/03
Ms	T	Wright	84 Ringwood Road	PERTH	PH3 2AB	Compass Cottage	17/05/03	328	24/05/03
Mrs	M	Elkins	44 Temperence Steps	~~SALISBURY~~ TO2 8JA-1	SP3 4GJ	Castle Cottage	19/07/03	486	26/07/03
Mr	I L	Wilson	7 King Street	~~PAIGNTON~~	TQ3 8BN	Compass	06/09/03	295	13/09/03
Mr	T	Hedley	43 York Street	LOWESTOFT	NR32 3NQ	Sundial	20/09/03	420	27/09/03
Mrs	S	O'Sullivan	388 Woodford Drive	LONDON	E12 3NO	Drimmin	06/09/03	280	13/09/03
Ms	J	Norris	51 Southdown Rise	LIVERPOOL	L32 1NE	Lantern Cottage	04/10/03	189	11/10/03
Mrs	D	Fisher	29 Bennetts Lane	LEICESTER	LE2 1NQ	Harbour Lights	15/02/03	210	22/02/03
Mr	A K	~~Jackson~~	~~17 Ragland Lane~~	~~COVENTRY~~	~~CV3 7WR~~	~~Compass Cottage~~	~~08/03/03~~	~~195~~	~~15/03/03~~
Mrs	F R	Whitmarsh	39 Perrymead	BRIGHTON	BH3 1SJ	Castle Cottage	24/05/03	429	31/05/03
Ms	M	Saunders	52 Lincoln Hill	WINCHESTER	SO21 4FH	Park Court	09/08/03	780	16/08/03
Mr	X	Jones	138 Newhall Drive	LEICESTER	LE4 5BJ	Harbour Lights	24/05/03	650	31/05/03
Mrs		Godfrey	45 Acorn Avenue	BATH	BA1 3LA	Harbour Lights	09/08/03	530	16/08/03
Mrs	L	Spencer	21 Burnham Road	CAMBRIDGE	CB4 9SF	Torfrey	04/10/03	270	11/10/03
Mr	D	Martin	6 Bourne Lane	PLYMOUTH	PL3 4CC	Sea Holme	21/06/03	420	28/06/03
Mrs	K	Elkins	22 Winchester Road	HULL	HU6 7ME	Mizzen	15/06/03	210	22/06/03

Please add these records to the datafile

Please key in the following standard document to merge with the datafile KEYS. Insert merge codes where indicated by * and use a justified right margin. Print one copy of the standard document and also print documents to all those whose holiday takes place in May.

* Title   * Initials   * Surname
* Street
* Town
* Post code

Dear * Title * Surname

* Property

Thank you for your balance payment of £* balance in respect of the rental fee for the above property. We are pleased to confirm that * Property will be available for you from * Start date to * Finish date inclusive.

The property will be ready for occupation from 3.00 pm. We ask that you vacate the property by 10.00 am on the day of leaving.   (Emphasise this sentence)

Full property details, keys and direction instructions are enclosed.

We hope you have a very enjoyable holiday.

Yours sincerely

Joseph Elliott
Manager
Eves

Exercise 4.20

Recall the datafile stored under HOLIDAYS and follow the instructions given. A worked example of this exercise can be found in the worked examples on the CD-ROM.

Handwritten instruction: Recall this datafile stored under HOLIDAYS. Amend as shown. Sort the amended data file by ascending order of Rental £. Save as FLOOD. Print one copy ensuring at least three records are on each page.

Handwritten note (pointing to Rental £ column): Please add this field to each record

Title	Initials	Surname	Street	Town	Postcode	Property	Start Date	Finish Date	Rental £
Mrs	H	Wilkins	42 Linthorpe Way	BRISTOL	BS2 4NK	Drimmin	0/10/02	08/10/02	425
Ms	N	Viner	10 Charmouth Road	~~CAMBRIDGE~~ *Rugby / ROMFORD*	~~CB2 2NP~~ *RG6 2SR / RM67 3WX*	~~Park Court~~	~~23/08/03~~	~~06/09/03~~	335
Mr	P	Pascal	65 Copythorne Road			Sea View Cottage	23/08/03	30/08/03	970
Ms / ~~Mrs~~ *Miss*	W	Tyrell	73 Oakhill Drive	OXFORD	OX8 2NP	Torfrey	05/07/03	12/07/03	439
	B	McWilliams	Rose Cottage	HULL	HU3 4ST	Castle Cottage	02/06/03	09/06/03	459
Mr	D	Gardner	21 Russell Square	NOTTINGHAM	NG3 4UB	Lantern Cottage	02/11/02	09/11/02	290
Dr	M	Ashley	80 Harlow Drive	KESWICK	CA12 3VB	Compass *Drimmin* ~~Fortune Cottage~~	02/08/03	09/08/02	675
Mrs	J	Howich	121 Rosslyn Road	BATH	BA2 3NO	Fortune Cottage	02/08/03	09/08/03	800
Mr	*Q G*	Wrench	22 Ashley Avenue	MANCHESTER	M21 4NR	Fortune Cottage	23/08/03	30/08/03	800
~~Mrs~~	C	~~Zarrabi~~	~~94 Longfellow Road~~	~~HULL~~	~~HU1 7CH~~	~~Mizzen~~	~~02/01/03~~	~~10/01/03~~	~~249~~
Mr	P	Singh	47 Lake Close	KESWICK	CA12 7PY	Mermaid Cottage	26/04/03	03/05/03	470
Mr	J	Capstan	61 Moorland Drive	YORK	YO1 2ML	Samphire House	16/03/03	23/03/03	250
Mrs	A F	Pointen	7 Mount Pleasant	SCARBOROUGH	YO12 6GV	Harbour Lights	24/05/03	31/05/03	445
Dr	K B	Ridgeley	7B Parkham Crescent	PORTSMOUTH	PO2 8BN	Sundial	15/07/02	22/07/02	577
Mr	C D	Ballantyne	38 Centry Drive	WINCHESTER	SO2 7NP	*Castle Cottage (See Home)*	02/06/03	09/06/03	640
Mrs	N P	Wing	30 Liversham Close	SOLIHULL	B90 2LS	Coastguard	26/04/03	03/05/03	577
Mrs	J	Castle	58 Holwell Road	IPSWICH	IP29 5NL	Mizzen	19/07/03	26/07/03	340
Mrs	G S	Shaftesbury *Sherington Spencer*	6 Greenbank Place	GUILDFORD	GU3 7AP	Samphire House	15/06/03	22/06/03	432
Mr	I A		121 Oldway Road	TRURO	TR3 9JL	Sea Holme	27/08/03	03/07/03	590
Mrs	E K	Lathem	62 Acer Drive *Avenue*	BELFAST	BT16 3NA	Drimmin	16/03/03	23/03/03	290
Mr	S I	Thomas	76 Prospect Road	PETERBOROUGH	PE1 6SF	Mermaid Cottage	17/05/03	24/05/03	425

Title	Initials	Surname	Street	Town	Postcode	Property	Start Date	Finish Date	Rental £
Miss	A Y	Greenslade	46 Newlands Road	LIVERPOOL	L21 8BY	Drimmin	06/09/03	13/09/03	335
Ms	V	McKillick	3 Summer Way	IPSWICH	IP32 7NQ	Torfrey	07/06/02	21/06/02	990
Mrs	R	Patel	74 Highway Road	EDINBURGH	~~EH2 4CX~~ EH1 6LM	Harbour Lights	05/07/03	12/07/03	420
Ms	L	Mayo	9 Heather ~~Close~~ Road	CHIPPENHAM	BA48 3NP	Lantern Cottage	21/06/03	28/06/03	500
Mr	S	Peterson	22 Livingstone ~~Close~~	ELLESMERE	SY32 7SL	Harbour Lights	31/01/03	03/02/03	178
Ms	T	Wright	84 Ringwood Road	PERTH	PH3 2AB	Compass Cottage	17/05/03	24/05/03	378
~~Mr~~ Mrs	L K ~~Elkins~~	Etherington	44 Temperence Steps	~~DEVIZES~~ SALISBURY	SP3 4GJ	Castle Cottage	19/07/03	26/07/03	345
Mr	I L	Wilson	7 King Street	PAIGNTON	TQ3 8BN	Compass	06/09/03	13/09/03	345
Mr	T	Hedley	43 York Street	LOWESTOFT	NR32 3NQ	Sundial	20/09/03	27/09/03	470
Mrs	S	O'Sullivan	388 Woodford Drive	LONDON	E12 3NO	Harbour Lights	06/09/03	13/09/03	330
~~Ms~~	~~J~~	~~Norris~~	~~51 Southdown Rise~~	~~LIVERPOOL~~	~~L32 1NE~~	~~Lantern Cottage~~	~~04/10/03~~	~~11/10/03~~	~~235~~
Mrs	D	Fisher	29 Bennetts Lane	LEICESTER	LE2 1NQ	Harbour Lights	15/02/03	22/02/03	260
Mr	A K	Jackson	17 Ragland Lane	COVENTRY	CV3 7WR	Compass Cottage	08/03/03	15/03/03	245
Mrs	F R	Whitmarsh	39 Perrymead	BRIGHTON	BH3 1SJ	Castle Cottage	24/05/03	31/05/03	477
Ms	M	Saunders	52 Lincoln Hill	WINCHESTER	SO21 4FH	Sea Holme	09/08/03	16/08/03	830
Mr	X	Jones	138 Newhall Drive	LEICESTER	LE4 5BJ	~~Harbour Lights~~ Torfrey	24/05/03	31/05/03	700
Mrs	J	Godfrey	45 Acorn Avenue	BATH	BA1 3LA	Harbour Lights	09/08/03	16/08/03	580
Mrs	W	Cruikshank	92 Lindhurst Road	READING	RG1 5TH	Compass	12/02/03	22/02/03	470
Mr	K	Archer	10 Prospect Road	HULL	HU4 7EM	Drimmin	13/9/03	26/09/03	300
Mrs	L	May	41 Bloomfield Road	TRURO	TR6 9SU	Sundial	4/10/03	11/10/03	420
Mrs	S	Marsh	9 Newbridge Road	ELY	CM14 6JZ	Torfrey	21/6/03	28/06/03	550

Please add these records to the datafile

Please key in the standard document to merge with the datafile FLOOD. Insert merge codes where indicated by * and use a ragged right margin. Print one copy of the standard document and also print documents to all those who had booked Drimmin for their holiday.

* Title * Initials * Surname
* Street
* Town
* Post code

Dear *Title * Surname

* Property
According to our records you have booked the above property for the period *Start date to *finish date.

Unfortunately *Property has been badly damaged by flooding. This means we are unable to honour your booking.

We can offer you an alternative property. This is called Rainbow Cottage and is situated close to the beach. Full details are enclosed with this letter.

If this is not acceptable to you then we will of course refund your rental payment of *rental in full. Please let us have your decision as soon as possible.

We apologise for the inconvenience this will cause.

Yours sincerely

Joseph Elliott
Manager
Enc

Please emphasise this sentence

Consolidation practice

The following consolidation exercises will help you prepare for the Mailmerge examination. Try to complete each set of consolidation pieces in the usual time allowed for this exam, that is 1 hour and 30 minutes.

Remember to check your work carefully, and correct any errors before printing. Don't forget to print the datafile and the standard letters showing the merge codes. Worked examples to these exercises can be found on the CD-ROM.

Mailmerge consolidation 1

Recall this datafile stored under CONSOLIDATION. Amend as shown. Sort the amended datafile into alphabetical order of Surname. Save as Credit 1. Print one copy ensuring that at least three records are printed on each page.

Please add this field to each record → Revised Limit £

Title	Initials	Surname	Street	Town	Postcode	Credit Check	Card Limit £	Date Issued	Revised Limit £
Mr	P A	Johnson	3 Mizzymead Rise	ABINGDON	OX14 4DA	Yes	10,000 → 10,500	01/06/01	12,000
Mrs	S	Willard	12 Frimley Road	WAKEFIELD	WF1 9NA	Yes	2,000	29/08/86	2,500
Mr	I	Gilvear	29 Bush Road	CHELMSFORD	CM1 2NX (BS10 7UG)	Yes	4,500	05/04/89	4,750
Ms	L	Rathe	48 Roxwell Avenue	YEOVIL → BATH	(BA1 3SP)	No	1,500	27/12/02	2,000
Mrs	R	Neale	5 Quaker Court	WALSALL	WS3 4QW	No	2,000	10/1/03	3,000
Mr	H	Layton	9 Wellington Close	LONDON	SE17 0IN	Yes → No	4,500 / 1,000	30/3/02	5,500
Ms	C	Marshall	6 Churchill Road	HORNCHURCH	RM11 2AX	No → Yes	6,000	09/02/00	6,250 / 1,500
Ms	D	Shilvock	22 Hazelmere Gardens	LEICESTER	LE3 8FU	Yes	12,000	24/03/96	14,000
~~Mr~~	~~P~~	~~Bowbrick~~	~~57 Rocky Lane~~	~~SLOUGH~~	~~SL3 7RB~~	~~Yes~~	~~5,000~~	~~31/01/96~~	~~5,750~~
Mr	W	Piper	121 Chelmsford Road	SHREWSBURY	SY5 6LP	Yes	3,000	02/06/98	3,250
Ms	J	Higham	3 Agar Road	EASTLEIGH	SO5 2BQ	No	1,500	16/01/03	1,750
Mrs	F	Seward	76 Garthorne Road	ALTON	GU34 5AH	Yes	7,500	26/07/99	8,750
Mr	N	Mainwood	5 Wyken Road	WHITBY	YO21 1LT	Yes	4,000	02/04/01	4,250
Mrs	I	Cartmell	7 Church Street	HEREFORD	HR1 8UL	Yes	8,750	09/05/02	9,250
Mr	Y → T	Dixon	56 Montgomery Close → Gardens	COVENTRY	CV1 8RP	Yes	3,500	07/11/02	4,000
Mrs	F	Spendley	4 Lime Road → Gardens	BATH	BA9 7YX	Yes	7,000	09/10/99	8,000
Ms	P	Langley	79 Bellotts Road	STEVENAGE	SG2 9RB → GL16 4HD	Yes	9,750	12/08/97	10,000
Mr	A	Bennett	5 School Avenue	GLOUCESTER	GL3 7GB	Yes	4,500	23/07/96	4,750
Mrs / Mr	V	Hunt / Johnson / ~~Hanson~~	3 Drove Lane	BRISTOL	BS33 7KA	Yes	5,500	22/09/99	6,250
Mrs	O	Hunt	66 Buckingham Road	MANCHESTER	M28 6TJ	No	1,000	27/01/03	1,500
Mr	E	Haffner	74 Woodside Avenue	CHELTENHAM	GL99 6LM	Yes	2,750	14/08/88	3,750

Title	Initials	Surname	Street	Town	Postcode	Credit Check	Card Limit £	Date Issued	Revised Limit £
Mrs	M	Clifford	44 ~~Oxton~~ *Forgham* Road	SHREWSBURY	SY3 2BB	Yes	10,500	04/03/97	12,500
~~Ms~~ Ms	D	~~Reynolds~~	3 Wentworth Road	~~MACCLESFIELD~~	~~SK11 7LH~~ SK11 7LH	~~Yes~~	6,750	17/05/98	7,750
Mrs	K	Lester	56 Staveley Road	TAMWORTH	B66 3EV	Yes	5,250	28/10/99	6,500
Mr	W	Hollingdale	38 Canon Street	PINNER	HA66 9MP	No	1,000	02/01/03	1,750
Mr	J	Staniforth	29 Whitfield Close	BRIGHTON	BN3 7GB	Yes	3,250 *12,750*	05/09/01	4,750
Mrs	S	Barry	9 Egerton Road	STOURBRIDGE	DY7 6BB	Yes	~~2,750~~	01/05/01	12,900
Mr	K	Fordham	93 Arundel Road	TAMWORTH	B77 8YG	Yes	2,000	14/03/99	2,500
Mrs	P	Clarke	19 Copper Street	TYNEMOUTH *TAUNTON*	NE28 1CZ *TA1 3RT*	Yes	3,500	21/08/98	4,250
Ms	I	Brown	61 Corsley Lane	*BATH*	*BA1 3KL*	Yes	7,500	30/10/96	6,500 *7,500*
Mrs	L	O'Neill	35 Station Road	MANCHESTER	M2 7DS	Yes	*6,500* ~~8,250~~	04/02/99	7,500
Mr	D	Tapp	5 Dorcester Close	LEICESTER	LE43 6AN	Yes	3,250	25/08/99	4,000
~~Mrs~~	~~G~~	~~Ried~~	~~14 Farren Road~~	~~THETFORD~~	~~IP26 3GP~~	~~No~~	~~1,500~~	~~18/01/03~~	~~2,000~~
Mr	L	Wale	29 Mayfield Avenue	TAUNTON	TA4 7LE	Yes	11,000	07/03/95	13,000
Mrs	J	*Langley* ~~Langdon~~	13 Forest Drive	EASTLEIGH	SO5 8JJ	Yes	8,000	18/03/96	9,000
Ms	I	Larkin	46 Latimer Road	WALSALL	WS4 5BN	Yes	7,500	23/05/98	8,500
Mrs *Ms*	A	O'Sullivan	3 Chaucer Road	LIVERPOOL	L33 7GJ	Yes	6,250	31/05/98	6,500
Mrs	D	White	61 West Avenue	LEEDS	LS1 3AK	Yes	4,750	15/07/02	5,000
Mr	D O	Loughlin	3 Burnham Road	BRISTOL	BS9 7SY	Yes	7,250	27/05/97	9,000
Mrs	J	Holly	42 Greenbank Place	TAUNTON	TA3 8AN	No	1,000	15/01/03	1,750

Handwritten additions:

Mr	M	Allard	1 Kingsway	IPSWICH	IP2 6 LJ	Yes	10,500	17/03/89	12,750
Ms	B	Jones	53 Manor Road	PORTSMOUTH	PO7 9QT	Yes	7,500	20/06/92	8,250
Ms	M	Zarrabi	49 Richmond Mews	YORK	YO5 6FZ	Yes	4,750	01/11/97	6,500

Please add these records to the datafile

Please key in the following standard document to merge with the datafile CREDIT1. Insert merge codes where indicated by * and use a ragged right margin. Print one copy of the standard document and also print documents to all those who have a credit limit of more than £9,999.

Our ref GC/03

* Title * Initials * Surname

* Street

* Town

* Postcode

Dear * Title * Surname

PLATINUM CARD OFFER

According to our records you have been a holder of our standard credit card since * date issued. Your current credit limit is £ * card limit.

We would now like to offer you the opportunity of becoming one of our special Platinum card holders. This special card is only issued to a small number of our customers.

With the Platinum card you receive extra benefits. These include free insurance for all your credit cards, and an exceptionally low interest rate. We will also increase your credit limit to £ * revised limit.

If you would like to take advantage of this offer please contact us within 14 days of the date of this letter.

We look forward to hearing from you. (Emphasise these words)

Yours sincerely

Alex Perry

Manager

Please key in the following records as a datafile suitable for use with the THEATRE letter. Save and print one copy. Save as TICKETS.

Mr Vikram Deboos
64 North Street
BRISTOL
BS12 8QT
Swan Lake
20 August
£60

Mrs Kerry James
4 Penn Lea Road
SALTFORD
BS9 7JF
Swan Lake
22 August
£80

Mrs Maggie Birchall
32 Clifton Place
BATH
BA1 4HW
Nutcracker Suite
5 September
£40

Miss Jayne Marchant
11 Ashley Road
BRISTOL
BS14 2VZ
Swan Lake
20 August
£80

Mr Peter Jarvis
62 Saville Row
BRISTOL
BS12 4HB
Swan Lake
20 August
£60

Mr Greg Latimer
5 Otega Terrace
BRISTOL
BS17 8LS
Nutcracker Suite
5 September
£60

Mr Andy Dean
1 Horseshoe Drive
BRISTOL
BS1 8SE
Nutcracker Suite
5 September
£50

Ms Deborah Fenton
7 Oldfield Gardens
BATH
BA1 3YT
Swan Lake
22 August
£60

Mrs Venetia Hargreaves
42 Larch Avenue
BATH
BA1 5BN
Swan Lake
22 August
£80

Mrs Molly Peters
22 Langdon Road
BRISTOL
BS19 4XZ
Swan Lake
24 August
£80

Please key in the following standard document to merge with the datafile TICKETS . Insert merge codes where indicated by * and use a justified right margin. Print one copy of the standard document and also print documents to all those who have purchased tickets for Swan Lake on the 20 August. Save as THEATRE.

Our ref SL/CF/208
* Name
* Address
* Town
* Postcode

Dear * Name

Thank you for your cheque for * Amount. We are pleased to confirm that two tickets have been reserved for the performance of * Performance on * Date.

The tickets may be collected from the box office at your convenience. We would be grateful if you could ensure they have been collected by 7.00 pm on the day of the performance.

please emphasise this sentence

We hope you have a very enjoyable evening.

Yours sincerely

Chantel Fabrice
Bookings Officer

Mailmerge consolidation 2

Recall this datafile stored under CONSOLIDATION. Amend as shown. Sort the amended datafile by ascending order of Credit Limit. Save as Credit2. Print one copy ensuring that at least three records are printed on each page.

Please add this field to each record →

Title	Initials	Surname	Street	Town	Postcode	Credit Check	Card Limit £	Date Issued	Additional Cardholder
Mr	P~~A~~	Johnson	3 Mizzymead Rise	ABINGDON	OX14 4DA	Yes	10,000	01/06/01	K Johnson
Mrs	S	Willard ~~Gulliver~~	12 Frimley Road	WAKEFIELD	WF1 9NA	Yes	2,000	29/08/86	P Willard / C Gulliver
Mr	I	~~Gulliver~~	29 Bush Road	CHELMSFORD	CM1 2NX	Yes	4,500	05/04/89	C Gulliver
Ms	L	Rathe	48 Roxwell Avenue	YEOVIL	BS10 7UG	No	1,500	27/12/02	S Rathe
Mrs	R	Neale	5 Quaker Court	WALSALL	WS3 4QW	No	2,000	10/1/03	Q Neale
Mr	H	Layton	9 Wellington Close	LONDON	SE17 0IN	Yes	4,500	30/3/02	B Layton
~~Ms~~	C	~~Marshall~~	~~6 Churchill Road~~	~~HORNCHURCH~~	~~RM11 2AX~~	~~Yes~~	~~6,000~~	~~09/02/00~~	F Marshall
Ms	D	Shilvock	22 Hazelmere Gardens	LEICESTER	LE3 8FU	Yes	12,000	24/03/96	None
Mr	P	Bowbrick	57 Rocky ~~Lane~~ Road	SLOUGH	SL3 7RB	Yes	5,000	31/01/96	L Bowbrick
Mr	W	Piper	121 Chelmsford Road	SHREWSBURY	SY5 6LP	Yes	**8,000** ~~3,000~~	02/06/98	C Piper
Ms	J	Higham	3 Agar Road	EASTLEIGH	SO5 2BQ **BA6 4RT**	No	1,500	16/01/03	J Higham
Mrs	F	Seward	76 Garthorne Road	~~ALTON~~ **BATH**	~~GU34 5AH~~	Yes	7,500	26/07/99	None
Mr	N	Mainwood	5 Wyken Road **Lane**	WHITBY	YO21 1LT	Yes	4,000	02/04/01	S Mainwood
Mrs	I	Cartmell	7 Church ~~Street~~	HEREFORD	HR1 8UL	Yes	~~8,750~~ **4,500**	09/05/02	T Cartmell
Mr	Y	Dixon	56 Montgomery Close	COVENTRY	CV1 8RP	Yes	~~2,500~~	07/11/02	H Dixon
Mrs	F	Spendley	4 Lime Road	BATH	BA9 7YX	Yes	7,000	09/10/99	R Spendley
Ms	P	Langley	79 Bellotts Road	STEVENAGE	SG2 9RB	Yes	9,750	12/08/97	W Langley
Mr	A	Bennett	5 School Avenue	GLOUCESTER	GL3 7GB	Yes	4,500	23/07/96	A Bennett
Mr	~~H~~ S	Hunt	3 Drove Lane	BRISTOL	BS33 7KA	Yes	5,500	22/09/99	None
Mrs	O	Hanson	66 Buckingham Road	MANCHESTER	M28 6TJ	No	1,000	27/01/03	P Hanson
Mr	E	Haffner	74 Woodside Avenue	CHELTENHAM	GL99 6LM	Yes	**3,500** ~~2,750~~	14/08/88	F Haffner

Title	Initials	Surname	Street	Town	Postcode	Credit Check	Card Limit £	Date Issued	Additional Cardholder
Mrs	M	Clifford	44 Okus Road	SHREWSBURY	SY3 2BB	Yes	10,500	04/03/97	None
Ms	D	Reynolds	3 Wentworth Road	MACCLESFIELD	SK11 7LH	Yes	6,750	17/05/98	None
Mrs	K	Lester	56 Staveley Road	TAMWORTH	B66 3EV	Yes	5,250	28/10/99	J Lester
Mr	W	Hollingdale	38 Canon Street	PINNER	HA66 9MP	No	1,000	02/01/03	A Hollingdale
~~Mr~~	~~J~~	~~Stanforth~~	~~20 Whitfield Close~~	~~BRIGHTON~~	~~BN3 7GB~~	~~Yes~~	~~3,250~~	~~05/09/01~~	~~E Stanforth~~
Mrs	S	Barry	9 Egerton Road	STOURBRIDGE	DY7 6BB	Yes	2,750	01/05/01	None
Mr	K	Fordham	93 Arundel Road	TAMWORTH	B77 8YG	~~Yes~~ No	~~2,000~~ 1,000	~~14/03/99~~ 12/01/03	Y Fordham
Mrs	P	Clarke	19 Copper Street	TYNEMOUTH	NE28 1CZ	Yes	3,500	21/08/98	N Clarke
Ms	I	Brown	61 Corsley Lane	BATH	BA1 3KL	Yes	7,500	30/10/96	None
Mrs	L	O'Neill	35 Station Road	MANCHESTER	M2 7DS	Yes	8,250	04/02/99	C O'Neill
Mr	D	Tapp	5 Dorcester ~~Close~~ Place	LEICESTER	LE43 6AN	Yes	~~3,250~~ 4,500	25/08/99	R Tapp
~~Mrs~~	~~G~~	~~Ried~~	~~14 Farren Road~~	~~THETFORD~~	~~IP26 3CP~~	~~No~~	~~1,500~~	~~18/01/03~~	~~V Ried~~
Mr	L	Wale	29 Mayfield Avenue	TAUNTON	TA4 7LE	Yes	11,000	07/03/95	M Wale
Mrs	J	Langdon	13 Forest Drive	~~EASTLEIGH~~ Swindon	~~SO5 8H~~ SN1 5BY	Yes	8,000	18/03/96	G Langdon
Ms	I	Larkin	46 Latimer Road	WALSALL	WS4 5BN	Yes	7,500	23/05/98	P Larkin
Mrs	A	O'Sullivan ~~White~~ Black	3 Chaucer Road	LIVERPOOL	L33 7GJ	Yes	6,250	31/05/98	O'Sullivan White Black
Mr	D	Loughlin	61 West Avenue	LEEDS	LS13 AK	Yes	4,750	15/07/02	O ...
Mr	D	Loughlin	3 Burnham Road	BRISTOL	BS9 7SY	Yes	7,250	27/05/97	P Loughlin
Mrs	J	Holly	42 Greenbank Place	TAUNTON	TA3 8AN	No	1,000	15/01/03	L Holly
Mr	M	Richard	12 Castle Street	SWINDON	SN6 5PB	Yes	4,500	17/06/02	B Richard
Mrs	C	Phillips	27 Thornbank Place	BRISTOL	BS16 8FH	Yes	9,000	21/02/99	C Phillips
Mr	S	Ross	7 Miles Road	MANCHESTER	M42 5LJ	Yes	3,750	01/11/02	P Ross

Please add these records to the datafile

Please key in the following records as a datafile suitable for use with HOLIDAY BOOKINGS memo. Save as Annual leave and print one copy. Do not key in the words in brackets.

John Langley
Accounts Assistant
20 (days entitlement)
8 (days booked)
12 (days left)
Accounts Department

May Hsiaso
Human Resources Supervisor
25 (days entitlement)
15 (days booked)
10 (days left)
Human Resources Department

Kathy Green
Accounts Supervisor
25 (days entitlement)
10 (days booked)
15 (days left)
Accounts Department

Derek Kirby
Design Manager
25 (days entitlement)
15 (days booked)
10 (days left)
Design Department

Darius Zarrabi
Admin Assistant
25 (days entitlement)
20 (days booked)
5 (days left)
Administration Department

Eddie Clarke
Accounts Assistant
20 (days entitlement)
8 (days booked)
12 (days left)
Accounts Department

Lucy Hopkins
Accounts Manager
30 (days entitlement)
25 (days booked)
5 (days left)
Accounts Department

Sara Metcalfe
Design Assistant
22 (days entitlement)
20 (days booked)
2 (days left)
Design Department

Martin Brookes
Sales Manager
20 (days entitlement)
10 (days booked)
10 (days left)
Sales Department

Carly Jones
Admin Assistant
25 (days entitlement)
19 (days booked)
6 (days left)
Administration Department

Please key in the following standard document to merge with the datafile CREDIT2. Insert merge codes where indicated by * and use a ragged right hand margin. Print one copy of the standard document and also print documents for all those who have a credit limit of £4,500.

Our ref ACH/AP

* Title * Initials * Surname
* Street
* Town
* Postcode

Dear * Title * Surname

Replacement Cards

Please find enclosed your replacement credit card, together with one for your additional cardholder * Additional cardholder. You are advised to check and sign these cards immediately and keep them somewhere safe. Please destroy your existing cards.

The issue date for the cards is * Date issued and your credit limit is £ * Card limit £. If you would like to increase your credit limit please contact one of our advisors. Decisions are normally made within 24 hours.

You may be interested to learn more about the services we offer our credit card holders. We hope you find the enclosed leaflet informative. It also tells you about our terms and conditions.

Yours sincerely

Alex Perry
Manager
Enc

Please emphasise this sentence

Please key in the following standard document to merge with the datafile Annual Leave . Insert merge codes where indicated by * and use a justified right margin. Print one copy of the standard document and also print documents to all those who have 12 or more days holiday entitlement left to book and work in the Accounts Department.

Memorandum

To * Name, * Job title

From Sandy Mayo, Human Resources Manager

Ref SM/HE

HOLIDAY ENTITLEMENT ← Please emphasise this heading

I am now arranging temporary cover for holidays taken by staff in the * Department. According to my records your holiday entitlement is * Entitlement. You have booked * days booked days.

It would be most helpful if you could book the remaining dates by the end of next week. Your remaining entitlement is * days left. I am enclosing a list of your booked dates.

Allocation will be made according to the date of request. Therefore, if you have any essential days you need to take off, then it is advisable to make your request as soon as possible.

Thank you for your co-operation in this matter.

Enc

Taking the examination

This section tells you exactly what the examiner will be looking for when marking your work. It does this by showing you the most common errors in documents submitted for the examination, together with hints on how to resolve these errors.

It also includes two examination practice exercises for you to complete to prepare you for the OCR examination.

Document 1

This task requires you to recall an existing datafile and make various amendments. These will include adding and deleting records, adding a new field to each record and sorting the datafile. The instructions ask you to print a copy of the amended datafile and to ensure that at least three records are printed on each page.

This task is very straightforward. The main problem here is proof-reading. As the amendments are dotted around the pages, it is useful if you use a ruler to go down each record to check whether there are any changes. If there are, once you have made them, tick the record to show that you have carried out the work.

Look at the following two documents. Figure 4.34 is correct, Figure 4.35 contains some errors. Can you spot them?

Title	Initials	Surname	Street	Town	Postcode	Property	Start Date	Balance	Total Rental
Ms	V	McKillick	3 Summer Way	IPSWICH	IP32 7NO	Torfrey	07/06/02	940	990
Dr	K B	Ridgley	7B Parkham Crescent	PORTSMOUTH	PO2 8BN	Sundial	15/07/02	527	575
Mrs	H	Wilkins	42 Linthorpe Way	BRISTOL	BS2 4NK	Drimmin	01/10/02	480	550
Mr	D	Gardner	21 Russell Square	NOTTINGHAM	NG3 4UB	Lantern Cottage	02/11/02	250	300
Mrs	C	Zarrabi	94 Longfellow Road	HULL	HU1 7CH	Mizzen	03/01/03	189	239
Mr	S	Peterson	22 Livingstone Close	ELLESMERE	SY32 7SL	Harbour Lights	31/01/03	128	178
Mrs	D	Fisher	29 Bennetts Lane	LEICESTER	LE2 1NQ	Harbour Lights	15/02/03	210	260
Ms	J	Marchant	12 Oakland Road	SALISBURY	SP3 5GH	Compass Cottage	01/03/03	250	300
Mr	A K	Jackson	17 Ragland Lane	COVENTRY	CV3 7WR	Compass Cottage	08/03/03	195	245
Mrs	E K	Lathem	62 Acer Drive	BELFAST	BT16 3NA	Drimmin	16/03/03	240	290
Mr	P	Singh	47 Lake Close	KESWICK	CA12 7PY	Mermaid Cottage	26/04/03	420	470
Mrs	N P	Wing	30 Liversham Close	SOLIHULL	B90 2LS	Coastguard	26/04/03	382	432
Mr	S I	Thomas	76 Prospect Road	PETERBOROUGH	PE1 6SF	Mermaid Cottage	17/05/03	375	425
Ms	T	Wright	84 Ringwood Road	PERTH	PH3 2AB	Compass Cottage	17/05/03	328	378
Mrs	A F	Pointen	7 Mount Pleasant	SALCOMBE	EX32 8AN	Harbour Lights	24/05/03	395	445
Mrs	F B	Whitmarsh	39 Perrymead	BRIGHTON	BH3 1SJ	Castle Cottage	24/05/03	429	479
Mr	X	Jones	138 Newhall Drive	LEICESTER	LE4 5BJ	Harbour Lights	24/05/03	650	700
Miss	B	McWilliams	Rose Cottage	EXETER	EX2 1KS	Castle Cottage	02/06/03	325	375
Mr	C D	Ballantyne	38 Centry Drive	WINCHESTER	SO21 7NP	Sea Holme	02/06/03	390	440
Mrs	G S	Shaftesbury	8 North Road	GUILDFORD	GU3 7AP	Samphire House	15/06/03	540	590
Ms	L	Mayo	9 Heather Court	CHIPPENHAM	BA48 3NP	Lantern Cottage	21/06/03	318	368
Ms	W	Tyrell	73 Oakhill Drive	OXFORD	OX8 2NP	Torfrey	05/07/03	520	570
Mrs	R	Patel	74 Highway Road	EDINBURGH	EH2 4CX	Harbour Lights	05/07/03	389	439
Mrs	J	Captain	58 Holwell Road	IPSWICH	IP29 5NL	Mizzen	19/07/03	480	530
Mrs	L	Elkins	44 Temperence Steps	DEVIZES	SP3 4GJ	Castle Cottage	19/07/03	486	536
Mr	I A	Spencer	121 Oldway Road	TRURO	TR3 9JL	Sea Holme	27/07/03	1250	1230
Dr	M	Ashley	80 Harlow Drive	KESWICK	CA12 3VB	Compass	02/08/03	625	675
Mrs	J	Howich	121 Rosslyn Road	BATH	BA2 3NO	Fortune Cottage	02/08/03	750	800
Ms	M	Saunders	52 Lincoln Hill	WINCHESTER	SO21 4FH	Sea Holme	09/08/03	780	830
Mrs	J	Godfrey	56 Acorn Avenue	BATH	BA1 3LA	Harbour Lights	09/08/03	530	580
Ms	N	Viner	10 Charmouth Road	CAMBRIDGE	CB2 9NP	Park Court	23/08/03	1240	1500
Mr	P	Pascal	65 Copythorne Road	ROMFORD	RM7 3WA	Sea View Cottage	23/08/03	650	700
Mr	Q	Wrench	22 Ashley Avenue	MANCHESTER	M21 4NR	Fortune Cottage	23/08/03	750	800
Miss	A Y	Greenslade	46 Newlands Road	LIVERPOOL	L21 8BY	Drimmin	06/09/03	285	335
Mr	I L	Wilson	7 King Street	PAIGNTON	TQ3 8BN	Compass	06/09/03	295	345
Mrs	S	O'Sullivan	388 Woodford Drive	LONDON	E12 3NO	Drimmin	06/09/03	280	230
Mr	T	Hedley	43 York Street	LOWESTOFT	NR32 3NQ	Sundial	20/09/03	420	470
Ms	J	Norris	51 Southdown Rise	LIVERPOOL	L32 1NE	Lantern Cottage	04/10/03	189	239
Mrs	N	Barker	34 King's Circus	EXETER	EX2 8WL	Lantern Cottage	01/11/03	200	250

Figure 4.34 Correct version

Title	Initials	Surname	Street	Town	Postcode	Property	Start Date	Balance	Total Rental
Ms	V	McKillick	3 Summer Way	IPSWICH	IP32 7NO	Torfrey	07/06/02	940	990
Dr	K B	Ridgley	7B Parkham Crescent	PORTSMOUTH	PO2 8BN	Sundial	15/07/02	527	575
Mrs	H	Wilkins	42 Linthorpe Way	BRISTOL	BS2 4NK	Drimmin	01/10/02	480	550
Mr	D	Gardner	21 Russell Square	NOTTINGHAM	NG3 4UB	Lantern Cottage	02/11/02	250	300
Mrs	C	Zarrabi	94 Longfellow Road	HULL	HU1 7CH	Mizzen	03/01/03	189	239
Mr	S	Peterson	22 Livingstone Close	ELLESMERE	SY32 7SL	Harbour Lights	31/01/03	128	178
Mrs	D	Fisher	29 Bennetts Lane	LEICESTER	LE2 1NQ	Harbour Lights	15/02/03	210	260
Mr	A K	Jackson	17 Ragland Lane	COVENTRY	CV3 7WR	Compass Cottage	08/03/03	195	245
Mrs	E K	Lathem	62 Acer Drive	BELFAST	BT16 3NA	Drimmin	16/03/03	240	290
Mrs	N P	Wing	30 Liversham Close	SOLIHULL	B90 2LS	Coastguard	26/04/03	382	432
Mr	P	Singh	47 Lake Close	KESWICK	CA12 7PY	Mermaid Cottage	26/04/03	420	470
Mrs	T	Wright	84 Ringwood Road	PERTH	PH3 2AB	Compass Cottage	17/05/03	328	378
Mr	S I	Thomas	76 Prospect Road	PETERBOROUGH	PE1 6SF	Mermaid Cottage	17/05/03	375	425
Mrs	Z	Pointen	7 Mount Pleasant	SALCOMBE	EX32 8AN	Harbour Lights	24/05/03	395	445
Mrs	F B	Whitmarsh	39 Perrymead	BRIGHTON	BH1 1SJ	Castle Cottage	24/05/03	429	479
Miss	B	McWilliams	Rose Cottage	EXETER	EX2 1KS	Castle Cottage	02/06/03	325	375
Mr	C D	Ballantyne	38 Centry Drive	WINCHESTER	SO21 7NP	Sea Holme	02/06/03	390	440
Mrs	G S	Shaftesbury	8 North Road	GUILDFORD	GU3 7AP	Samphire House	15/06/03	540	590
Ms	L	Mayo	9 Heather Court	CHIPPENHAM	BA48 3NP	Lantern Cottage	21/06/03	318	368
Mr	J	Lewis	16 Bellotts Road	YORK	YO7 6CG	Sundial	21/06/03	400	450
Mrs	R	Patel	74 Highway Road	EDINBURGH	EH2 4CX	Harbour Lights	05/07/03	389	439
Ms	W	Tyrell	73 Oakhill Lane	OXFORD	OX8 2NP	Torfrey	05/07/03	520	570
Mrs	J	Captain	58 Holwell Road	IPSWICH	IP29 5NL	Mizzen	19/07/03	480	530
Mrs	L	Elkins	44 Temperence Steps	SALISBURY	SP3 4GJ	Castle Cottage	19/07/03	486	536
Mr	I A	Spencer	121 Oldway Road	TRURO	TR3 9JL	Sea Holme	27/07/03	1250	1230
Dr	M	Ashley	80 Harlow Drive	KESWICK	CA12 3VB	Compass	02/08/03	625	675
Mrs	J	Howich	121 Rosslyn Road	BATH	BA2 3NO	Fortune Cottage	02/08/03	750	800
Mrs	J	Godfrey	56 Acorn Avenue	BATH	BA1 3LA	Harbour Lights	09/08/03	530	580
Ms	M	Saunders	52 Lincoln Hill	WINCHESTER	SO21 4FH	Sea Holme	09/08/03	780	830
Ms	N	Viner	10 Charmouth Road	CAMBRIDGE	CB2 9NP	Park Road	23/08/03	1240	1500
Mr	P	Pascal	65 Copythorne Road	ROMFORD	RM7 3WA	Sea View Cottage	23/08/03	650	700
Mr	Q	Wrench	22 Ashley Avenue	MANCHESTER	M21 4NR	Fortune Cottage	23/08/03	750	800
Mrs	S	O'Sullivan	388 Woodford Drive	LONDON	E12 3NO	Drimmin	06/09/03	280	230
Miss	A Y	Greenslade	46 Newlands Road	LIVERPOOL	L21 8BY	Drimmin	06/09/03	285	335
Mr	I L	Wilson	7 King Street	PAIGNTON	TQ3 8BN	Compass	06/09/03	295	345
Mr	T	Horton	43 York Street	LOWESTOFT	NR32 3NQ	Sundial	20/09/03	420	470
Ms	J	Norris	51 Southdown Rise	LIVERPOOL	L32 1NE	Lantern Cottage	04/10/03	189	239

Figure 4.35 Incorrect version

Error 1

The sort has been carried out incorrectly. It has been sorted by ascending order of total rent, whereas the instruction asked for the order of start date.

Solution

Ensure that you sort by the correct column. Check that you are keying in the correct values into the sort table. In particular, with this sort, the value box in the sort option stated that the **type** of the material contained in the 'Total Rental' column was 'Text'. This is of course incorrect, the **type** of the material contained in the Total Rental column is '**Number**'.

If you are at all unsure of how to set up a sort, refer to page 197.

Error 2

Several records are missing. These include J Marchant, J Lewis and N Barker.

Solution

There are several causes for this problem. It might be that these are the three records that should have been added, or it might be that these should have been deleted. You must check you have made all the amendments very carefully.

Error 3

The record for Mrs Pointen has not been amended. The initials for this record should have been changed to AF.

Solution

Again, this all comes down to careful proof-reading. You must ensure that you check your records very carefully.

Document 2

This task requires you to create a small datafile. You will enter 10 records and each record will contain 7 fields.

Look at Figures 4.36 and 4.37 below. Figure 4.36 is correct, Figure 4.37 contains some errors. Can you spot them?

Title	Initials	Surname	Job Title	Department	Payroll	Salary
Mr	P	Griffin	Manager	Sales	3339	£28,000
Mrs	H	Orwell	Manager	Design	2981	£29,000
Mr	A	Hanson	Supervisor	Production	3988	£18,500
Miss	F	Payne	Assistant	Sales	1899	£15,500
Mr	E	White	Assistant	Design	2977	£13,500
Mr	G	Pike	Assistant	Production	3977	£12,500
Ms	L	Johnson	Supervisor	Warehouse	3731	£14,500
Mrs	N	Singh	Manager	Accounts	4655	£28,000
Mr	I	Hussain	Supervisor	Accounts	4621	£18,500

Figure 4.36 Correct version

Title	Initials	Surname	Job Title	Department	Payroll	Salary
Mr	T	Griffin	Manager	Sales	3339	£28,000
Mrs	H	Orwell	Manager	Design	2981	£29,000
Mr	A	Hanson	Supervisor	Production	3988	£18,500
Miss	F	Pain	Assistant	Sales	1899	£15,500
Mr	E	White	Manager	Design	2977	£13,500
Mr	G	Pike	Assistant	Production	3977	£12,700
Ms	L	Johnson	Supervisor	Distribution	3731	£14,500
Mrs	N	Singh	Manager	Accounts	4655	£28,000
Mr	I	Hussain	Supervisor	Accounts	4621	£18,500

Figure 4.37 Incorrect version

Error 1

There are a number of typographical errors in Figure 4.37. This means that your query may not produce the correct number of merged documents.

Solution

You can check that your datafile is correct by carrying out the merge and then checking this against the examination paper. It will not take long to work out who should have received the merge documents. If you have not printed sufficient merge letters, then you know that you have either made a query error or a typographical error. You can easily check the query options. If this is not the case, then go through your records very carefully to ensure that the text has been entered correctly.

Another problem may be that you have not entered the same datafile names in your merge document as are contained in your datafile. Remember, with this task you must form your own field names. This can sometimes be confusing. The best way to avoid problems with this is to look at the standard document draft contained in the examination paper before you start to create your datafile. Now use the field names given in this document for your datafile. This way you will avoid any errors.

Documents 3 and 4

Error 1

It is easy to forget to print a copy of the standard document when you are in a hurry to get the merge letters completed.

Solution

As soon as you have completed keying in the standard document, press Print as soon as you have checked it. This way, you know the standard document has been printed and so you can forget all about it (apart from ensuring you hand it in of course!).

Error 2

Your merge letters are not correct.

Solution

You may have keyed in the fields incorrectly, or given the incorrect query option. You must check these very carefully before merging documents. If you cannot remember how to set up queries or merge fields in your documents see page 181.

Error 3

There a number of typographical errors.

Solution

Proof-read your work very carefully before printing. This is particularly the case with mailmerge as you do not want to waste masses of paper printing incorrect merges.

Examination practice

To help you prepare for the examination, two full examination papers follow. Try to complete these in exam conditions, ie finish in the 1 hour and 30 minutes allowed, including printing. Do not ask for help or refer to this book for information on how to do things. Try not to talk to anyone whilst working on these tasks. If you can do all of these then your work will give you a good indication of whether you are ready to sit the real exam. Once you have completed the tasks, you can check your documents with the worked examples on the CD-ROM.

When you are working through these exercises you will need to remember the following:

- To find out which field names to use when setting up the datafile, look at the standard document that goes with it.
- Remember you must print copies of the datafiles and the standard documents showing the merge codes.
- It can be difficult to ensure that all amendments have been made on the datafile. Tick off each amendment as you make it.
- If your merge query does not work immediately don't panic! Work through the options again, checking that you have entered all the information correctly.
- Remember to spellcheck your work after you have finished each document.
- Consistency is very important. Make sure that all your work, including spacing between paragraphs, numbers, etc., shows a consistent display.

If you can complete all the work within the time without too many errors then you should now try working on some old examination papers. These will give you a feel for the type of examination paper you are likely to face. You must not become too complacent, even if you are consistently doing well in practice papers, as the examination itself can make you nervous and this is when it is easy to make mistakes.

The key to success in the examination is proof-reading your work carefully, referring back to the examination paper to check that you have keyed in the correct words, not the ones you think are there or should be there!

Handwritten instruction (callout box):

Recall this datafile stored under PRODUCT. Amend as shown. Sort the amended datafile by alphabetical order of Surname. Save as PRODUCT1. Print one copy ensuring that at least three records are printed on each page.

Handwritten note with arrow pointing to the Product Code column:

Please add this field to each record

Title	Initials	Surname	Street	Town	Postcode	Item	Value £	Payment Method	Product Code
Mr	R	Peters	11 Maybrick Road	TRURO	TR3 8AN	Toaster	15.00	Cheque	TR65
Mrs	A	Turner	7 Herbert Road *(amended: 24 ... Mount Road)*	EXETER	EX7 6NO	Kettle	20.00	Cheque *(amended: Cash / Credit card)*	KT32
Ms	D	Sinclair	7 Mount Road	RUGBY	CV21 4HB	Coffee grinder	18.00	Cash	CG12
Mr	V	Frecknall	67 Commercial Road	PORTSMOUTH	PO5 3ET	Food processor	59.00	Cheque	FP14
Mrs	M	Wade	43 Morris Lane	BRISTOL *(amended: ELY; CAMBRIDGE crossed)*	BS1 5JN	Toaster *(amended: Food processor)*	15.00 *(amended: 59.00)*	Credit card	TR65 *(amended: FP14)*
Mrs	T	Gale	21 Heath Park	CAMBRIDGE	CB3 6QL	Coffee grinder	18.00	Debit card	CG12
Mrs	E	Morling	125 Kingston Road	LINDFIELD	RH14 3BJ	Coffee grinder	18.00	Debit card	CG12
Ms	A	Newall	37 Commercial Road	SALISBURY	SP5 8AJ	Espresso maker *(amended: Coffee Percolator)*	48.00 *(amended: 32.00)*	Cash	EM06 *(amended: CP20)*
Mr	F	Ettridge	86 Westburn Mews	MALVERN	WR14 6OY	Hand blender	22.00	Cash	HB29
Mrs	W P	Tribe	54 Lyndhurst Road	LONDON	SE5 6NA	Toaster	15.00	Cheque	TR65
Mr	C	Scarborough	6 Portsmouth Road	KETTERING	NN16 4SM	Sandwich toaster	12.00	Debit card	ST10
Mrs	R	Colley	8 Dove Street	DERBY	DE9 4DQ	Food processor	59.00	Credit card	FP14
Mr	J	Mackintosh	4 Falstaff Road	LEEDS	LS3 7YB	Hand blender	22.00	Cash	HB29
~~Mrs~~	~~G~~	~~Martin~~	~~23 Manor Drive~~	~~REDDITCH~~	~~B98 3VK~~	~~Coffee percolator~~	~~32.00~~	~~Cheque~~	~~CP20~~
Mr	B	McMahon	22 Nayling Avenue	BASINGSTOKE	RG22 5GH	Kettle	20.00	Credit card	KT32
Mrs *(amended: Mr)*	L	Tozer	39 Aylwin Street *(Lane)*	LIVERPOOL	L83 2WD	Coffee grinder	18.00	Cheque	CG12
Mrs	S	Cook	12 Enville Road	COVENTRY	CV3 8BN	Toaster	15.00	Debit card	TR65
Mrs	R	Johnson	101 Lakeside Road	YORK	YO4 5KJ	Food processor	59.00	Credit card	FP14
Mrs	J	Pybus	Eastley Road	SPALDING	PE11 7HM	Hand blender	22.00	Cash *(amended: Cheque)*	HB29
Mrs	N	Britten *(amended: Beaumont)*	4 Oxford Street	STOWMARKET	IP15 6AG	Coffee percolator	32.00	Cheque	CP20

Examination practice 1

225

Title	Initials	Surname	Street	Town	Postcode	Item	Value £	Payment Method	Product Code
Mr	P	Sollich	45 Severn Road	FAREHAM	PO16 8UB	Sandwich toaster	12.00	Cash	ST10
Mrs	T	Turnidge	62 Harley Street	EXETER	~~EX4 7NQ~~ EX22 4GH	Kettle	20.00	Cash	KT32
Mr	O	Kennedy	54 Thomas Street	TAUNTON	TA2 3NL	Toaster	15.00	Debit card	TR65
Mr	M	Payne	33 Pera Mews ~~Road~~ Park	BRISTOL	BS22 5EK	Hand blender	22.00	Cheque	HB29
Ms	H	Shellard	1 Southdown Road	TRURO	TR4 6NG	Espresso machine	48.00	Credit card	EM06
Ms	N	Ellis ~~Dinning~~ Davis	76 Parade Street	BRIXHAM	TQ5 7PW	Kettle	20.00	Cheque	KT32
Mr	AC	Dinning	83 Aspley Avenue	STROUD	GL43 7ZL	Coffee grinder	18.00	Cash	CG12
Mrs	B	Elkheim	69 Rosslyn Road	BIRMINGHAM	B38 2NS	Sandwich toaster	12.00	Debit card	ST10
~~Mrs~~	~~A~~	~~Sutton~~	~~3 Park Avenue~~	~~EXMOUTH~~	~~EX16 3JM~~	~~Toaster~~	~~15.00~~	~~Credit card~~	~~TR65~~
Mr	S	Wing	55 Osbourne Drive	SHEFFIELD	S33 6AS	Coffee percolator	32.00	Cheque	CP20
Mr	P	Jackson	55 Coronation Road	YORK	YO4 3AS	Hand blender	22.00	Cash	HB29
Mr	T	Seagar	9 The Oval	PORTSMOUTH	PO3 5NA	Kettle	20.00	~~Credit card~~ Debit Card ~~Cash~~	KT32
Mrs	F	Simmonds	4 Newbridge Road	LAUNCESTON	EX5 7DL	Sandwich toaster	12.00	Cash	ST10
Mrs	D	Redfern	83 Lyndhurst Road	CARDIFF	CF5 2HA	Coffee grinder	18.00	Debit card	CG12
~~Mr~~	~~B~~	~~Stock~~	~~6 Richmond Place~~	~~YORK~~	~~YO3 6TR~~	~~Food processor~~	~~59.00~~	~~Credit card~~	~~FP14~~
Mr	E	Wilmot	67 Ringwood Road	BRISTOL	BS22 5AE	Food processor	59.00	Cash	FP14
Ms	K	Longham	43 Brook Road	STROUD	GL7 9WK	Kettle	20.00	Credit card	KT32
Mr	A	Portnall	10 Charlton Mews	LONDON PAIGNTON	SW17 5EB	Hand blender Toaster	22.00 15.00	Debit card	HB29
Ms	R	Bletso	3 Julian Road	~~TORQUAY~~ TORQUAY	TQ2 3RT	~~Sandwich toaster~~ Toaster	~~12.00~~ 15.00	Cheque	~~ST10~~ TR65
Mr	L	Hagman	64 Mile End Road	PORTSMOUTH	PO5 7CS	Coffee percolator	32.00	Cash	CP20
Mrs	G	Greene	7 Victoria Terrace	SWINDON	SN11 6PX	Sandwich Toaster	12.00	Cash	ST10
Mr	R	Berry	94 Marsden Road	CARDIFF	CF4 2LM	Hand blender	22.00	Debit card	HB29
Ms	F	Latham	16 Empire Road	HULL	HU1 3XY	Toaster	15.00	Cheque	TR65

Please add these records to the datafile

Please key in the following records as a database suitable for use with Offer letter. Save and print one copy. Save as Jewellery.

Mr J Kahn
22 Park Drive
MANCHESTER
M62 3RL
Daisy
Bracelet
DAB23

Miss L Sumner
7 The Larches
TUNBRIDGE WELLS
TN16 7FV
Daisy
Necklace
DAB26

Mr G Kent
29 Brook Road
BELFAST
BT3 61A
Iris
Necklace
IRN70

Ms J Ready
46 Baker Road
YORK
YO1 7DP
Daisy
Bracelet
DAB 20

Mrs S James
7 Weymouth Square
DORCHESTER
DR6 8SD
Iris
Bracelet
IRN69

Mrs P Kenyon
4 Sion Park Road
BURY ST EDMUNDS
IP22 4KJ
Iris
Necklace
IRN62

Mr P Cross
94 Lansdown Road
LOWESTOFT
NR32 6BY
Daisy
Necklace
DAB27

Mrs T Sagar
12 Beacon Drive
ROMFORD
RM6 5LJ
Iris
Bracelet
IRN63

Ms B Raj
49 Russell Street
SCARBOROUGH YO33 9NM
Daisy
Necklace
DAB28

Mr S Ashley
32 Cartmell Road
LIVERPOOL
L2 4PP
Daisy
Bracelet
DAB16

Please key in the standard document to merge with the datafile Product1. Insert merge codes where indicated by * and use a ragged right margin. Print one copy of the standard document and also print documents to all those who have purchased a kettle.

* Title   * Initials   * Surname
* Street
* Town
* Postcode

Dear * Title * Surname

Faulty Product

Emphasise this sentence

According to our records you purchased a Phoenix brand * Item, *Product code product code, recently.

Unfortunately, a fault has been identified with this product. Please return your product to your nearest store for a full refund of £ * Value.   Alternatively, we will exchange the item for one of a similar value.

We apologise for the inconvenience this will cause you.

Yours sincerely

Marcus Romero
Sales Manager

Please key in the standard document to merge with the datafile _____. Insert merge codes where indicated by ✱ and use a ragged right margin. Print one copy of the standard document and also print documents to all those who have purchased a Daisy Necklace.

✱ Name
✱ Street
✱ Town
✱ Postcode

Dear ✱ Name

Jewellery Offer

We note from our records that you recently purchased a ✱Range Diamond ✱Item. You may be interested to learn we have just added diamond earrings to the range.

As a valued customer we are giving you the opportunity to purchase these at a reduced price of £599. This represents a saving of 25% of the recommended retail price.

If you would like to add these earrings to your collection please call us. You should quote reference ✱ reference when placing your order.

Yours sincerely

Margaret Steadman
Manager

Examination practice 2

> Recall this datafile stored under PRODUCT. Amend as shown. Sort the datafile by ascending order of Payroll. Save as Staff. Print one copy ensuring that at least three records are printed on each page.

> Please add this field to each record →

Title	Initials	Surname	Street	Town	Postcode	Start Date	Payroll	Salary	Branch
Mr	R	Peters	11 Maybrick Road	TRURO	TR3 8AN	01/08/99	1289	£16,500	Truro
Mrs	A	Turner	7 Herbert Road	EXETER	EX7 6NO	27/04/01	1464	£12,500	Exeter
Ms	D	Sinclair	7 Mount Road	RUGBY	CV21 4HB	05/12/98	1211	£14,000 ~~£8,500~~	Rugby
Mr	V	Frecknall	67 Commercial Road	CAMBRIDGE	CB5 3KR	18/02/00	1381	£5,750	Cambridge
Mrs	M	Wade (Connelly ~~Gate~~)	43 Morris Lane	NORTHAMPTON	NN2 5XP	28/03/02	1762	£14,000	Nottingham
Mrs	T		21 Heath Park	CAMBRIDGE	CB3 6QL	30/09/01	1478 ~~1487~~	£4,800	Cambridge
Mrs	E	Morling	125 Kingston Road	RUGBY	CV21 7YV	10/10/97	1100	£22,000	Rugby
Ms	A	Newall	37 Commercial Road (Park)	LONDON	SE12 6JM ~~NE32 5SE~~	31/01/99	1292	£14,500	Kensington
Mr	F	Ettridge	86 Westburn Mews	NORTHAMPTON	NN1 3UM	02/06/95	1002	£9,500	Northampton
Mrs	W	Tribe	54 Lyndhurst Road	LONDON	SE5 6NA	12/12/98	1212	£10,100	Oxford Street
Mr / Mrs	C	Scarborough	6 Portsmouth Road	KETTERING	NN16 4SM	23/11/02	1789	£3,500	Northampton
Mrs	R	Colley	8 Dove Street	ELY	CB17 8QR	14/05/97	1148	£7,750	Cambridge
Mr	J	Mackintosh	4 Falstaff Road	BRISTOL	BS12 9QN	12/10/98 ~~28/04/99~~	1302	£11,400	Bristol
Mrs	G	Martin	23 Manor Drive	BATH	BA19 8HG	17/03/98	1245	£18,900	Bristol
~~Mr~~	~~B~~	~~McMahon~~	~~22 Neyling Avenue~~	~~BASINGSTOKE~~	~~RG22 5GH~~	~~13/02/00~~	~~1377~~	~~£14,500~~	~~Kensington~~
Mrs	L	Tozer	39 Aylwin Street	NEWMARKET	IP29 8NW	21/02/01	1495	£12,300	Cambridge
Mrs	S	Cook	12 Enville Road	KEYNSHAM	BS18 7GN	28/03/99	1263	£5,800	Bristol
Mrs	A (~~X~~)	Johnson	101 Lakeside Road	RUGBY	RG6 2MW	07/02/99	1326	£7,500	Rugby
Mrs	J	Pybus	Eastley Road	EXETER	EX19 7BW (CB17 6PB)	15/10/01	1499	£14,500	Exeter
Mrs	N	Beaumont	4 Oxford Street	~~STOWMARKET~~	~~IP15 6AG~~	29/01/02	1654	£12,750	Cambridge

Title	Initials	Surname	Street	Town	Postcode	Start Date	Payroll	Salary	Branch
Mr	P	Sollich	45 Severn Road	LONDON	SW6 8GC	01/03/99	1378	£15,000	Oxford Street
Mrs	T	Turnidge	62 Harley Street	EXETER	EX4 7NO	12/10/97	1183	£17,000	Exeter
Mr	O	Kennedy	54 Thomas Street	SWINDON	SN4 3WD	29/08/96	1045	~~£4,750~~ £7,500	Bristol
Mr	M	Payne	33 Pera Mews	BRISTOL	BS22 5EK	05/04/99	1367	£8,900	Bristol
Ms	H	Shellard	1 Southdown Road	NORTHAMPTON	NN7 9JD	02/06/95	1101	£14,600	Northampton
~~Ms~~	N	Ellis	~~76 Parade Street~~	~~BRIXHAM~~	TQ5 7PW	27/07/94	0193	£13,200	Exeter
Mr	A	Dinning	83 Aspley Avenue	TRURO	TR15 8SN	24/11/99	1382	£18,000	Truro
Mrs	B	Elkheim	69 Rosslyn Road	KETTERING	NN16 5JL	13/01/93	0189	£3,500	Northampton
Mrs	A	Sutton / Wiggett / Wing	3 Park Avenue	EXMOUTH	EX16 3JM	31/03/97	1065	£14,500	Exeter
Mr	S	Jackson	55 Osbourne Drive	LONDON	SE4 7HG	02/10/98	1221	£12,200	Oxford Street
Mr	P	Jackson	55 Coronation ~~Avenue~~ Road	TRURO	TR4 8YR	04/11/99	1326	£11,500	Truro
Mr	T	Seegar	9 The Oval	RUGBY	RG3 7NA	21/03/89	0192	£18,000	rugby
Mrs	~~F~~ K	Simmonds	4 Newbridge Road	LAUNCESTON	EX5 7DL	10/02/00	1277	£6,750	~~Truro~~ Exeter
Mrs	D	Redfern	83 Lyndhurst Road	CAMBRIDGE	CB5 2HA	12/08/99	1928	£11,500	Cambridge
Mr	B	Stock	6 Richmond Place	LONDON	SW14 6PL / BA3	02/05/01	1729	£14,500	Kensington
Mr / ~~Mrs~~	E	Wilmot / Davies / ~~Longham~~	67 Ringwood Road	~~BRISTOL~~ Bath	~~BS22~~ 5AE	09/06/02	1284	£18,000	Bristol
	K		43 Brook Road	PAIGNTON	TQ2 3NW	17/05/01	1729	£22,000	Exeter
Mr	A	Portnall	10 Charlton Mews	LONDON	SW17 5EB	30/09/02	1533	£14,500	Kensington
Ms	R	Bletso	3 Julian Road	TORQUAY	TQ2 3RT	06/02/98	1082	£8,500	Exeter
~~Mr~~	~~L~~	~~Hagman~~	~~64 Mile End Road~~	~~RUGBY~~	~~RG5 7GS~~	~~14/10/00~~	~~1944~~	~~£7,500~~	~~Rugby~~
Mrs	R	Morrison	3 North View Road	Ely	CB2 4HJ	21/06/00	1627	£10,500	Cambridge
Mr	P	Grant	15 Acer Drive	Rugby	RG4 6BP	29/01/03	1992	£15,000	Rugby
Mrs	L	Murray	12 Lyndhurst Road	Truro	TR4 5KJ	06/02/02	1894	£12,000	Truro

Please key in the following records as a datafile suitable
for use with the Targets memo. Save and print one copy.
Save as Dinner.

Steve
Ross
285,000
Grand Hotel
Swindon
7.30 pm
21 August

Paul
Birch
290,000
Grand Hotel
Swindon
7.30 pm
21 August

Laura
McDonald
265,000
Royal Hotel
Oxford
8.00pm
21 August

Chris
Connelly
215,000
Grand Hotel
Swindon
7.30 pm
12 August

Dave
Richburn
325,000
Grand Hotel
Swindon
7.30 pm
12 August

Carol
Clarke
270,000
Royal Hotel
Oxford
8.00 pm
21 August

Sue
Clayton
330,000
Grand Hotel
Swindon
7.30 pm
12 August

Colin
Grahame
305,000
Royal Hotel
Oxford
8.00 pm
21 August

Ian
Blackett
275,000
Grand Hotel
Swindon
7.30 pm
21 August

Paula
Maidley
215,000
Grand Hotel
Swindon
7.30 pm
12 August

LLYFRGELL COLEG MENAI LIBRARY
LLANGEFNI MÔN ANGLESEY LL77 7

Please key in the standard document to merge with the datafile Staff. Insert merge codes where indicated by * and use a justified right margin. Print one copy of the standard document and also print documents to all staff who work in the Exeter branch.

Memorandum

To   * Title * Initials * Surname
From   Peter Salt
Ref   PRIPS

Personnel Records ◄——— Emphasise this heading

We are currently updating all our staff records. We have the following information held on our database. Could you please check the information and amend if necessary.

Your address is   * Street   * Town   * Postcode.
Your Payroll number is   * Payroll.
You began work with us on the * Start date.

We would like to confirm that all data is held in accordance with the guidelines set out in the Data Protection Act.

Thank you for your co-operation in this matter.

ST NO		14.99
CC NO		051695
		652.5
		10.11.04
		DUJ

Please key in the standard document to merge with the datafile Dinner . Insert merge codes where indicated by * and use a justified right margin. Print one copy of the standard document and also print documents to all those who are invited to the Grand Hotel on the 21 August.

Memorandum

To   * First name   * Surname

from   Gerald Monk   Regional Manager

Ref   ST/GH

QUARTERLY TARGETS

Congratulations! You have not only met your second quarter's target, but have exceeded it by over 10%. You have sold * Value of Phoenix brand products. In order to show our appreciation we would like you, and a guest, to attend our Regional Dinner. The details of this event are as follows:

Venue   * Venue * Town
Date   * Date
Time   * Time

Please let me know as soon as possible whether you are able to attend this event. It would be helpful if you could let me have a note of the name of your guest in advance of the evening.